# DANCING
## TO A
## BLACK MAN'S
## TUNE

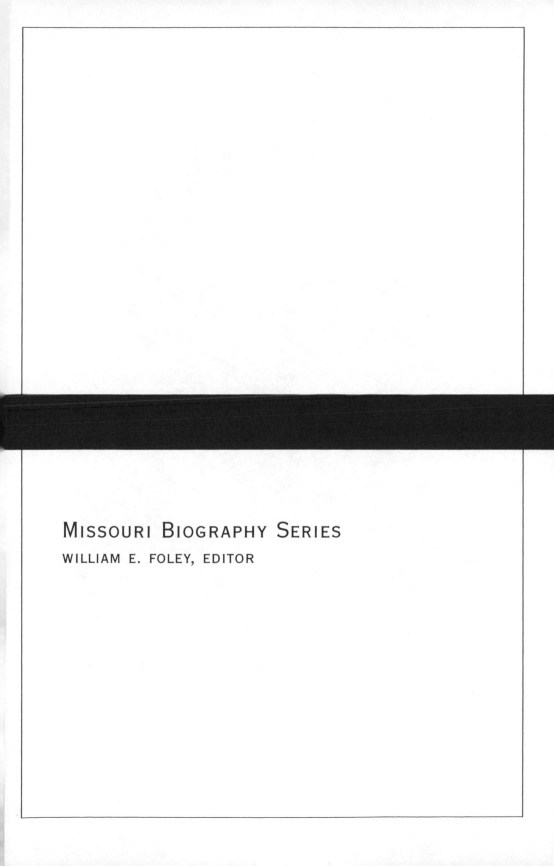

# Missouri Biography Series

WILLIAM E. FOLEY, EDITOR

# DANCING TO A BLACK MAN'S TUNE

## A LIFE OF SCOTT JOPLIN

SUSAN CURTIS

UNIVERSITY OF MISSOURI PRESS

COLUMBIA AND LONDON

Copyright © 1994 by
The Curators of the University of Missouri
University of Missouri Press, Columbia, Missouri 65201
Printed and bound in the United States of America
5  4  3  2  1        08  07  06  05  04

Library of Congress Cataloging-in-Publication Data

Curtis, Susan, 1956-
    Dancing to a black man's tune : a biography of Scott Joplin /
Susan Curtis.
        p.  cm.— (Missouri biography series)
    Includes bibliographical references and index.
    ISBN 0-8262-1547-5 (pbk.; alk. paper)
    1. Joplin, Scott, 1868-1917. 2. Composers—United States—
Biography. I. Title. II. Series.
ML410.J75C87   1994
780'.92—dc20
    [B]                                                    93-46116

                                                    CIP
                                                    MN


☉™ This paper meets the requirements of the American
National Standard for Permanence of Paper for Printed
Library Materials, Z39.48, 1984.


TEXT DESIGN: ELIZABETH FETT
TYPESETTING: CONNELL-ZEKO TYPE & GRAPHICS
PRINTING AND BINDING: THOMSON-SHORE, INC.
TYPEFACE: SCHNEIDLER


FRONTISPIECE: Scott Joplin around 1911, photo courtesy
Music Division, New York Public Library for the Performing
Arts, Astor, Lenox and Tilden Foundations

For my husband,
Charles Ross Cutter

# CONTENTS

# PREFACE

Every book has a beginning—something that prompts a writer or scholar to seek out materials on a particular subject, to pursue a new angle of vision on a familiar topic, and to tell a story of interest to others. This book arose from two seemingly unrelated sources—one very personal and the other more traditionally academic. I have been interested in Scott Joplin for nearly twenty years, but my scholarly initiation into the history of music and popular culture is of much more recent vintage. Neither source, however, can be ignored, for both contributed a great deal to my appreciation of this great Missourian—the King of Ragtime.

My personal interest in the subject arises from a childhood in which piano music played an important role. My grandfather, George Wesley Curtis, born in 1886, considered it essential for girls to learn how to play the "pianny" and milk cows as preparation for womanhood on an Iowa farm—probably necessary skills in his youth, when farmers were relatively isolated and largely self-sufficient. As a result, he bought a piano for my sister and me and listened patiently and appreciatively as we struggled to learn how to play his favorite hymns. I took lessons from Lloydene Steen, an accomplished pianist and music teacher in our community, who introduced me to a wide variety of classical and popular music and hymns. In all truth, Mrs. Steen deserved a better student than I, but by the time I was in high school, I could play passably well and derived great satisfaction from "thumping" on our old upright.

At about that time, *The Sting* and its soundtrack were taking the country by storm. Like many Americans, I was as enchanted by the music as amused by the film and eagerly acquired not only a recording of the soundtrack but also the sheet music to the various Joplin rags it featured. None of my training quite prepared me for the difficulty of the music. The rhythms, the octave chords, and the general complexity all left me exasperated but awestruck. I knew I was in the presence of greatness. In one stroke, Scott Joplin became for me one among the pantheon of musical gods. The seeds of my future interest were thus planted.

The more formal, academic origins of this project lie, perhaps ironically, in my first book, *A Consuming Faith: The Social Gospel and Modern American Culture.* I feel reasonably confident that that book discussed some important issues that help explain how people steeped in the Protestant Victorian tradition of nineteenth-century America eventually accepted and participated in a twentieth-century modern secular culture. But even as I made the final revisions, I realized that my study of social gospelers and their lives and ideas represented a small part of a much larger problem in American cultural history. All the subjects were white, and most were middle class. What was true for them might not have been true for people of other races, ethnic backgrounds, or classes. And to understand "American" culture at the turn of the century, one could not overlook the complex relationship between the diverse people who sought identity and meaning in the United States.

I also realized that I wanted to articulate and elaborate more fully the assumptions that underlay *A Consuming Faith,* adding important racial and regional dimensions for consideration. One of the most important of these assumptions was the belief that culture and society have a dialectical relationship to one another. That is, each is dependent on the other, but neither *determines* the other. A study of culture that focuses on either values or artistic expression cannot afford to lose sight of social conditions and relations that shaped their creators. But, like many of the "new" cultural historians, I reject any dogmatic Marxist scheme that posits a deterministic relationship between "base" and "superstructure." In *A Consuming Faith,* I studied a group of thinkers, teachers, writers, and activists, who, as purveyors of middle-class ideals, occupied a position of influence in American life. Their class position and cultural expression mutually reinforced one another. (This was, nevertheless, a source of pain to many social gospelers, driven as they were by conscience to challenge what they perceived to be an unjust society.) I wondered how society and culture interacted in the lives and works of people who were not part of the middle class, not white, and not interested in reinforcing their subordinate position.

The use of terms like *dominant* and *subordinate* points to another issue I wanted to explore more fully: namely, the cultural foundations of social power. The terms emerged from theoretical insights of the British Culture Studies under the leadership of Edward P. Thompson and Raymond Williams, both of whom were, in turn, influenced by the thought of Italian Marxist Antonio Gramsci. According to this school, power in society is maintained not only or even most importantly through sheer force, but also through the construction of widely accepted beliefs, codes, and ideals that inscribe desired behavior that benefits those in power. As various studies in this tradition have shown, articulation of such ideals, values, beliefs, and attitudes helps define the boundary between acceptable and unacceptable thought and action and tends to reinforce existing social relations. The result is the confirmation of the "hegemonic" position of those with power—both material and cultural. Thus, the arena of culture is anything but neutral and, in fact, represents one of the key locations for contest and debate that result in historical shifts.

I wanted to see if it was possible to explore the personal and social consequences of an individual from a more marginal group creating cultural expressions that challenged the dominant worldview and eventually shaped the contours of cultural change. Would cultural inclusion translate into social acceptance? Would participation in the culture of the dominant classes compromise the avant-garde aspirations of the subordinate? Could a piece of music have more than one meaning, depending on the audience?

In order to do justice to those questions, I knew I would have to face more directly the theoretical problem of the creation, intention, and reception of cultural expression. It was apparent to me that in the case of social gospelers, the texts they produced— whether sermons, novels, social criticism, or legislation—took on a life of their own once they left the hands of their authors. The producers may have wanted to convey particular notions and to achieve specific outcomes, but once their work was in the public arena, it was subject to widely divergent interpretations and led to various results, not all of which were intended by the writers. As linguistic theorists recently have informed us, these results can be ascribed, in part, to the lack of fixity between language and object—between "signifier" and "signified"—that creates the condition for multiple meanings, misunderstanding, and inappropriate appropriations of ideas, and that thwarts the intentions of the author. Thus, communication, on which much of culture rests, can be seen as contested ground, where meanings are negotiated rather than given.

Added to my conception that culture can inscribe and reinforce structures of power, this view of cultural contestation has led me to try to imagine a model for thinking about cultural life in a diverse society. I have settled on the term *conversation* because it implies give-and-take, uneven and unequal participation, and it leaves room for those not participating who, nevertheless, get on with the business of living. In a good conversation, the subject is agreed upon, but each participant brings his or her own perspective, experience, and insight to bear, and disagreements often arise. One group or another may have the last word—sometimes through sheer volume, sometimes because of seemingly irrefutable arguments—but it is by no means the only or universally accepted word. "Conversation," thus, should not be mistaken as a camouflage for "consensus." I *do* wish to understand terms, values, and attitudes that were shared widely by Americans of different backgrounds, but I want to explore them as topics on which there were heated debates and multiple understandings. At the turn of the century, as now, diverse groups made up American society. It seems as important to me to find the common ground of public culture—however partial and/or illusory it may turn out to be—shared by society's members as it is to identify experience and meaning specific to a race, class, gender, or ethnic group.

Given this agenda, I began groping toward my next project by expanding the scope of my inquiry into culture to include art, music, architecture, fiction, and popular culture and by seeking the work of influential cultural creators, some of whom were not white, middle class, or Protestant. More than once, I came across the name of Scott Joplin, and in the back of my mind I remembered not only my own admiration for his music but also a wonderful lecture on ragtime I had heard at the University of Missouri that made me think Scott Joplin might be the perfect vehicle for the questions I wanted to ask. The lecture was given by David Thelen, who, inimitably, had presented ragtime as a critical example of cross-race, cross-class resistance to the stifling imperatives of modernity in Sedalia, Missouri, in the 1890s. He had made Joplin come alive as a key actor in the drama of modernization, and perhaps more impressively, he had made Joplin's music seem relevant and significant to a classroom full of undergraduates raised on a musical diet that consisted largely of rock, bluegrass (it *was* Missouri), and disco (it was also the early 1980s). After looking at a few biographies, I became convinced that Joplin's life deserved a closer examination—one in which his experience could also serve as a way of addressing race and class dimensions of cultural history. The desire of the University of Missouri Press to include a biography of Joplin in its series on famous Missourians coincided with my growing interest in the King of Ragtime, and the rest, as they say, is history.

The book that has emerged from these two sources—personal and academic—is both biographical and interpretive. My intention has been to add depth to our knowledge and understanding of Scott Joplin by contextualizing him in the various communities in which he lived and worked. It also has been to place Joplin's activities and productions in the cultural world of turn-of-the-century America. I thus address the previous biographies of Joplin and the debate about culture in those years of transition.

The book opens with an introduction to the sources and historiographical debates surrounding Joplin and American culture in the Gilded Age. It is intended for a scholarly audience and may well be of less pertinence for general readers more interested in learning about Joplin. The remaining chapters are organized mostly chronologically, but each also explores a particular, salient theme. Chapter 1, for example, chronicles Joplin's childhood in northeastern Texas within the context of Reconstruction. The persistence of slave traditions and the pervasiveness of racist violence and prejudice probably left a mixed imprint on an African American child like Joplin. He undoubtedly learned early that race divided American society and created hardship for his people, but he also must have learned lessons of strength and beauty from family, friends, and neighbors who confronted that reality. Both truths found their way into his music, which spoke to a powerful white world and drew from African American cultural sources.

Chapter 2 picks up, chronologically, where the first chapter leaves off—the early 1890s—when Joplin worked as an itinerant musician. It focuses, however, on the Chicago World's Fair, at which Joplin is believed to have performed. Since no source corroborates the oral histories, which place Joplin in Chicago in 1893, I have explored the importance of the fair itself for promoting the conditions in which ragtime music could flourish. I also look at the coincidence of the cultural extravaganza and economic disaster, and argue that the depression helped unhitch cultural imperatives like hard work and self-control, which affected the reception of ragtime, its meaning, and its place in a period of cultural uncertainty.

Chapter 3 focuses on the community of Sedalia, Missouri, where Joplin first became a local celebrity and, after the publication of *Maple Leaf Rag,* achieved national fame. The main theme of this chapter involves the complicated relationship between a thriving African American community and a dominant white community in a booming commercial center. I modify the typical picture of Joplin as a figure from the underclass and red-light district by identifying his circle of friends, their activities and achievements, the neighborhood in which he lived and worked, and the relationship he developed with his chief publisher, John Stark. Local newspapers and manuscript census reports of the time suggest that African Americans and whites in the 1890s and early 1900s were in the process of negotiating the terms of a relationship to move beyond Jim Crow laws and lynch mobs. Joplin's music fit into a larger process whereby African Americans participated in the making of cultural codes embraced by themselves and others in the community.

In chapter 4, I depart from a strict chronology to reflect on the emerging music industry in which Joplin and Stark were important players. I explain how technological as well as commercial changes made possible the mass production and national dissemination of music by African Americans like Joplin, thereby allowing for the incorporation of African American cultural expression in the mainstream of American entertainment. I also show how advertising of Joplin's music—like that for much popular sheet music—conveyed ambiguous racial messages even as it claimed for Joplin the status of King of Ragtime and the markings of a "classical" composer. The business of the music industry furthered the incorporation of African American music even as it perpetuated many of the stereotypical images that relegated African Americans to second-class status in the United States.

Chapter 5 picks up the chronological narrative once more, following Joplin's later experiences in St. Louis and New York. While both moves represent Joplin's efforts to penetrate larger and more lucrative markets in order to permit more full-time devotion to composition, they also point up the ongoing frustrations faced by African Americans in early-twentieth-century society. As this chapter shows, however, not all the disappointments are attributable to racism. As Joplin tried to make his way in Harlem, the emerging capital of black culture in America, he was rebuffed by some members of the African American community because of his rural, southern roots and his classical aspirations. Here, I explore regional variations in a community too often viewed as monolithic.

I devote the final chapter to an assessment of the legacy of Scott Joplin. I place Joplin's achievements in the context of early-twentieth-century America and comment on Joplin's music and experience as part of a conversation about appropriate social relations—between classes, races, and the sexes—about meaningful cultural values, and about the nature of "American" culture in a rapidly evolving society. Joplin's experience complicates any simple representation of American culture and reflects the ambiguities of a "double consciousness" inherent for African Americans in American life. Joplin must be seen as much more than just a hero for African Americans. An examination of his experience can help all Americans understand the way cultural meanings are constructed and the frustrating reality that cultural inclusion does not necessarily translate into social equality.

# Acknowledgments

It is a pleasure to acknowledge the many people whose assistance and support have made this an enjoyable and enlightening project. I thank the directors and staffs of the following institutions, who made sources easily accessible: the State Historical Society of Missouri in Columbia, Missouri; the Missouri Historical Society in St. Louis; the State Fair Community College Library and Maple Leaf Room in Sedalia, Missouri; Barker Texas History Center at the University of Texas in Austin; the Texarkana College Library; and the Lilly Library in Bloomington, Indiana. The staff of the Purdue University inter-library loan office helped me greatly by tracking down innumerable hard-to-find sources. I also want to thank my friend and teacher, Lloydene Steen, who made available to me her collection of turn-of-the-century sheet music, from which I learned a great deal about the packaging and marketing of popular music in that era. As my piano teacher, Lloydene also instilled in me a love for beautiful music that, in part, prompted me to investigate the King of Ragtime.

The following people read and commented on earlier drafts of various chapters of this work: Harold Woodman, David Roediger, Charles R. Cutter, and Tom Pendergast. Their comments and insights improved this work immeasurably, but I take sole responsibility for any errors. In addition to a careful reading of the entire manuscript, John Stauffer gave me much-needed assistance in the selection and reproduction of many of the images that illustrate the text. I am grateful to Gerald Early, who included my essay on Joplin and Sedalia, Missouri, in his Black Heartland Project.

Thanks go to my colleague, Randy Roberts, who introduced me to Beverly Jarrett, editor-in-chief of the University of Missouri

Press. William Foley, the editor of the Missouri Biography Series, and Beverly offered unfailing support and encouragement from the time I first proposed this biography until it was accepted for publication. It has been a pleasure working with the excellent staff of the University of Missouri Press. I am grateful for the fine work done by Sara Fefer, who guided me through the many stages of the production process and whose editorial suggestions improved the manuscript.

For her constant love and support, I thank my mother, Lieselotte Curtis. And to my husband, Charles R. Cutter, who has brought a special kind of music to my life, I dedicate this work.

# DANCING
## TO A
## BLACK MAN'S
## TUNE

# INTRODUCTION

When Scott Joplin syncopated his way into the hearts of millions of Americans at the turn of the century, he helped revolutionize American music and culture. His ragged rhythms and lilting melodies made people want to tap their feet, slap their thighs, or dance with happy abandon. As Americans embraced his music, they participated in a dramatic transformation of American popular culture—their Victorian restraint gave way to modern exuberance. And whether in the elegant parlors of comfortable, respectable American homes or in the honky tonks and cafes of America's sporting districts, ragtime music accompanied a reorientation of cultural values in America in the twentieth century. The excellence and appeal of his compositions earned for Joplin the generally accepted title King of Ragtime.

But the King hardly lived a regal life. The son of freedmen in northeastern Texas, Joplin grew up amid toilers and sharecroppers, never too far removed from their years in bondage. Indeed, Texas during Reconstruction was not the most congenial place for an African American with high aspirations. Consequently, as a teenager, Joplin left his childhood home and began a career as an itinerant musician. He traveled from one community to another throughout the Mississippi River valley and performed in clubs, dance halls, and saloons. By the time he landed in Sedalia, Missouri, where he first achieved fame, Joplin had a world of musical experience behind him, but, like many of his African American contemporaries, he lacked the technical skills and personal connections to make a permanent record of his musical works. He struggled throughout his career to find financial backers for his most ambitious compositions. And in 1917, as the

1

United States prepared to enter the Great War in Europe, Joplin died in a ward for the insane at the Manhattan State Hospital in New York City.

It is precisely the incongruity between his life and achievements in late-nineteenth- and early-twentieth-century America that makes Joplin a fascinating and historically significant subject. Americans who cakewalked and two-stepped to his ragtime melodies literally danced to a black man's tune, but it is clear that in every other respect, African Americans occupied an unenviable position in American society and called none of the political or economic tunes of the age. Even in the emerging popular music industry, where African American compositions and rhythmic innovations set the tone for trends, African Americans did not dominate that industry as years passed. Scott Joplin, who contributed many a sensational hit and whom fame and fortune mostly eluded, offers a glimpse into the cultural world at the turn of the century. His life and career help illuminate the complex interaction of cultural strain, social negotiation, and musical inventiveness that shaped the contours of modern American popular culture, and they reveal the personal costs of such fundamental cultural and historical change.

As an African American artist in America's Gilded Age, Joplin merits examination in his own right, and he has received considerable attention. During his lifetime, and immediately following his untimely death, most biographical accounts celebrated his achievements but conveyed inaccurate biographical information. Contemporary news stories treated him as something of a curiosity—an African American composer of popular piano rags who had aspirations to write serious music. Their inattention to the details of his family, childhood, and training probably reflected an unwillingness to take him seriously enough as a composer to believe that his work would outlast the next season's sensations, although it might have resulted from the difficulty of obtaining such information—especially after 1917.[1] Years after his death, Brunson Campbell and Rudi Blesh kept alive the memory of Joplin's accomplishments in biographical sketches that relied on personal recollections and interviews with aging family members and friends. Their accounts, invaluable as they are for impressions of his character and talent and important details of his early career, nevertheless perpetuated unsubstantiated anecdotes and apocryphal stories about the King of Ragtime. Except among a relatively small circle of ragtime enthusiasts, Joplin gradually faded again from Americans' collective musical memory.[2]

Joplin's music resurfaced in the early 1970s, and this time two historical factors worked in its favor: the increased interest in the cultural legacy of African Americans following the civil rights movement and the central role of mass media in American life. The quest for the works and lives of unheralded Americans—women, workers, minorities, and marginalized ethnic groups—which became the agenda of New Left scholars and "new" social historians, led to the legitimization of studying obscure historical figures like Scott Joplin.[3] In this climate, Joshua Rifkin, a professor, musicologist, composer, and performing pianist, recorded an album of Joplin rags in 1970 and acknowledged the "awakening of interest in black culture and history during the last decade," which offered "a perfect opportunity to discover the beauties of [Joplin's] music and accord him the honor that he deserves."[4] Little more than a year later, T. J. Anderson reconstructed *Treemonisha,* one of Joplin's operas; Anderson's reconstruction premiered in Atlanta in the 1971–1972 opera season. He later commented, "My attitude toward Joplin is not the same as it was thirty years ago. We see him now as one of the most important creators of his generation, certainly comparable to Schoenberg. Yet most people knew nothing about Joplin when he was alive—other than as a composer of rags."[5] Both Rifkin and Anderson, it would seem, found Joplin's music in their quest for African American contributions to American culture, and their celebration of his work resulted in a quickened interest in Joplin and ragtime.

The mass media of film, however, gave Joplin's work national notice and acclaim. Joplin compositions such as *The Entertainer, Solace,* and *Pineapple Rag* provided the musical backdrop for *The Sting,* a box-office success, starring Paul Newman and Robert Redford. Though the movie was set in the 1930s, some thirty years after Joplin originally composed the rags and well after ragtime had fallen from popular favor, Americans in the 1970s ignored (or, more likely, were unaware of) the anachronism and enthusiastically embraced the music and its creator. In the wake of *The Sting*'s success, it was not at all uncommon to hear the lilting strains of *The Entertainer* on top-forty radio programs or to find recordings and sheet music of Joplin's work readily available.

Likewise, Joplin and ragtime became the subjects of a number of scholarly inquiries in the aftermath of the movie's and its soundtrack's success. Most of the biographies of Joplin followed in the tradition begun by Rifkin and Anderson: they told the untold story of a forgotten African American musician. Addison W. Reed's 1973 dissertation on the life and works of Scott Joplin, for example, not only hailed Joplin's originality and race pride, but also took pains to identify the obstacles to black achievement.[6] James Haskins's biography, which appeared five years later, provided much-needed documentation on Joplin's life and openly expressed the author's personal interest in the King of Ragtime. "Like most other blacks," he wrote in the introduction, "I was pleased when Scott Joplin was 'rediscovered,' and I read avidly the books and the articles about him that began to appear in abundance even in the mass audience magazines, to say nothing of the music periodicals."[7] That interest took him to census records and periodical literature to try to fill in the gaps of Joplin's life left by previous biographers. Of importance to both Reed and Haskins was the compilation by Vera Brodsky Lawrence of all Joplin's published works. Lawrence recovered the original versions of his compositions and made them accessible to students and fans newly acquainted with his Missouri style of ragtime.[8]

In the years between Reed's dissertation and Haskins's book, a number of books more focused on ragtime music appeared. Peter Gammond's *Scott Joplin and the Ragtime Era* provided little new information on the musician's life but offered an interpretation of the importance of his music. Gammond identified Joplin as one of three "classic" ragtime composers, whose work far surpassed the trite rags churned out on Tin Pan Alley. His analysis of Joplin's music suggested that it should be examined as serious music and differentiated from the cruder works of Joplin's contemporaries, a point underscored a few years later by Edward Berlin, whose examination of the early-twentieth-century debate over ragtime revealed a decided focus on ragtime songs rather than on the piano compositions.[9] In addition to these scholars, David Jasen, Trebor Tichenor, John Edward Hasse, William Schafer, and Johannes Reidel have offered musicological interpretations of ragtime, with some references to Joplin, but little exploration of the particulars of his life. They generally emphasize the African American origins of the form, rhythms, and melodies of ragtime music as an American genre.[10]

Taken together, scholarship on Joplin in the past two decades has accomplished a great deal. It has resurrected the life and work of a thwarted and forgotten African American artist and made his music familiar to a new generation of American music lovers. This revived interest has enriched all Americans, but it speaks particularly to African Americans seeking to recover the stories and voices of their ancestors. Moreover, analyses of ragtime have placed that genre within the larger context of American music and have begun to consider the significance of ragtime as a broader social and cultural phenomenon. Ragtime was a music that was heard in various, but particular, social settings; it was produced and distributed within specific financial constraints; it inscribed and embodied important nonmusical values; and its promoters presented ragtime using language and images that bore critical racial, ethnic, cultural, and class assumptions.

Unfortunately, to a large extent, the literature on Joplin and the studies of popular music have remained separate. The biographers of Joplin are more interested in recounting the specific conditions and achievements of the musician's life than in exploring the context in which he lived and worked. Likewise, those who study ragtime typically devote a section or a chapter to Joplin and the Missouri style of ragtime but leave him suspended when they go on to discuss other styles or issues in which Joplin did not figure. The result is an incomplete picture of both Scott Joplin and the social/cultural world of turn-of-the-century America.

What is needed, then, is a way of synthesizing the celebratory studies of Joplin with the analyses of popular music into a single discussion that amplifies our understanding of both. Such a project, however, faces certain pitfalls that must be addressed at the outset. The most obvious problem lies in the tension between the chronological imperative of biography and the thematic schema employed in most monographic studies. The former has a built-in form and logic that is determined by the actual events of the life of the individual being considered, and the latter demands greater freedom to make connections across time. The challenge is to maintain a balance between chronology and interpretation—to examine the life of a man in the context of processes and forces beyond his immediate control. Beyond this strategic question, two conceptual problems require attention, each of which shall be addressed in turn. The first involves the analysis of music as a historical source, and the second involves ethnicity and "Americanness."

## MUSIC AND HISTORY

One of the challenges in studying a figure like Scott Joplin is to find sources from which to reconstruct his life and thought. He produced numerous musical manuscripts, including one opera that has survived into our own time, but he left very little in the way of private personal texts—a few letters, a handful of newspaper interviews, responses to census takers' questions, and the recorded memories of people who knew him. The techniques and sources of social history can help locate him as an individual in particular social settings—an African American in northeastern Texas during Reconstruction, at the Chicago World's Fair, in a bustling Missouri town in the 1890s, in Harlem in the early twentieth century— but they cannot reveal much about his thought. One is forced to rely on his chief cultural expression—his music.

The problem with relying on music is knowing how to treat it as a source. Music has textual, social, and artistic dimensions, but it defies easy analysis. Unlike a novel, its representation of "reality" or its utopian fantasies may not be explicitly stated (especially in compositions without lyrics) and therefore may be more difficult to decode as a text. Unlike a painting, it is not confined to a single canvass to which the viewer can return again and again. Each performance of music varies according to the whims, idiosyncrasies, and technique of the performer(s), and improvements in technology have made possible a wide range of renditions of any given piece of music. Of all the fields of culture, music is perhaps the most difficult to use as a historical source because the audial experience is so fleeting, and the meaning is so elusive.

Music is a source that forces one into the murky territory at the intersection of intellectual, cultural, and social history. As a form of abstract expression that provides an outlet for emotion, ideals, spiritual conviction, and stylized representations of reality, music permits some investigation of a composer's thought. Compositions with lyrics make this analysis easier, because they contain specific ideas that are then attached to a given combination of melody and rhythm. These thoughts may invoke specific issues—social, political, religious—that are then either called into question or reinforced by the lyrics and the music. Moreover, music offers a window into a particular cultural milieu because of the forms used, conventions adhered to or rejected, and the conversations about it that follow its public performance. In a sense, music becomes part of a larger cultural discussion by prompting commentators to articulate what it means to them and what they think it means to their society. Finally, music demands some kind of social analysis because it is transmitted in particular social settings and conveys values and ideals that may be widely held and part of a particular way of life. It is a social art because it depends on performers (who must interpret the music through the medium of notation) and on an audience (who interpret the performers' interpretation).[11] Furthermore, the social dimension of art includes an examination of the reproduction, dissemination, and marketing of music as a form of entertainment within a given economic and social framework.

In short, the full significance of music as a historical source cannot be understood unless the social context and the composer's position in society are examined as closely as the ideas openly or implicitly expressed in the composition. As a result, the study of music as a subject and as a source for historical analysis requires the consideration of both its "meaning" and its "experience."[12]

Here the problem becomes thorny. For knowing what music means is an enormously complex problem, which generations of musical commentators, educators, and critics consistently have acknowledged even as they offer ways of appreciating music. Most agree that music is some kind of language, but they also agree, ironically, that it is indecipherable. A speaker at the Society for Ethical Culture in Chicago in 1893, for example, remarked to an audience at the Grand Opera House that Music is "the only universal language. It does not have to be translated in order to be understood." Likewise, Walter Raymond Spalding, in *Music: An Art and a Language* (1920), insisted that "to define . . . what music is, will be forever impossible. . . . It is a peculiar mysterious power." He illustrated this point with an anecdote about Beethoven. "When once asked the meaning of a sonata of his," Spalding wrote, he "played it over again and replied, 'It means that.'" Similarly, a few years later, writing *Music in Everyday Life* (1935) at the behest of the Carnegie Corporation, Eric Clarke wrote, "Music . . . is a language which conveys ideas and feelings that words cannot."[13] Typical of these approaches is a view that music belongs to the ideal realm and that it is mysterious and inarticulate, but inexplicably, accessible to all.

Perhaps Aaron Copland put it best in *What to Listen For in Music:*

> All music has an expressive power, some more and some less, but . . . all music has a certain meaning behind the notes and . . . the meaning behind the notes constitutes, after all, what the piece is saying, what the piece is about. This whole problem can be stated quite simply by asking, "Is there a meaning to music?" My answer to that would be, "Yes." And "Can you state in so many words what the meaning is?" My answer to that would be, "No."[14]

Recognizing that the ultimate, deep meaning of a composition may remain a mystery, historians nevertheless can explore its more accessible dimensions in order to speculate on the place of musical and artistic expression in the process of social and historical change. Three particular approaches have been useful in helping one explore the difficult problem of music and its meaning in the past.

The first is a musicological approach and can be used to identify a music's rhythmic and melodic antecedents, its form and structure, and the influences on the composer. Did the composer use some kind of formula of chord progressions and repeated phrases? Does the piece bear the marks of the composer's mentor or musical idol? Is it similar to or different from other pieces that appeared at about the same time? Answers to such questions reveal the musical elements and some clues about their origins. In the case of Joplin, for example, musicologists have identified the antecedents of his music in the rhythms of African American slave music, the melodies of black church music, and the influence of untutored improvisors. Whatever genius he may have displayed found expression in established forms and made use of particular musical and rhythmic elements.[15]

A second approach treats music as a text, subject to literary and critical analysis. Such an examination provides insight into the kinds of words used, the values they embrace, attitudes toward the song's subject, and beliefs. This approach has been used by Sandra Sizer to unpack late-nineteenth-century gospel songs and by James Dormon to illuminate racist attitudes inscribed in popular "coon songs" of the 1890s. Others, notably Edward Berlin and Nicholas Tawa, have treated sheet music itself as a textual artifact to be studied for messages—cultural, musical, commercial—contained on the jacket, in the advertisements for other songs, and in the presentation of the author and the composition itself.[16]

The underlying premise in the work of these authors is that the cultural context conditions the expression of ideas in a musical, lyrical, or commercial idiom. While not disagreeing with the thrust of such interpretations, scholars must be cautious of accepting overly simplistic analyses of these complex texts. As linguistic theorists have argued convincingly in recent years, words themselves are slippery and open to multiple definitions, which might make it difficult to claim one particular meaning for any given word or phrase in a lyric or an advertisement. The author may have intended one meaning; different audiences may have inferred others. A good example is the reference to "jig" piano in some advertisements for ragtime music. In our day, "jig" carries racist connotations that may not have been understood at the time the ads were written and so must be ignored in favor of the word's usage at the turn of the century. Moreover, even if we assume a greater fixity in language than actually exists, how exactly culture shapes individuals is debatable.[17]

In spite of these problems, this critical approach is indispensable. One can, for example, study words and phrases by comparing them with their uses in other contexts. Likewise, images can be contextualized by noting ways that similar objects, depictions, and symbolic evocations function in different media. And a sense of prevailing attitudes and beliefs provides a sounding board for ideas expressed in the words or images used on the covers of sheet music.

The third model seeks the meaning of music in its sociology—that is, when and by whom it was experienced and the economics of its production and dissemination. That music is a social experience is undeniable, for the composer's ideas expressed musically must be filtered through the conventions of notation and directions, the interpretations of a performing musician, and the audience's reception of and response to the audial experience.

Interest in the sociology of music first arose in the 1930s, when a number of critical thinkers began to question the earlier, loftier interpretations of music as an unknowable and mysterious art form. Like many American intellectuals in the 1930s who became intrigued by the concept of culture in the midst of economic disaster, Elie Siegmeister turned a critical gaze on the field of music. Why, he wondered, was music perceived as a form of expression outside history and social experience? Whose interests were served by the myth that music transcended economic conditions and social setting? Siegmeister believed that uncritical attitudes toward music perpetuated and strengthened an antidemocratic structure of power. He thought it problematic, for instance, that antilabor groups sponsored concerts with such works as Beethoven's Ninth Symphony on the program—the half-hour diatribes against organized labor, which preceded the concerts, seriously undermined the music's proclamation that "Alle Menschen werden Brueder!" and it was the music, he believed, that was drained of its most important message. He also explored the business of music in the field of jazz.[18]

Though Siegmeister's was an important plea for a sociological study of music, Theodor Adorno's essays on music have become the standard starting point for the sociology of music. A prominent member of the Frankfurt School, Adorno saw music—especially popular music—as a product of the capitalist, industrial system. His was part of the Frankfurt School's general critique of modern mass culture. In his effort to demonstrate the industrialization (and hence, degradation) of art by an insatiable market imperative, he pointed to similarities within popular musical genres. "Hits"—like those from New York City's infamous Tin Pan Alley—were standardized products, produced and reproduced inexpensively with little or no artistry. This mass culture denied individuality, creativity, and human liberation; indeed, dominant groups used it to hold sway over those subordinate to them.[19]

While the conclusions of more recent studies in the sociology of music have tempered Adorno's conclusions, his view has not been abandoned altogether.[20] Recent authors are generally more willing to acknowledge the individuality of some popular pieces of music, though they may root their interpretations of it in a social class analysis. Christopher Ballantine, for example, argued in *Music and Its Social Meanings* that "social structures crystallize in musical structures" and "the musical microcosm replicates the social macrocosm."[21] According to this argument, something within a given society calls into being certain expressions that speak with force to those experiencing the prevailing social conditions, but that does not necessarily reduce music—even popular music—to the status of a mass-produced article indistinguishable from other such "products."

The most important insights offered by the sociological approach include the recognition that musicians depend on social relations for the success of their art and that theirs is, indeed, a business that involves production, packaging, advertising, and marketing. Moreover, insofar as music inscribes certain values—some of which impinge on social relations and expectations—music can comment on and even promote or critique particular social structures. Consequently, part of the meaning of music lies in its relationship to the prevailing social conditions under which it was conceived and produced.

Taken together, the musicological, cultural, and sociological approaches to the historical study of music form a matrix within which some sense of the meaning of Joplin's music and the experience of the composer and his contemporaries can be understood. This approach offers a way to explore the relationship between the social setting of the late nineteenth century and the abstract expression of ragtime, recognizing that each dimension will shed light on the others. Thus, identifying the significance of Scott Joplin's work reveals a great deal about social and cultural forces in the process of transforming the United States in the late nineteenth century. It also clarifies the structures of power within which Joplin's music was created and disseminated and from which many, like Joplin, wanted to depart.

## "AN AMERICAN, A NEGRO": ETHNICITY IN AMERICA

The final issue to consider involves Joplin's role as an American composer of African American descent. Joplin experienced what W. E. B. Du Bois referred to as "double consciousness, this sense of always looking at one's self through the eyes of others, of measuring one's soul by the tape of a world that looks on in amused contempt and pity. One ever feels his twoness,—an American, a Negro; two souls, two thoughts, two unreconciled strivings; two warring ideals in one dark body, whose dogged strength alone keeps it from being torn asunder."[22] Like many African American artists, educators, and public figures, Joplin carried the burden of his race into his professional work. He was conscious of setting the values and experiences of his people to a music derived from their heritage. At the same time, however, he kept one eye on the standard of the dominant society on which he depended for a livelihood.

Joplin's music, consequently, cannot be easily categorized as "African American." Indeed, in the early twentieth century, some music commentators considered ragtime the quintessential American music. Hiram K. Moderwell, for example, writing in the *New Republic* in 1915, argued that ragtime was "the one original and indigenous type of music of the American people" and "a type of music substantially new in musical history. . . . I am sure that many a native composer could save his soul," he argued, "if he would open his ears to this folk music of the American city." Likewise, foreign commentators like Arnold Bennett of the London *Times* urged Americans to find in ragtime the inspiration for an original "national" music. "Ragtime," he wrote in 1913, "represents the American nation." In that same year, Charles Wakefield Cadman seemed to respond to the call by composing a trio in D Major for violin, cello, and piano in which the last movement was described as "idealized ragtime." Thus ragtime in the world of popular entertainment as well as its manifestations in serious music was linked by many to American music.[23]

At the same time, ragtime clearly was identified as "Negro music"—a label that inspired either enthusiasm or scorn by black and white Americans alike. Some white Americans denounced ragtime as primitive and African, hardly representative of the heritage of all the nation's citizens, and some African Americans resented the association between their race and a music held in contempt by some of the leading musicians in the country. The editor of *The Negro Music Journal* in 1903, for example, complained that ragtime was an obstacle to the advancement of African Americans in the United States. He argued that such music "does not portray [the Negro's] nature, nor is its rhythm distinctly characteristic of our race."[24] Many, however—both black and white—believed that Negro music in general, and ragtime in particular, constituted America's only folk music, which had arisen from the experiences and traditions of people in North America. Kelly Miller, writing in *The Voice of the Negro* in 1906, noted that "Negro melody has been called the only autochthonous music of the

American continent." While focusing first on the popularization of "plantation melodies," Kelly went on to herald the rise of ragtime music in America as "another stage of Negro music." Like the plantation songs, ragtime was "not African, but American."[25]Similarly, Scott Joplin believed that ragtime was one of the African American's chief contributions to American culture.[26]

The problem posed by this kind of labeling may seem unimportant. After all, ragtime *did* originate with African Americans in the United States, so it was both African American and American. But because of the social and cultural implications of the designation, it was of no small consequence—at the turn of the century or now—to classify and categorize such music. As long as ragtime could be pigeonholed as "Negro music," it was easier to trivialize and dismiss it, and recognition, opportunities, and economic advancement could be denied to African American composers. Moreover, as ethnic music, ragtime existed outside the mainstream and contributed to an African American identity as "other" or "not us"—from the perspective of native-born white Americans, who then dominated most cultural institutions.

One of the chief aims of this book is to explore the relationship between African American and American culture as well as to understand the ambiguities of these terms in the twentieth century. Neither fully existed outside the other; in important ways, each depended for its existence on the other. Americans in the late nineteenth century—as Americans at many different times in the past—sought to identify the distinctive characteristics of their culture. What *was* American culture? Likewise, African Americans, though perhaps conscious of a special experience in North America, hoped to find their place in the larger society while retaining something of their own value system and art. At important points, the aims, aspirations, and works of both groups intersected. Indeed, as early-twentieth-century cultural commentators noted, authentic American motifs had to incorporate the sounds, rhythms, and images of its "folk"—the rough equivalents of European peasants with a rich cultural tradition that arose from their humble toil, their close association with the land, their lack of formal education, and their simple appreciation of joy and sorrow, bounty and hardship. In the United States, African Americans and Indians were considered to be the likeliest bearers of this kind of folk tradition.

In part, then, this is a book about the relationship between ethnicity and Americanness. As many studies of immigrants and blacks in America rightly have pointed out, ethnicity involves the struggle to maintain a way of life and a system of beliefs that may not coincide with those of the surrounding culture. In this view, assimilation represents the breakdown of ethnic character and is, in a sense, to be regretted. As Werner Sollors has argued, however, ethnicity itself is an "invention." As he writes in *The Invention of Ethnicity*, it is

> not so much an ancient and deep-seated force surviving from the historical past, but rather the modern and modernizing feature of a contrasting strategy that may be shared far beyond the boundaries within which it is claimed. It marks an acquired modern sense of belonging that replaces visible, concrete communities whose kinship symbolism ethnicity may yet mobilize in order to appear more natural.[27]

Recognizing ethnicity as an invention and a process of constant redefinition of identity, Sollors does not deny the reality or the power of ethnic consciousness. Rather, he links them to modernity. In the modern, mobile setting, where people from around the globe move from one nation to another, becoming naturalized citizens yet clinging to older cultural traditions, ethnic identity takes on added importance. That identity, he argues, results partly from biological origins—"descent"—and partly from the embrace of available values and personal signposts—"consent." The result is a fluid and evolving ethnic identity articulated against the backdrop of an equally fluid mainstream culture.[28]

Such a process, by definition, identifies otherness. Because a group has certain characteristics, beliefs, values, and customs, it can be distinguished from the other groups around it. Some differences may be exaggerated in order to make the distinctions even clearer. Looking back from the distance of several decades, it is easy to assume that a specific ethnic group had fixed traits that, if no longer completely intact, have been eroded by contact with the surrounding or dominant groups. The result, however, can be a distortion of the actual experiences of people living in a diverse society.

In the case of African Americans at the turn of the century, the issue of ethnicity is complicated by a number of particular historical circumstances. The most important of these arose from the social reordering after the Civil War. While the Union's victory in 1865 sealed the promise of the Emancipation Proclamation, it did not ease former slaves' transition from bondage to citizenship. Reconstruction entailed more than the readmission of the former Confederate states into the Union. As Eric Foner has shown, it was a drama of great social significance, in which African Americans played major roles. Their participation in the political process and the demands they placed on former masters gave Reconstruction part of its shape and direction.[29]

In the years following 1877, when political reconstruction came to an end, white and black Americans continued to negotiate the terms of their society and to define the boundaries of their culture. The "race question," which occupied many columns in the leading reform journals in the Gilded Age, can be seen as an important part of the debate over both black ethnicity and the nature of American culture, for the upshot of the race question involved the extent to which former freedmen and their descendants could become full-fledged and equal participants in American life. Were African Americans inherently unequal, forever consigned to some second-class status, as unreconstructed white supremacists, eugenicists, and racists argued? Would education help make up the deficit caused by the experience of slavery and lead to integration and equality? If so, would it be Booker T. Washington's faith in industrial training and Victorian striving that closed the gap between the races or W. E. B. Du Bois's insistence on higher learning that led the race through the dark days of post-Reconstruction oppression? And as important as these questions were to the debate, another problem formed its subtext: would the definition of American identity be altered by the incorporation of African Americans into the wider society?

The question of Americanness had intrigued citizens in the New World since the eighteenth century, when J. Hector St. John Crevecoeur had posed his now famous query: "What then is the American, this new man?" in his *Letters from an American Farmer.* But it took on a new urgency in post–Civil War America as millions of immigrants poured into the United States from all parts of the world and as former slaves officially became part of the nation's citizenry.

Though always a diverse population, Americans in the nineteenth century had perceived themselves primarily as a Protestant people with an Anglo-Saxon heritage, and cultural leaders from such a background had dominated the literary and cultural institutions that gave written, expressive, and concrete form to that identity.[30] Of course, many, like Crevecoeur, had recognized that people from different backgrounds came together in the New World, where they were "melted into a new race of men," which implied that certain characteristics were distilled into an essential American character. But in the changing social scene of the late 1800s, the growing presence of Catholics, Jews, nonbelievers, and people of different races produced considerable anxiety among the cultural and political elite about the future of that American character.[31]

One constant in the quest for American identity was a conviction that the promise of the United States—indeed of the New World generally—lay in its freedom from European decadence and corruption. In no small measure, the American identity rested on an ethnic assumption of "otherness." Unlike Europeans, Americans were *not* ruled by despots, they did *not* divide their society into distinct, nearly impenetrable, social strata, and their barely tamed continent yielded a people virtuous, hard-working, and close to nature. As more than one commentator noted, travelers to the United States did not come to see the monuments and ruins of a decayed past: the lure of America was the grandeur of its land—forests, mountains, and lush prairies—the promise of its future, and the openness of its democratic society. By the late nineteenth century, however, industrial development and large cities blighted the natural environment, and the opulence surrounding captains of industry undermined the egalitarian hope of democracy.

The race question and the question of American identity, then, coincided, resulting in a tumultuous critical debate over American art. Judging from the subjects of articles in leading periodicals of the 1890s and early 1900s, Americans obsessively tried to define the distinguishing marks of their art, architecture, literature, educational system, and music.[32] A writer in *The Outlook* in 1905 noted, for example, that the United States had begun to "develop its own distinctive musical traits. . . . the same traits of unconventionality and boldness, of freedom and cosmopolitanism, that have characterized the American way of reading and writing literature, and of viewing and painting pictures."[33] Even a decade later, however, not everyone agreed with this assessment. Henry F. Gilbert, writing in the *Musical Quarterly* in 1915, argued, "We certainly do not have *American* composers [because] we have hardly as yet developed an American race." Americans had developed a distinctive spirit, which had been captured by the great writers of the nineteenth century, and Gilbert hoped that that spirit would eventually help "our composers to kick over the traces of European traditions and to treat American subjects, to use fragments of melody having an American origin as a basis for musical structure."[34]

In the case of music, the two issues of race and nation came together forcefully during and after Antonin Dvorak's stay in the United States. Writing in 1893, a year after his arrival, the great Bohemian composer declared, "I am now satisfied that the future music of this country must be founded upon what are called the negro melodies. This must be the real foundation of any serious and original school of composition to be developed in the United States. . . . These beautiful and varied themes are the product of the soil. They are American."[35] Dvorak's own *New World Symphony* contained passages inspired by the melodies that had so impressed him. Within weeks of Dvorak's comment, responses appeared, ranging from anger at the prospect of developing an "African school of music" to enthusiastic support.[36] Whenever the subject of an American school of music came up in the following decade or two, the question of what role Negro music should play invariably arose as well.[37]

In this context of uncertain cultural nationalism, Scott Joplin arrived on the American musical scene. Forgetting for a moment how the next two decades unfolded, we can imagine that as Joplin began to produce piano compositions in the late 1890s and early 1900s, he saw himself contributing musically both to a protean American school of music and to the cultural accomplishments of his race. As we shall see, Joplin's experience testifies to the difficulty of both aims.

In many respects, Joplin is an ideal subject for a study of American music at the turn of the century. First, his life framed perfectly a critical cultural "moment" in American history. His birth in 1868 coincided with the ratification of the Fourteenth Amendment to the Constitution, which set in motion the struggle for equal treatment under the law for African American citizens, and which eventually was used to protect the interests of big business in the 1890s and early 1900s. Official legal racial diversity and large-scale industrial development, both of which emerged from the Fourteenth Amendment, irrevocably altered prevailing social relations in the United States. Likewise, Joplin's death in 1917 in the midst of America's decision to enter the Great War in Europe marked the culmination of social and cultural changes begun in the post–Civil War decades. By examining his life in the context of American history, we shall focus on the critical formative years between Reconstruction and World War I, when modern American culture took shape.

Joplin's life is instructive for a second reason—as an African American, he offers an important perspective on culture formation. Hardly representative of the musical elite, Joplin was a social outsider striving for acceptance and hoping to play an influential role in the culture of his nation. Recognizing that he did not feel himself limited to writing "race music," we can explore the attitudes toward, affinity for, and loyalty to the dominant culture by one of its subordinate citizens. Finally, Joplin's peripatetic existence allows us to examine several cultural arenas—the rural South; small-town America; America's World's Fairs; and cities— through the eyes of a hopeful observer and participant.

Scott Joplin, the King of Ragtime and the founder of a distinctive Missouri style of ragtime music, will be a teacher, like the protagonist of his opera *Treemonisha*. Through examining his life, we can hope to learn how Americans at the turn of the century came to terms with a racially diverse citizenry, struggled to reformulate an American culture, and incorporated African American music into their national heritage. Through the great Missouri composer, we can begin to understand how dancing to a black man's tune involved a complex process of artistic creation, unequal social power, racial discrimination and advancement, and the formation of American culture.

## CHAPTER 1

# RECONSTRUCTING A CHILDHOOD; RECONSTRUCTING THE NATION

The story of Scott Joplin begins like a whisper in the pine forests of northeastern Texas—the message is hard to understand, but its very lack of clarity draws us closer and compels us to listen more carefully. A child of a despised race, born in one of the backwaters of the South to former slaves, Joplin entered the world without fanfare, lacking even a perfunctory notice of his birth in the local newspaper. As he grew to maturity, his comings and goings, successes and disappointments failed to excite the interest of prominent people in the community. But his memory was kept alive by those on the fringes of that community who were touched by his musical originality and ability, by friends and relatives who remembered the talented boy who taught himself to play the piano, then stubbornly refused to treat his playing as a pastime while he earned his way with manual labor. The historical record is not silent, but like a whisper, it forces us to strain to hear in the sources a word or a phrase that makes Joplin more comprehensible, instructive, and alive. Before the composer of *Maple Leaf Rag* burst upon the American musical scene, talented but modest, musically daring but personally reserved, an African American child was born in the piney woods of Texas on November 24, 1868.

Scott Joplin was a child of Reconstruction. He was born at a moment when Americans endeavored to heal their nation's wounds and to forge a new nation. Through much of his life, he would have to contend with the social conditions, racial prejudices, and cultural barriers that took shape during the crucial years following the Civil War. Joplin, the second son of Jiles and Florence Joplin, was freeborn, but they had experienced slavery firsthand.[1] Both the region and the time of his birth offer critical insights into the life and music of Scott Joplin. Joplin was born near the Texas-Arkansas border. He spent his formative years in the rich cotton country of the Red River valley, a region profoundly affected by slavery, slave culture, and the vicious aftermath of the Civil War.

## THE JOPLIN FAMILY IN MID-CENTURY TEXAS

Jiles and Florence Joplin were among the mass of African American citizens who struggled to make a good life for themselves and their children in mid-century Texas. Typical of many African Americans in the Lone Star State, Florence Givens and Jiles Joplin had come to northeastern Texas from other parts of the South before the Civil War. Florence, a free black woman from Kentucky, accompanied her father, Milton, and her grandmother, Susan, to Texas sometime before the Civil War.[2] Jiles's owner, Charles Moores, brought him to northeastern Texas in 1850 from South Carolina.

Jiles was still a child when he arrived in Bowie County, Texas. Little is known of his early life in Texas, though probably, because of his age, he initially was spared from grueling field labor. According to family lore, Jiles became an adept musician and played the fiddle for dances in his masters' households. Since he eventually took the surname of Joplin, it has been argued that at some point he became part of the Warren Hooks estate and eventually a gift to his daughter, Minerva Hooks, who in the late 1850s married Josiah Joplin. Unlike the vast majority of slaves in Texas, however, Jiles was granted his freedom several years before the Emancipation Proclamation was honored in the state. He settled down to farming in Cass County—it must have been difficult for a free black man to travel far in Texas in the tense years before the war. There he met Florence Givens, and in 1860 they married. Their first son, Monroe, was born sometime in the next couple of years as the nation exploded into civil war.[3]

Jiles Joplin and Florence Givens represent the diversity among African Americans in antebellum Texas. After the region achieved independence from Mexico in 1836, its vast expanse of arable land attracted southern planters, who brought their slaves from the older regions of the South and started over in cotton country. Even before the United States annexed Texas in 1845, the extreme northeastern counties of Bowie, Red River, and Harrison had experienced rapid growth in population—both black and white. By 1845, the three counties together contained 21 percent of all the slaves in the state.[4] In the next fifteen years, Texas—especially areas of it like the Red River valley with its access to river transportation—continued to attract planters like Charles Moores and Warren Hooks. But increasingly after 1850, slaveowners in other parts of the South saw Texas as a refuge from the threat of war and the loss of slaves. Even in the midst of the secession crisis, slaveowners spirited their chattel into Texas as a way of preventing their slaves from escaping to Union forces when war came. By 1861, Texas had become home to nearly two hundred thousand slaves from all parts of Dixie.[5]

The Civil War actually affected Texas very little. Although some Texans volunteered to fight for their way of life and sacrificed their bodies or lives to the Southern Cause, no battles were fought in the Lone Star State. Commerce may have been slowed, but because the chief products of northeastern Texas were cotton and lumber, both easily stockpiled and stored, farmers and planters in that part of the state suffered relatively little. When the South admitted defeat in April 1865, it must have been difficult for many Texans to accept. Unlike most other Southerners, Texans did not see their fields lying in ruins, their homes plundered and burned, and their lands and state impoverished and defeated. Texans resisted the politics of Reconstruction that followed in the wake of the war partly because they had not faced such horrors. Many devoted their energy and anger to the cause of salvaging as much of the old social system as they could.[6]

Reconstruction itself presented enormous political and social challenges throughout the South. After the relatively mild terms of Presidential Reconstruction under the direction of Andrew Johnson, Radical Republicans in Congress placed greater demands on former Confederate states in a simultaneous effort to punish Southerners for trying to destroy the nation and to provide some guarantees of protection to former slaves. The first three years after the Civil War were marked by confusion, acrimony, and, in some parts of the South, persistent violence, as Americans debated the proper terms of readmission to the Union and the character of social relations in a world without slavery. Southerners, resentful at being subjected to a second set of criteria for readmission, often took out their anger on African Americans. And in the end, the political process could not guarantee that former slaves and their children would be able to live free from violence, injustice, and intimidation.[7]

The states where Joplin spent his childhood—Arkansas and Texas—demonstrate how two very different experiences with Reconstruction nevertheless produced a similar outcome for African Americans. Arkansas was the first Southern state to be readmitted to the Union under the Congressional plan for reconstructing the nation; Texas was the last. In April 1868, both houses of the Arkansas legislature unanimously ratified the Fourteenth Amendment to the United States Constitution, which guaranteed citizenship and equal protection of the law to all Americans, regardless of race. Texans held out until February 1870 before they grudgingly granted citizenship to former slaves. In spite of these differences, however, neither Arkansas nor Texas extended adequate protection or assistance to the new citizens. Indeed, in the region that spanned both states along the Red River valley, Reconstruction years were dangerous ones for African Americans.[8]

On November 24, 1868, the very day Scott Joplin was born, Powell Clayton, the governor of Arkansas, addressed the General Assembly on the "Condition of the State." "We are in the midst of civil commotion," he began, and then recited the "dark catalogue of crimes" that had prompted his decision to declare martial law in the recently reconstructed state. In the cluster of counties in southwestern Arkansas that bordered on the state of Texas— cotton country adjacent to the Red River—the Ku Klux Klan was terrorizing African American citizens, former Union supporters, sheriffs, and agents for the Freedmen's Bureau. African Americans in the field were "brutally murdered," civil authorities gunned down on public roads, and county sheriffs shot or threatened with violence. "In many of these counties," Governor Clayton had declared two weeks earlier, "a perfect reign of terror now exists." To make matters worse, "bands of outlaws from Texas and Louisiana" had invaded southwestern Arkansas and had begun "committing murders and depredations upon the citizens." The Arkansas governor believed the terror had started once federal troops were withdrawn from the "reconstructed" state. Without their protection, Arkansas citizens—especially the recently enfranchised African Americans—bore the brunt of antireconstruction sentiment in both states.[9]

At the same time, across the Red River in northeastern Texas, a different Reconstruction scenario was under way. Texans officially had delayed emancipation of their slaves by more than two months after the end of the Civil War, and some held their slaves in bondage months after "Juneteenth"—June 19, 1865—when the state officially recognized the end of slavery. The planter who owned Susan Merritt in Rusk County, for example, had continued to work his slaves well into September, when "a gov'ment man" came to the plantation and informed the slaves of their freedom. Merritt recalled that "massa make us work sev'ral months after that. He say we git 20 acres land and a mule but we didn't git it." Others in the county used force and terrorism to maintain the institution of slavery. They shot and hanged African Americans who tried to run to nearby Harrison County, where emancipation had been acknowledged.[10] Having escaped the bloodshed and destruction of Civil War battles, Texans resisted the outcome of the war and were determined to cede as little as possible to the freedmen and freedwomen. According to an official for the Freedmen's Bureau, the army and the bureau had been unable to prevail in Texas, and the result was that African Americans "are frequently beaten unmercifully, and shot down like wild beasts, without any provocation."[11]

Jiles and Florence Joplin left no written or oral recollection of their experiences in the years following the Civil War, but many of their regional neighbors did. Their accounts corroborate the record of violence reported by whites. In nearby Rusk County, one former slave remembered,

> Lots of niggers was kilt after freedom, 'cause the slaves in Harrison County turn loose right at freedom and them in Rusk County wasn't. But they hears 'bout it and runs away to freedom in Harrison County and they owners have 'em bushwacked, that shot down. You could see lots of niggers hangin' to trees in Sabine bottom right after freedom, 'cause they cotch 'em swimmin' 'cross Sabine River and shoot 'em.[12]

A former slave from Harrison County, south of Cass, remembered hearing about the Ku Klux Klan in northeastern Texas. "They say they rode up and down the road in white suits," Wes Brady reported, "and that they would cut the arms and heads off of a Nigger just cause he was free. I don't know if they did or not, but the Nigger sho' was fraid of them."[13] Violence—actual or threatened—set the tone for black-white relations in northeastern Texas and southwestern Arkansas.

On both banks of the Red River, African American citizens—both those who were freeborn and former slaves—were learning the pleasures and pitfalls of liberation during the years of Reconstruction. Many celebrated exuberantly when they learned of their new status; others immediately made plans to move away from former owners and establish themselves on new land. Before Juneteenth in Texas, some slaves quietly slipped across the river into Hempstead County, Arkansas, to get a head start on freedom. But within a short time, Texas became known to freedmen and freedwomen in other parts of the South as a land of wide-open spaces—a place to begin a new life. Thousands flocked to the Lone Star State.[14] But whether content to stay in the place of their birth or eager to move to some distant land, African American aspirations were not the only factors in the post–Civil War South. Whites and blacks together negotiated the parameters and characteristics of a social system that endured and evolved over the decades. The facts of political Reconstruction pale before this effort to create the new, biracial society in which young people like Joplin made their way in the Gilded Age.

## CHILDHOOD LESSONS IN A TRANSFORMING REGION

Ever since Roscoe Conkling's startling confession in the 1880s that Radical Republicans in the 1860s had intended the Fourteenth Amendment to protect corporations as well as African American citizens, Americans rightly have questioned whether the party of Lincoln had the best interests of former slaves in sight during the politically tumultuous years of Reconstruction. African Americans in northeastern Texas may well have doubted the good intentions of their champions in the North as they listened to Radical Republicans' plans for postwar Texas. Few could have been thrilled with the radical desire to divide Texas into three separate states. For had Republicans had their way, West Texas would have been the province of white Republicans, the eastern coastal region would have been controlled by black Republicans, but northeastern and central Texas would have been left in the hands of "the disloyal elements"—the former Democratic slaveowners.[15] In other words, the part of the state with a population most in need of protection was the last concern of Radical Republicans in the Lone Star State.

While the radical dream of creating three states failed to materialize, its articulation is important for understanding the experience of African Americans in these years. Their desires did not always coincide with the political and social reality of postwar Texas. The African American children of Reconstruction Texas inherited a world in which the future was uncertain and social relations and cultural expectations were no longer clear. In the first few years following the war, blacks and whites together groped their way toward a biracial society and culture. The results of their quest became the lessons of Joplin's childhood.

Attempts to keep former slaves tied to farming—first through years of terror during Reconstruction and then eventually through sharecropping—are by now well known. But it is equally important to realize that in the first few years after the Civil War, no one was entirely sure what the Union victory actually meant. A common refrain heard in the narratives of former slaves in northeastern Texas were complaints about the unsettled quality of life right after the war. Will Adams, for example, remembered "lots of cryin' and weepin'" right after emancipation, because the former slaves "knowed nothin' and had nowhere to go." Others viewed their new freedom with guarded optimism, but they did not immediately strike out on their own without some kind of permission from a figure of authority. At the war's conclusion, for instance, Campbell Davis accompanied some of his fellow freedmen to the Provost Marshal in Shreveport, Louisiana, to "ask him what to do." Still others like Bill Collins reported widely different expectations on the part of black workers and their white employers. His brother agreed to chop cotton for a farmer near Nacogdoches for five dollars a month, but after five months had received no pay. His employer told him it would be "hard to get work any where as most of the Southerners thought [the freedmen] were supposed to work for nothing." A common response to the news of freedom was uncertainty.[16]

Former slaveowners were equally uncertain. Some white Texans became frightened that the end of slavery would result in their subjugation by former slaves. The *Tri-Weekly Star Gazette* of June 29, 1868, reported, "The reign of niggerdom has now commenced," a comment that captured the exaggerated fears of whites in Texas. "Negroes are in the House of Representatives to make a constitution for the white people," the newspaper lamented. "They threaten the white members with their 40,000 voters. They boldly say that they are to rule the country."[17] W. D. Wood recalled the "stunning effect" of Lee's surrender on the white people of Leon County. "A feeling of universal fear and terror possessed the whole community." Moreover, he lamented the effect of the ensuing military rule on formerly good relations between the races. "The negroes at once became insulting and impudent in their intercourse with the whites," he reported in *Reminiscences of Reconstruction in Texas*. They became "dissatisfied and hostile to the whites" and "abandoned their employers and their crops."[18]

Consequently, white Texans fought bitterly any effort to circumscribe their rights. They immediately attacked the compromise Constitution of 1868–1869, which affirmed the supremacy of the Federal Constitution, the full and equal citizenship of Negroes, and the need for black public education. Landlords in Harrison and Bowie counties, near where the Joplins lived and worked, hoped to maintain the old relations through political intimidation. In the months before the critical election of delegates to the 1868 constitutional convention, they threatened to compile lists of the names of freedmen who voted with "the Yankees," and they let it be known that anyone whose name appeared on the lists would not find employment. A year later the regional Republican newspaper, the *Jefferson Radical,* opined that African Americans who tried to vote in the South did so "at the risk of loss of employment, often of life itself." Such political intimidation, the editor believed, effectively had blocked the ratification of the Fifteenth Amendment in the state of Texas.[19]

Beyond the fear of political domination lay the equally critical concern over labor relations. Political Reconstruction created new opportunities for African Americans, but two facts remained relatively unaltered: white people owned the land and businesses, and black people, with few resources, had to work in order to survive. Thus, it was hard to avoid reestablishing a relationship based on dependence. During Presidential Reconstruction, white Texans moved quickly to compensate for the end of slavery. Like other Southern states, Texas established Black Codes that provided for corporal punishment of unruly laborers and for lopsided labor contracts. Moreover, Texans wanted to keep black women at work, so they stipulated that their contracts "shall embrace the labor of all the members of the family able to work."[20] In addition to Black Codes, white Texans also wrote laws that provided for stiff prison sentences for minor offenses and then made provisions for leasing convicts to labor for white employers. According to Eric Foner, "Blacks constituted about one third of the convicts confined to the state penitentiary, but nearly 90 percent of those leased out for railroad labor."[21] These actions, in a sense, reinstituted slavery under the guise of law and order.

In the area around Cass County, where the Joplins continued to labor, former planters were particularly eager to maintain the necessary labor force to run their cotton plantations and used their power or violence to achieve that end. Between 1865 and 1867, for instance, whites in Red River County murdered fifty African Americans who attempted to leave the area after emancipation. Similarly, in Titus County, a resident planter, Dave Timmins, paid a local outlaw to intimidate freedmen laborers who did not submit to his authority. When a Freedmen's Bureau agent arrived in Bowie County in 1866, he found by examining the ledgers of local planters that they routinely overcharged African Americans for food, supplies, and farming implements in order to help insure their dependence, a practice that often led to peonage.[22] Two years later, Bowie County planters hired a gunman to shoot freedmen who either tried to leave the county or balked at the terms of their contracts. Cullen Baker did "not hesitate to shoot . . . [freedmen] on the slightest complaint made by the employers." One of the Joplins' neighbors, Alex Humphrey, remembered "hiding out from a man called Cullen Baker" shortly after the war. "If you want to put my people on the run," he insisted, "just say 'Cullen Baker was seen in a neighboring community last night.' They'd hide out for two days."[23] In the same year Klan raids in all the counties bordering on Cass County became so vicious and regular that many African Americans deserted their homes and hid in the woods to avoid the violence.[24]

While force underlay white efforts to reestablish their authority in the region, it was not always required. Indeed, some former freedmen and freedwomen remembered their former masters affectionately and willingly stayed on the plantations to work for them. More than one echoed the sentiments of Gus Bradshaw, who believed that "Darkies got 'long better" as slaves than as freedmen.[25] Others, though perhaps less sanguine about slavery and their employers, also settled down to make a living on the land they knew as home. The Joplins, for example, though freed before the war, nevertheless remained in Cass County as one of five black families who worked for William Caves on a farm valued at three hundred dollars. Like the Joplins, the Crows, Shepherds, and Smiths were in their late twenties or early thirties in 1870, had young children, and were unable to either read or write. Only Susan and Milton Givens, Florence's grandmother and father, were older and less able to start a new life after freedom. Though young and presumably strong, the other families continued to work in the fields until better opportunities came along.[26]

Between political intimidation, force, and the need to support growing families, white and black Texans eventually forged a sharecropping system that defined labor relations under new postwar conditions. Many former slaves remembered working on shares for former masters or in nearby farmlands. A few, like A. M. Moore of Harrison County, managed to save enough money to buy their own land. By 1880, however, when the Census Bureau prepared a report on cotton production in the United States, only a very small proportion of African American farmers in Texas owned either the land they tilled or the home in which they lived. "The share system prevails very generally throughout the state," the census taker reported.[27]

Sharecropping necessitated both mutual dependence of and interaction between white landowners and black laborers. The common practice in northeastern Texas was that African American farmers who could furnish their own tools and supplies kept three-quarters of the cotton and two-thirds of the grain they produced, giving the remainder to the white owner. If, however, the share-cropper received food and implements from the owner, he kept only one-third of any crops produced. Any improvements made to the property belonged to the owner.[28] Though in theory each party contributed something—either labor or land and capital—to the arrangement, many African Americans recognized their disadvantage and reflected that knowledge in their demeanor toward their landlords. For example, a freedman in Harrison County believed that "if you behave yourself, [white people] will allus help you when you need it." He remembered some advice from his grandmother right after the war: "Don't run your mouth too much, and allus have manners with both white and black."[29] Another freedman from the region put it more bluntly: "The negro is classed below the white people. If white man don't treat him fair and square the negro cannot say anything, if he does the white people will hang him."[30] The effect, whether voluntary or grudging, was deference by African Americans toward white employers and neighbors.

Dependence on and deference toward whites may well have been among the lessons Scott Joplin learned while growing up in rural northeastern Texas. Aside from farming, few employment opportunities existed. Large-scale lumbering did not create jobs until the mid-1870s, when railroads connected the piney woods region of northeastern Texas with national markets.[31] Before then only a handful of small lumbering establishments, employing just a few hundred hands, had been built and capitalized in counties adjacent to Cass County.[32] So for a time at least, the Joplins, like other African Americans in the region, counted on a white landlord for their livelihood.

The chances of rising above this kind of second-class economic and social status were hampered by the lack of education in the black community of northeastern Texas. Illiteracy continued to plague the black population, and northeastern Texas lacked adequate resources for education. Indeed, counties in that area obtained fewer than 10 percent of the teachers needed to staff the public schools; the violence and primitive conditions made it difficult to attract teachers to that area. In 1870, only two African American girls attended public school in Bowie County, Texas, and the majority of African American citizens there above the age of ten could neither read nor write.[33]

Without education as an alternative, many African Americans continued to turn to superstitions and belief in the supernatural to make sense of their world. Their continued belief in "haunts" and ghosts made them especially susceptible to terrorism by white supremacists. Louis Cain, a freedman of northeastern Texas, explained the connection between black superstition and white domination eloquently, "Yes Son, if it had not been for them there ghost or what they called the Klu Klux Klan the negro would have gone on the war path, several times since the negro has been freed, but you know the negro is superstitious and they have always been afraid of them white sheets cause they look too much like dead people. They have influenced the negro more than anything in his life and ways here in his new country."[34] Years later, when Joplin wrote *Treemonisha,* an opera about plantation life in southwestern Arkansas, he identified superstitions, "luck bags," and "conjurors" as the chief obstacles to economic progress and social harmony for the black people who lived there. Like Cain, Joplin believed that fear of evil spirits would prove to be the undoing of his race, so he urged instead the embrace of formal education.

Dependence, deference, and fear, however, were not the only lessons Joplin and his generation mastered in the postwar rural South. They had before them examples of courage and character displayed by elders—family members and neighbors—who wrested a dignified existence from a grudging society and an economy dominated by unreconstructed Texans. To begin with, many African Americans hit the road within the first few years of freedom. According to Leon Litwack, former slaves followed roads in the South to a new life—they moved, even if only a short distance, to experience freedom and to improve their lot.[35] Even those who remained with former masters for a time often moved to different land within a few years. In Texas, as elsewhere, African Americans were elected to terms in the state legislature and as delegates to the constitutional convention in spite of the terror tactics designed to frighten their supporters from the polls. The Republican party sponsored a "Loyal League" to protect African American voters on election day, and as a result, citizens from such troubled areas as Harrison County sent African Americans to the legislature and to the constitutional convention.[36]

African Americans helped themselves in other ways as well. When the Ku Klux Klan became active in northeastern Texas, not all freedmen responded by hiding in the woods. According to a former resident, an African American man named Dick Walker from Jefferson, Texas, organized a "cullud militia," which struggled "to keep the Klux off the niggers" after the Federal troops had left Texas.[37] In nearby Upshur County, African Americans repaid

Klansmen's terrorism with an ambush of their own. According to Nancy King, a handful of freedmen went out one night when the Klansmen were out patrolling. "They run down a narrow road and tied four strands of grapevine 'cross the road, 'bout breast high to a hoss. The Kluxers come gallopin' down that road and when the hosses hit that grapevine, it throwed them [the Klansmen] every which way and broke some their arms."[38] Such actions gave black children examples of courage and initiative in the face of great danger.

In other less dramatic and less violent ways, African Americans in northeastern Texas presented children like young Joplin with examples of autonomy. They organized churches and occasionally schools. For example, within two years of Texarkana's founding in 1874, the Mt. Zion Baptist Church was built, and the next year, two African American Methodist congregations erected churches as well.[39] They also made a living on their own, which instilled the pride of ownership and accomplishment in themselves and their children. Betty Powers was only a few years older than Scott Joplin when her parents were freed. They "worked on shares" for a few years until they had saved enough money to buy their own land. "De land ain't clear," she remembered, "so we'uns all pitches in and clears it and builds de cabin. Was we'uns proud? There 'twas, our place to do as we pleases, after bein' slaves. Dat sho' am de good feelin'."[40]

And beyond these examples, young blacks of Joplin's generation could partake of a rich cultural heritage that had grown out of the experience of slavery. They organized barbecues and potluck picnics, dances, and community socials to break up the monotony of daily labor. Juneteenth and the Fourth of July were the most festive of these occasions. Some communities organized brass bands, which marched in parades to celebrate Emancipation Day. Parties marked the end of harvest season, and throughout the year, African Americans in northeastern Texas organized dances and cakewalks. After the founding of Texarkana, African Americans organized skating parties and balls, and some met regularly to discuss political issues of importance to their community. These events were largely segregated from white experience and featured African American leadership, organization, and cultural forms.[41]

Music lay at the heart of this culture. Longtime African American residents of northeastern Texas, who looked back on the 1860s and 1870s, often recalled the music that accompanied their lives, work, and celebrations. Whether for secular entertainment or for sacred worship, the music was emotional and rhythmic and often elicited a lively physical response. As one northeastern Texan put it, "Dey sing 'bout de joys in de nex' world an de trouble in dis. Dey first je's sung de 'ligious songs, den dey commenced to sing 'bout de life here an w'en dey sang of bof' dey called dem de 'spirituals.' De ole way to sing dem wuz to keep time wid de clappin' of de han's an pattin' of de feet."[42] Others recalled ring shouts that involved singing, clapping, and dancing. "De folks 'ud git in er ring an' march 'roun in tune ter der singing," Lou Austin remembered, "an den w'en dey git wa'amed up, dey shout an' clap an' dance an' sing."[43]

African American men and women of Joplin's generation learned a wide variety of songs. Some, like "Dem Golden Slippers" and "Sometimes I Feel Like a Motherless Child," eventually became part of the slave/folk music tradition in the United States after such choirs as the Fisk Jubilee Singers toured the country with their stylized renditions of these beautiful spirituals. African Americans in Joplin's neighborhood enjoyed less well known spirituals like "Oh How I Love Jesus," "We're Marching to Zion," and "Little Chil'ren, I Am Going Home." Perhaps Joplin knew the ring play "Ellen Yards, Seven Stars" that Simp Campbell of Harrison County considered one of his childhood favorites.[44] Music accompanied much of the activity of children, workers, and worshipers in the postbellum African American community.

African Americans in many lines of work sang or chanted to establish a constant pace for their efforts. In Arkansas in the 1930s, railroad workers still coordinated track laying with a chant from the 1870s. The foreman hollered "Little Rock!" as a signal to lift and move a rail onto the ties, and the crew answered "Memphis . . . Memphis . . . Memphis" until the rail was in place.[45] Jiles Joplin, who eventually gave up farming to work on the railroad in Texarkana, may well have used this chant or one like it while he labored. Vinnie Brunson of northeastern Texas believed that his people did virtually all their tasks to some kind of music. "De timber nigger he sings as he cuts de logs an keeps de time wid his axe," he asserted. "De women sing as dey bend over de washtub, de cotton chopper sing as he chops de cotton. De mother sing as she rocks her baby to sleep. De cotton picker sing as he picks de cotton, an dey all sing in de meetin's an at de baptizin' an at de funerals."[46]

While most of the music in the postwar African American community was vocal, it was often accompanied by simple instruments. Banjos made from sheepskin and wood with cat-gut strings, fiddles, and guitars were typical. Given their bonded past, it should come as no surprise that African Americans relied heavily on stringed instruments. One northeastern Texan remembered "We didn't know nothin' 'bout no piano or nothin' but the guitar and fiddle," and most others confirmed her statement.[47] According to family lore, Jiles Joplin played the fiddle, Florence played the banjo, and each of the children either sang or played some kind of stringed instrument.[48]

Scott Joplin's childhood was filled with the music of his people. Whether he was listening for them or not he must have heard many songs that had been passed down from generation to generation during the years of slavery as well as the newly minted chants created for work in an industrializing economy. Since many of his neighbors had come to northeastern Texas from other parts of the South, Joplin quite likely was exposed to a wide variety of melodies, rhythms, and musical traditions from across the Gulf Coast states and from cities like New Orleans, with its rich musical heritage. Together they formed his conception of music and helped establish his aesthetic standards as he matured and immersed himself in the creation of beautiful sounds.

As a child of a biracial society, however, Joplin was not limited to the music of the African American community. White people, for whose dances and entertainments African Americans like Joplin's father had played, expected to hear familiar waltzes, schottisches, polkas, quadrilles, and reels.[49] These, too, became part of the musical inheritance of the future composer.

Growing up in Cass and Bowie Counties in Texas, Scott Joplin learned to make his way in a world in transition from an agricultural society dependent upon the peculiar institution of slavery to the increasingly industrialized New South. His was a world in which some whites perverted the American political process, terrorized African Americans, and recognized their economic advantage in an effort to conserve an older way of life and in which others, more resigned to postwar conditions, offered employment to their African American neighbors. There blacks and whites together created a society that relied on agricultural production, cooperation, and interaction, and that was limited by relative isolation and consequent ignorance. In this world created out of the tatters of disunion, African American children learned the nature of their circumstances in a biracial society and dreamed of the possibility of greater freedom and volition. In the 1870s and 1880s, the effects of an industrializing American economy would alter this world even more and set the stage for the making of a new American culture.

## ON THE MOVE: THE JOPLINS IN TEXARKANA

Sometime in the 1870s, Jiles Joplin and his family moved to Texarkana, Texas, where he began working as a common laborer for the Texas & Pacific Railroad. Texarkana owed its existence to the construction of railroads in postwar Texas and Arkansas, and the city, in turn, offered African American families like the Joplins opportunities that fundamentally changed their lives. Since the 1860s, a handful of families had lived in Texarkana, the loose designation for a region in the piney woods where the exact borders dividing Texas, Arkansas, and Louisiana were not certain. As a city, however, Texarkana, Texas, officially came into existence on December 8, 1873, when the Texas & Pacific Railroad held a sale of lots at its eastern terminus in anticipation of its junction with the Cairo & Fulton Railroad in Arkansas. In early 1874, the Cairo & Fulton began selling lots on the Arkansas side of the state line, and within a year, the Arkansas legislature established Miller County in its extreme southwestern corner and named Texarkana, Arkansas, its seat.[50]

Jiles Joplin's new job brought many changes to his family. They left the countryside and farming to take up residence in a rapidly expanding city. As an employee of the railroad, Jiles made a good living for his family, which by 1880 included eight members. According to James Tucker of Harrison County, African Americans who worked for the railroads in northeastern Texas, made somewhere between $1.00 and $1.25 per day, the same wages paid to their white counterparts.[51] At this wage, supplemented by Monroe's earnings as a porter in a store and Florence's housekeeping income, the Joplins may have been earning about twice as much as they had on the farm.[52]

In addition to material improvement, the whole family gained greater access to a world beyond the horizons of northeastern Texas. By 1880, Texarkana boasted three newspapers—the *News,* the *Visitor,* and the *Index*—all of which included items of local interest as well as stories from other communities in Texas and the nation.[53] As early as March 1874, the Texas & Pacific and the Cairo & Fulton railroads had made contact, connecting Texarkana to St. Louis, Missouri. Within a few years, Texarkana was on the Cotton Belt line as well as a part of the Kansas City Southern system. The coming and going of trains gave Texarkanans—both black and white—a sense of movement and opportunity and brought them in contact with people, goods, ideas, and sounds from all parts of the country.[54]

Moving to Texarkana also meant some formal schooling for the Joplin children. Though the decentralization of the public school system in Texas in 1875 made it possible for remote communities like Texarkana to neglect public education of both black and white children, apparently some independent efforts resulted in schooling for the children of freedmen as well as the children of white citizens. Private schools and tutoring sometimes took the place of state-run schools. As late as 1884, the *Daily Texarkana Independent* carried advertisements for various private schools for white children, such as G. A. Hays's Texarkana Graded and Normal School, Texarkana High School, run by T. J. Patillo, and College Hill High School, under the direction of W. H. Butch.[55] At the same time, news reports indicate avid interest in the black community for free public schools for their children. In September 1884 a public meeting attracted the "leading colored representatives," who decided to use money allotted for a black public school to purchase a lot for a building to be constructed in the future. "Until the lot and building are paid for the colored people will not have any free school, but will employ a teacher by private subscription," the *Daily Texarkana Independent* reported. "This same course was taken by the white people two years ago, and the result is an elegant two-story school building, the property of the free schools of Texarkana."[56] They also began accepting applications for the principalship of the colored free school on the Arkansas side of the city. Moreover, a "Normal College for the colored people" in Pine Bluff, Arkansas, reportedly could boast an enrollment of 203 pupils in 1883, a fact used to attract new students the following year.[57]

According to the 1880 census, Scott and Robert Joplin were "going to school," and their sister Jose occasionally attended school. All three, their oldest brother, Monroe, and their father had learned to read, and Jose and Jiles both could write. Moreover, their neighborhood in Texarkana was occupied mostly by other African American working people—a railroad car porter, a brick-yard worker, a gardener—who were roughly the same age as Florence and Jiles and who were literate. Although officially few educational opportunities existed for the children of freedmen, the progress of these families provides evidence that African Americans made some kind of informal provision for instruction.[58]

Like her husband, Florence Joplin had changed her occupation upon reaching the city of Texarkana. In order to supplement her husband's income, Florence hired out as a domestic servant to white families in Texarkana, work which eventually redounded to the educational and musical benefit of her second son. From the Joplin home at the 600 block of Hazel Street, Florence Joplin walked but a short distance to reach the corner of Sixth and Laurel Streets, where she worked for W. G. Cook and his family. As an attorney, Cook was sufficiently wealthy to hire domestic help for his wife and to afford a piano. According to descendants of the Cook family, when Scott accompanied his mother to her work, he was given free use of the piano, an instrument on which he displayed amazing natural ability. In a short time he became known as something of a prodigy.

Word of Joplin's talent for piano playing spread through the community of Texarkana, which by 1880 numbered fewer than four thousand citizens on both sides of the state line. At about the age of eleven, Joplin had attracted the attention of a German music teacher, who gave him free lessons in sight-reading, harmony, and classical composition. Joplin never recorded the name of this teacher, and as a result, scholars can only speculate on his identity. Of the various theories put forward, Theodore Albrecht's identification of Julius Weiss seems the most thoroughly researched and plausible. If correct, Albrecht's thesis helps explain a great deal about Joplin's development.[59]

Julius Weiss, the only German music teacher in Texarkana in

1880, had been born in Saxony in the early 1840s and was reputed to have received a university education in music, which he probably completed sometime in the 1860s. He may well have left his homeland between 1866 and 1870 in order to avoid military duty in the wars for German unification. He came to Texarkana in the 1870s at the behest of Robert Woodring Rodgers, a local businessman and champion of public education, in order to tutor Rodgers's children. According to Rodgers family lore, Weiss taught all the boys to play the violin; all the girls took piano lessons from him; and he instructed at least one of the Rodgers children in German, astronomy, and mathematics. He left Texarkana sometime in 1884 after Rodgers's death, when Rodgers's widow no longer could afford to keep a private tutor.

Joplin's contact with a man like Weiss would have had important consequences for an African American in northeastern Texas. The educated German could open the door to a world of learning and music of which young Joplin was largely unaware. He undoubtedly introduced Joplin to the elements of opera and to works by classical composers. As an immigrant from a distant land, Weiss offered an example of the possibilities of travel and daring—of opportunities that lay beyond the hinterland of Texarkana. As a tenant and employee in the Rodgers household, he may have brought Joplin in contact with two of Texarkana's leading advocates of public schooling—Robert W. and Frances J. Rodgers—from whom Joplin may have absorbed an appreciation for the liberating potential of education.[60] Rodgers's efforts between 1874 and 1878 to provide private schools in the absence of state-run schools attracted attention, and in September 1878, he was appointed "Trustee of Texarkana, No. 1 School, Community No. 14" in anticipation of the coming school system. If Joplin's lessons took place in the Rodgers's parlor, as did the lessons of Weiss's other students, then the young African American may have known firsthand something of the Rodgers's commitment to education.

Scott's piano playing and education with his German music teacher apparently became a source of controversy within the Joplin family. On the one hand, the boy's talent attracted considerable attention and some opportunities to play music for pay, which must have been a source of pride for his parents. Indeed, according to Joplin family members, Jiles scraped together enough money to purchase an old square piano for his son, even though he eventually opposed Scott's singleminded devotion to music.[61] On the other hand, Jiles's opposition probably stemmed from the fact that Joplin's concentration on music took him away from some kind of practical employment, which would have supplemented the family's income in a more substantial way. Florence's encouragement of her son's musical ambitions angered her husband, and, as Joplin entered his teens, became the source of serious division within the family.[62]

In spite of the tensions at home, Joplin immersed himself in the musical life of the community. He played music at church gatherings and for secular entertainments. It is likely that he played waltzes, polkas, and schottisches for African American dances, but he was known for the originality of his music. One black Texarkanan who heard him play insisted that "Scott worked on his music all the time. He was a musical genius. He didn't need a piece of music to go by. He played his own music without anything." Another contemporary, Zenobia Campbell, remembered, "He did not have to play anybody else's music. He made up his own, and it was beautiful; he just got his music out of the air."[63]

The air in Joplin's Texarkana was rich with sounds—work songs, gospel hymns and spirituals, dance music, and the classical compositions to which his German music teacher introduced him. A young man like Joplin with an ear for music, natural ability on the piano, and a will to create original music may well have experimented with the various sounds to produce music that was at once familiar and danceable as well as novel and unique. Joplin may well have been in the process of inventing the kind of ragtime that became celebrated in the 1890s as a blend of African American and European forms and melodies. One of his contemporaries, Alexander Ford, believed that Joplin had been playing some of the strains of *Maple Leaf Rag* in Texarkana many years before he formally wrote it down.[64]

Joplin's years in Texarkana began the process of education and interaction with whites and blacks that enabled him to create a new and compelling form of music at the end of the century. Though the opportunities available in the city could open the mind of an African American boy from rural northeastern Texas to a way of life liberated from superstition, ignorance, primitive living conditions, and base poverty, they could not erase the fact of Joplin's race in a viciously prejudiced society. Even in a bustling commercial center like Texarkana, incidents of racial violence occasionally cropped up. In 1875, for example, the wife of an African American minister named Duncan sustained multiple injuries when someone with a shotgun opened fire on her for reasons unknown. A few months later, the *Texarkana Democrat* gleefully reported that "the boys had fine sport last Saturday, shooting at a negro, who had escaped from the sheriff of Bowie, and who was trying to get over the [state] line."[65] When Joplin was eleven, the aborted lynching of a black man accused of raping a white woman resulted in armed battle between blacks and whites—a battle that prompted the *Texarkana Visitor* to exclaim that "preparation for war could be seen on all hands."[66]

Living in the hub of the Red River valley cotton-growing country, the young musician undoubtedly knew the horrors of the recent past, the debt peonage of many people of color, and the fine line that separated deference and respectfulness toward whites from subjugation, self-deprecation, and oppression. He may have wanted more from life than he had seen in the African American community, but he could not ignore the barriers that separated the races in post-Reconstruction Texas.

Reconstruction had spawned both the opportunities and the limitations Joplin knew in Texarkana. And those opportunities and limitations continued to coexist in the 1880s as railroads extended the chance to move and deepened the dependence on cotton and landlords for many African Americans in that region. Both railroads and racial interaction in the Gilded Age contributed to the making of music and culture in the United States.

## RAILROADS AND THE AFRICAN AMERICAN EXPERIENCE

No one is certain precisely when Scott Joplin left Texarkana. Some longtime Texarkana residents claimed to remember him enrolled in high school in the late 1880s, while other sources remember him leaving the community when he was in his early teens— perhaps as early as 1882.[67] Even less certain than when he left was his destination. Until he resurfaced in the 1890s in Missouri, Joplin's whereabouts are unknown and difficult to verify. All that is known is that for a time—perhaps as many as ten or as few as five years—Joplin made his way around the southern heartland as an itinerant musician. He was part of a people on the move—no longer as civilians dislocated by war but as people in search of opportunities in a changing society.

Though not certain, it is likely that Joplin made his way by rail. The major lines that connected Texarkana to other parts of the South and Midwest had been completed by the 1880s, and they beckoned to opportunities beyond northeastern Texas. By the mid-1880s, Texarkanans could take the Cairo & Fulton to Memphis or St. Louis, the Texas & Pacific to Dallas, and the Texas & St. Louis to Mt. Pleasant, Texas, and St. Louis. And on any of these lines, an itinerant musician could stop in one of the myriad small towns to play in saloons or clubs and to take a break from the road.

The railroad played an important role in African American culture generally and in Joplin's music more particularly. First, the railroad offered the chance to move, and mobility underscored the reality of freedom. Virtually all accounts of slavery noted the presence of "pattyrollers," whose job consisted of restricting the unauthorized movement of slaves, and, as noted above, one major feature of Reconstruction Texas was the active presence of the Ku Klux Klan, gunslingers, and plantation owners, who combined to keep the freedmen in place. In spite of these restrictions, however, African Americans traveled away from the South and the past, and eventually they did so by taking trains. When William C. Handy, the Father of the Blues, struck out from his home in Alabama on a quest to become a famous musician, for example, he did so by riding in boxcars. African American musicians and entertainers in northeastern Texas organized short excursions on local rail lines and kept their passengers amused and diverted along the way. Likewise, traveling shows, like the Haverly Minstrels, Duprez and Benedict's Gigantic Famous Minstrels, the Cooper, Bailey & Co. Circus, and the Sells Brothers' Circus, all toured by rail.[68]

In addition to geographical mobility, railroads and trains offered social mobility as well. Although at times a mixed blessing, working for the railroad represented a step up from the uncertainty and isolated drudgery of farm labor. Harrison Boyd of Harrison County, for instance, gave up farm work, at which he earned ten to twelve dollars a month to work as a laborer for the Texas & Pacific Railroad between Marshall and Longview, Texas. His daily wages of a dollar and a half were supplemented by three drinks of whiskey every day. He believed that this new pay elevated his material position.[69] At the same time, working for the railroad did not free African Americans from discrimination. Harrison Boyd and Jiles Joplin may well have been among the petitioners from Bowie and Harrison Counties who protested to Governor Hubbard against the practice of using convict labor instead of free workers.[70] Some African American railroad workers lost their jobs as a result. But their petitions demonstrate the desirability of working for the railroad. When the elder Joplin urged his second son to give up his musical pursuits for something more lucrative and responsible, he suggested railroad work.

Thus, socially, railroads altered the existence of African Americans by bringing them in contact with people and places outside of the land of their birth. They represented an important part of the transition from a rural, agricultural past to an urban, industrial future. Moreover, railroads effected a more fully biracial and multiethnic nation by the early twentieth century, because with more massive movement northward, African Americans no longer were confined to southern states. Such movement and mixing, combined with the large influx of "new" immigrants, was critical for the debate over American culture that began to rage at the turn of the century.

Beyond these social ramifications, some scholars have noted more immediate cultural connections between the railroad and African American music. Railroads served as subjects for African American songs. Indeed, one of Joplin's earliest written compositions was *The Great Crush Collision,* which he dedicated to the Missouri, Kansas & Texas Railway. More significantly, however, some believe that the steady rhythm of trains and industrial work became embedded in African American musical forms such as ragtime and later jazz and stride piano. These post–folk musical forms rely on a steady rhythm played in the bass part by the left hand as a foundation for the rhythmically complex counterpoint of the treble played by the right hand. As Luther G. Williams writes of these separate but intertwined rhythms,

The left hand defined the beat and the harmonies. The regularity of its figures resonated in factory work, the assembly line, the printing press, domestic labor, dancing, and sexual intercourse. The right hand played the melody and fill-ins. Flexible and discursive, its cross-rhythmic figures seemed to comment plaintively on the activities represented by the left hand. In other words, the left hand depicted living conditions, while the right hand gave emotional reactions to them.[71]

And most importantly, the uniqueness of this kind of music derives from the presence of *both* steady and whimsical—standardized and individualized—components. Though African American in origin, it is a melding of various elements.

As an itinerant musician, Joplin became one of a growing number of traveling African American entertainers. Sometimes performing in cafes or saloons, sometimes in churches or on local stages, African American musicians of this variety brought color and novelty to the relatively isolated communities of the late nineteenth century. They experienced perhaps as fully as any group within the black community the ambiguity of being African American in the United States. As musicians they found themselves in great demand, but as members of the society, they faced barriers to full and equal participation.

African American minstrels, for example, helped perpetuate a form of entertainment that had become popular before the Civil War. A number of black troupes toured the country following the war, and they gave African American performers the opportunity to travel about the country and to add their own flourishes to a kind of show usually controlled by whites. Some African American performers such as Billy Kersands, Sam Lucas, James Bland, and James Bohee achieved fame as traveling entertainers in the United States and Europe. In 1882, Gustave and Charles Frohman organized Callender's Consolidated Spectacular Colored Minstrels, the largest Negro company to that time, and a year later Primrose and West Minstrels featured Billy Windom, a black tenor who wrote and performed his own songs. By the 1890s, three black minstrel troupes—Hicks & Sawyer Minstrels, Richards & Pringle Minstrels, and McCabe & Young Minstrels—were performing in the United States. Their shows, which included humor, dancing, and parody playlets, always featured some kind of African American music.[72]

Reviewers raved about the African American minstrel shows.

Commentators believed they drew larger audiences than white groups. P. T. Barnum, perhaps the greatest showman of the nineteenth century, called the Georgia Minstrels "extraordinary, and the best I ever saw." Even in stuffy Boston, they scored "a decided hit" and "were received with great enthusiasm."[73] Nevertheless, no matter how much white audiences enjoyed the humor, singing, and dancing, they would not grant the performers their due. The shows included well-trained musicians in large part because they could find no employment in better establishments or within the world of serious music. In small towns, especially in the South, the black showmen sometimes found themselves sleeping in railroad stations or on the hard floors of the stage on which they performed because whites were unwilling, and blacks were unable, to provide better accommodations. While the citizens of these towns might turn out to see the minstrels parade down the main street on the morning of their scheduled performance and pay to see the show in the evening, they had no desire to host unsupervised African Americans after dark.

Itinerant musicians not attached to minstrel shows fared no better. They could occasionally take advantage of opportunities to perform for whites on steamships or on trains to supplement their work as waiters, cooks, or laborers or to pay their passage. Traveling singing groups might make their way for a time in this manner. But the momentary delight of the white audiences did not translate into either social acceptance or equality. In the end, they were still treated as inferior citizens of the nation.

Particular and fortuitous circumstances in Joplin's life opened his mind and senses to new experiences and impelled him away from northeastern Texas. But even these experiences could not erase one of the fundamental realities of Reconstruction America: emancipation and constitutional amendments did not override white expectations of subordination, deference, dependence, and docility. As Joplin's generation would learn in the last two decades of the nineteenth century, freedom of movement, artistic expression, and economic opportunities could all be cut short by lynch mobs, discriminatory booking practices, and Jim Crow laws.

And yet in the midst of these stifling truths, African Americans began to produce a kind of music that all Americans—black and white—found hard to resist. Unmistakably African American, it nevertheless incorporated the rhythms and influences of an

industrializing economy dominated by white Anglo-Saxon Protestant values. Their music bore the marks of a rural, agrarian,
slaveholding past and the faster tempo of urban and industrial
life. In the years immediately following Reconstruction, the seeds
of modern American popular music began to germinate; they
already held the essence of the culture that would blossom at the
end of the century.

# CHAPTER 2

# 1893

## THE COLUMBIAN EXPOSITION, ECONOMIC DEPRESSION, AND THE EMBRACE OF RAGTIME

The White City must have been breathtaking to the twenty-four-year-old African American musician who arrived in Chicago sometime in the summer of 1893. The majestic buildings that had been built in Jackson Park to house the exhibits of the Columbian Exposition stood in marked contrast to the humble structures in the Mississippi valley towns where he had found employment for the past several years. Like many other visitors, Scott Joplin must have been dazzled by the bright electric lights, the towering ferris wheel, and the disparate peoples, tongues, and cultures that greeted him on the Midway Plaisance. Perhaps he wandered into the Missouri Building on his tour of the impressive array of buildings constructed to show off the arts, products, and virtues of the individual states. There Joplin likely would have found the Sedalia room, simple but elegant, furnished with carpets, draperies, a piano, and a chair—an inviting scene for a professional musician.[1]

Scott Joplin may or may not have been a part of the Chicago World's Fair. No independent evidence confirms personal anecdotes that place him at the exposition. If he performed in some establishments in Chicago's sporting district, no advertisements hawking his talents have surfaced. If he played the piano at one of the cafes along the Midway Plaisance, no one remembered him by name, even though other African American entertainers escaped anonymity. He wrote no letters or cards that have survived, and

The Missouri Building at the World's Columbian Exposition in Chicago, 1893

he only obliquely referred to 1893 as an important year for the embrace of ragtime by white Americans—and that reference appeared two decades after the fact.

In spite of this dearth of corroborating evidence, however, biographers have insisted that Joplin was in Chicago for at least part of 1893. They speculate that there the African American itinerant musician met Otis Saunders, who became a lifelong friend. Moreover, it is believed that Joplin formed his first band in Chicago. The exposure to other African American piano thumpers, they argue, nourished Joplin's own developing style, and the contacts he made provided direction for the maturing musician's life. For these reasons, biographies of Joplin have included some discussion of the World's Columbian Exposition as a formative experience in the musician's life.[2]

It is undoubtedly fair to assume that Scott Joplin experienced the World's Fair and was profoundly influenced by it. In addition to the personal impact of the exposition on Joplin, however, there are other reasons for a biographer to pause on this extraordinary year of 1893. In 1893 Americans witnessed two dramatic events that shaped the contours of American culture in the coming decades. The Columbian Exposition, held in Chicago and organized to celebrate four hundred years of progress in the New World, proclaimed American achievements in the arts and sciences and provided a forum for American popular entertainment. But before anyone had a chance to celebrate the grandeur of the cultural spectacle in Chicago, the stock market failed and plunged the nation into one of the worst economic depressions of the nineteenth century. The Columbian Exposition, described by one observer as "the coming of age of American industry," represented the triumph of capitalist ingenuity and American culture; the depression demonstrated how fragile that triumph could be.[3]

Both the World's Fair and the economic downturn wrought important changes in America's cultural life and created the conditions in which Americans embraced ragtime music. The fair, with its varied exhibits from around the country and the world presented a wide range of artistic and cultural expressions that could be studied, categorized, or even emulated. These options took on added significance in the wake of the depression as the economic disaster called into question prevailing cultural assumptions in the United States. For example, widespread failures—by even the most stalwart of Victorian businessmen—and climbing unemployment rates among workers desperate to labor challenged the validity of Americans' belief that hard work and self-control resulted in success and security. Economic frustration and cultural uncertainty fed off one another, with the result that Americans looked about for new ways of defining themselves and their way of life. As a kind of music that grew in popularity in the years following 1893, ragtime must be examined within the context of these two events and as an example of the changing components of American culture and identity.

Ragtime music was not a part of the official program of the Columbian Exposition. Despite many ragtime musicians' status as anonymous entertainers on the raucous Midway Plaisance or in the city's tenderloin district, Americans were captivated by the strains of this syncopated music and thronged Jackson Park in 1893. As Scott Joplin put it in 1913, "There has been ragtime music in America ever since the Negro race has been here, but the white people took no notice of it until about twenty years ago."[4] Ragtime music—or "jig piano," as it may have been known familiarly—was one of the exotic sounds Americans remembered as part of their experience at the Fair, and at that point it was associated almost exclusively with African American performers. Joplin's comment indicates that he and other African American itinerant musicians had been improvising what would eventually be called ragtime long before 1893, but it was the penetration of white consciousness at the Columbian Exposition that sent ragtime on its way toward the mainstream of American popular music.[5]

The incorporation of an essentially African American music into the realm of popular music epitomizes a crucial part of the cultural reorientation of the 1890s—a quest for authenticity that led many middle-class whites to search for an American folk tradition.[6] More than one commentator believed that only African American slaves and native American Indians resembled European peasants as a source of folk culture and music. Plantation songs and Indian chants thus served as inspiration for American composers hoping to lay claim to a uniquely American music and may help account for the attraction of white Americans to black ragtime music.[7] Ironically, white middle-class Americans looked to the songs of two despised social groups for a glimpse of "authentic" American expression as a way of defining themselves as a people and a nation.

This selection had important consequences for African Americans like Scott Joplin. It created, on one hand, many new opportunities to play his music in places other than honky tonks or bordellos. As emblems of the American folk, Joplin and his music offered middle-class Americans a chance to participate in—perhaps to imitate—that authentic, revitalizing musical experience. But in another way, the quest for a folk tradition, one that was not a "natural" part of most Americans' lives, reinforced the position of those who had inherited, perpetuated, and embroidered on it as outsiders. Thus, as vital links between an authentic past and a cultural identity in the making, Joplin and other ragtime musicians found themselves, curiously, welcomed and kept at a distance, embraced and rejected.

## A BLACK MUSICIAN IN THE WHITE CITY

Scott Joplin's name appeared on none of the official musical programs of the World's Fair. Indeed, he, like many itinerant musicians of the day, had come in search of steady work in the sporting district of the city, where saloons, cafes, gambling houses, and brothels did a brisk business with out-of-towners looking for more than intellectual stimulation at the fair. But in spite of their position on the periphery of the fair, Joplin and his ragtime cohort introduced millions of Americans to a kind of music that they soon clamored to hear. Before the fair was over, ragtime cast a long shadow over the official musical program of the White City.

Like the designation "white city" for the cluster of snowy structures grandly arranged in Jackson Park, the musical program of the fair inscribed particular cultural, racial, and class assumptions as its creators hoped to enlighten and uplift the multitude. Theodore Thomas, the celebrated conductor of the Chicago Symphony Orchestra, served as the coordinator of music at the exposition and envisioned an impressive schedule of concerts by orchestras, choral societies, and soloists performing the works of the European masters. The bulletin of exposition concerts submitted before opening day to such popular music magazines as *The Etude,* for example, included performances by the Boston Symphony Orchestra, the St. Paul–Minneapolis Choral Association, and the New York Liederkranz Society and a program featuring works by Bach, Handel, Mendelssohn, Brahms, Rubinstein, and Wagner. Overwhelmingly classical in its orientation, the program was to be punctuated by "daily popular orchestral concerts" performed by noted military bands of which John Phillip Sousa's was the most prominent. The decision, weighted heavily in favor of European, classical music, asserted a standard that excluded work by American composers generally and African American composers altogether.[8] As music that appealed to the cultivated and patrons of classical music—by and large white Anglo-Saxon Americans—it was, perhaps, the ideal musical accompaniment for a "white city."

Unexpectedly, however, the crowds of Americans that sacrificed a great deal to make the pilgrimage to Chicago to see the great World's Fair were not particularly interested in hearing "serious" music or in being "uplifted" by the strains of music written by white, European composers. A visitor from Missouri, writing in late May to the readers of his hometown newspaper, put it succinctly: "Classic music is not popular in the west." Fairgoers, he insisted, were doing their best "to oust Theodore Thomas and a sheriff in Kansas is after Damrosch."[9] In July, *The Etude* acknowledged that musicians at the exposition were "the leaders in musical life" and that their performances were "of the highest order," but it reported that ticket sales for the concerts were abysmal. The New York Symphony Orchestra, the writer complained, "played to only about 50 people, and vacant seats are the rule."[10] Just a few weeks earlier an editorialist in the *Chicago Tribune* insisted that the "people should . . . be given more music. The regular concerts, excellent as they are only appeal to musicians and connoisseurs, and to this extent they answer their purpose admirably, but the people want more outdoor music." The author contrasted the failure of the official musical programs with the howling success of the midway, where people were drawn to "the gay colors, fascinating sights, and music of every description from the Dahomey tom-toms to the German garden bands."[11] By late summer, following Thomas's resignation as music director, the music program fell into disarray. Indeed, in the middle of August, the exposition orchestra was divided into two parts and ordered to give popular concerts. "To judge by the conduct of the men," noted one observer, "they felt it to be an imposition to be asked to furnish popular music for the vulgar crowds."[12]

However disappointed the exposition musicians may have been, midway performers, like Joplin, were eager to provide popular music, and visitors could not seem to get enough. Whether provided by the military bands engaged by fair organizers or by entertainers on the midway, popular music and rhythms pervaded the grounds of the exposition. Moreover, beyond the official confines of the fair, music could be heard in the sporting district of the city at all hours. Early in May, police had tried to shut down businesses that served as fronts for illegal games of chance, and they closed saloons, arrested prostitutes, and silenced brass bands and mandolin orchestras. But it was not long before business was thriving again, and the police could do little to staunch the flow of humanity into the entertainment district.[13]

Popular music and diversion created a climate that appeared to encourage the mingling of people from diverse backgrounds. At the fair, "the clicking turnstiles" that registered "over a hundred thousand visitors every day" certainly increased the odds that a varied assortment of people would come together inside Jackson Park.[14] Visitors like Grace Mathews from Sedalia, Missouri, came away from the fair with an impression of great diversity. As she reported in a letter to the *Sedalia Bazoo*—a letter significantly titled "The White City"—the midway "looked like Bedlam," where the "customs of all nations [were] illustrated."[15] Had observers like Mathews been inclined to so comment, however, they might have noticed that little in the American exhibits and few of the faces in the crowd reflected the African American presence in the New World. It was a white city in more ways than one.

The fair, as a cultural event, inscribed the superiority of "white" over "black." The white buildings, as temples of cultural and scientific achievement, contrasted sharply with the dark, rude huts of the people of color on the midway. Moreover, the midway itself was arranged in such a way that the white—more "advanced"—people were closest to Jackson Park, while the dark—more "primitive"—were furthest away. The physical arrangement reinforced a sense of hierarchy—those closest to culture were white; those furthest away were shades of black. Finally, without a special exhibit devoted to African Americans, citizens of the Dahomey village served as the chief representatives of the race at the fair, and that implied an association between black skin and lack of development.[16]

During the fair and after its closing, Frederick Douglass gave voice to the contradictions African Americans had observed in the White City. As a commissioner from Haiti, Douglass witnessed the inauguration ceremonies of the exposition, but as he later wrote, "There was one thing that dimmed their glory. . . . Although there are eight millions of men of African descent in this country, not one of them seems to have been worthy of a place on the platform of these inaugural ceremonies."[17] None of the exhibits had been reserved to feature the cultural and social contributions of African Americans to the upbuilding of the New World, and none of the individual exhibitors had seen fit to incorporate African American arts. Furthermore, none of the commissioners, committee members, guides, or guards were African Americans. Later in the year, Douglass and Ida B. Wells began promoting a booklet, *The Reason Why the Colored American Is Not in the World's Columbian Exposition,* to expose the concerted efforts to deny African Americans any role at the fair. They intended to distribute it to foreign visitors to explain the absence of their people from the exposition.[18]

A year later, Douglass penned a second pamphlet entitled *Why*

*Is the Negro Lynched?* in which he posited a relationship between the neglect of African Americans at the fair and social injustice in day-to-day relations between the races. He argued that the neglect of African American intellectuals and the representation of the race by primitive Africans sent an insulting message as to the intellectual and cultural potential of African Americans—a message that seemed to justify persecution of a "savage" race. "What a commentary is this upon the liberality of our boasted American liberty and American equality!" he concluded. "It says to the lynchers and mobocrats of the South, go on in your hellish work of Negro persecution. You kill their bodies, we kill their souls."[19] Moreover, the connection between African Americans and African tribesmen was not lost on white writers. It became the focus of offensive humor in a series of cartoons in *Harper's Weekly* in which a fictitious African American family at the fair is explicitly compared to foreign people of color. One cartoon, for example, featured Mr. Johnson stopping to shake hands with one of the men in the Dahomeyan village while his wife hollers, "Ezwell Johnson, stop shakin' Han's wid dat Heathen! You want de hull Fair ter t'ink you's found a Poo' Relation!"[20]

If viewed from the perspective of a venerable leader like Frederick Douglass, the World's Columbian Exposition was indeed troubling for African Americans. Even the day set aside for African Americans at the fair provided additional fodder for degrading cartoons and commentary. The *World's Fair Puck,* for example, contained "Darkies' Day at the Fair," a cartoon and verse that lumped "Congo's Sable Kings" with "their Yankee friends" in a visual and verbal parade of insulting stereotypes. The caricatures featured thick, broad smiles, sloping foreheads, spears, musical instruments, and a "family" resemblance among all the people of color regardless of their nationality. The "Grand Parade of the United Sons of Ham" was led by the remnants of a black brass band, and the destination was a table, where all could receive a slice of "Ice Cold Water Million." Some African American leaders had urged their community to stay away, and with the exception of about one thousand fairgoers, it did.[21]

Considering the perspective of a musician like Scott Joplin, however, complicates the matter considerably. Joplin was too perceptive to have missed the discrimination against his people noted by Douglass, Wells, and other prominent African American

"THE JOHNSON FAMILY VISIT THE DAHOMAN VILLAGE
MRS. JOHNSON: 'Ezwell Johnson, stop shakin' Han's wid dat
Heathen! You want de hull Fair ter t'ink you's found a Poo'
Relation?'" from *Harper's Weekly,* August 19, 1893

leaders, but he himself realized significant triumphs at the fair.
His music reached and apparently touched a class of people who,
under other circumstances, either would not have had occasion
to hear it or would have deliberately avoided it. At the fair, Joplin
met musicians from around the country and the world from whom
he could absorb ideas about rhythm, melody, and performance
techniques. And as an African American from a southern state,
he could discover social expectations and race relations different
from those he had experienced in northeastern Texas and the small
towns in the Mississippi River valley. Illinois had passed an antidiscrimination law in 1885 to compensate for the U.S. Supreme
Court's striking down of Reconstruction-era civil rights legislation
two years earlier. On the basis of the Illinois law, several cases
against Chicago businesses had come forward by 1893. Joplin may
have observed a relatively affluent African American community
in the southern part of the city and noticed African American

members of the police force and the local chapter of the Knights of Labor.[22] By contrast, states throughout the South had begun passing new legislation designed to segregate the races, and incidents of violence against African Americans in the South rose dramatically.[23] Given his past, the fair may well have given Joplin hope for better things to come.

For Joplin, the World's Fair may have offered employment, but probably more importantly it gave him the chance to hear some of the best popular African American musicians in Chicago in the 1890s. There he reportedly heard "Plunk" Henry Johnson and Johnny Seymour, whose style of playing entranced the handsome young itinerant musician as well as the audiences that thronged to hear them. In addition to hearing great African American musicians, Joplin also made some lasting friendships. For example, it

Cartoon from *World's Fair Puck* commenting on the day devoted to African Americans at the World's Columbian Exposition, photo courtesy the Library of Congress

is believed that in Chicago Joplin met and became friends with Otis Saunders. It was Saunders, a Missourian, who eventually took Joplin to Sedalia and encouraged him to learn more about formal composition. One can imagine that the two aspiring African American musicians, both from former slave states, marveled at the sights and sounds of Chicago and the White City and at the popularity of their music.

Inspired, perhaps, by the creative atmosphere of 1893 and by the demand for popular music, Joplin formed his first band in Chicago. It probably included a cornet, a clarinet, a tuba, and a baritone horn. Moreover, he began developing his skills at notation, writing arrangements of popular pieces for his band. By the time of the closing of the exposition, Joplin must have been full of ideas for arranging and performing music that Americans wanted to hear.[24] He may have taken heart at the success of other black entertainers in the city. For example, *Creole Show,* which had an all-black cast, stayed the whole season in Chicago during the fair and experimented successfully with introducing African American numbers and dispensing with burnt cork.[25] And after the fair, Joplin and Saunders spent two years traveling around the Midwest performing their own compositions. According to one biographer, by 1895, the two musicians "were convinced that Scott Joplin had a new music that the public wanted."[26]

Joplin's experience forces us to modify Frederick Douglass's analysis somewhat, for social exclusion and discrimination occurred within a context of profound cultural reorientation that allowed some room for African American participation. While Americans in Chicago—and later in their own hometowns—looked askance at the genteel music that dominated the official music programs of the exposition, they lacked a ready-made cultural alternative to it. They eventually endorsed popular entertainment, of which African American ragtime was a significant type, and they thereby created additional opportunities for African American participation in the cultural life of the United States.

The way middle-class Americans articulated their experience of this emerging popular culture and music, however, would suggest a certain ambivalence about their choice. They discussed popular entertainment in terms of the exotic, the unfamiliar, and the daring—characteristics that both attracted and repulsed them. In 1893, and in the years that followed, Americans defined the parameters of an acceptable popular music, the terms of which opened up great opportunities for black musicians and at the same time maintained unflattering stereotypes of African Americans. The experience of black Americans in the White City portended the ambiguous position of African Americans in American life in the next couple of decades.

## ON THE FRONTIER OF MODERN CULTURE

The American Historical Association, in its infancy in 1893, held its annual meeting in Chicago while the World's Columbian Exposition was open. The fair offered American historians the perfect opportunity to reflect on the development of national institutions in the centuries since Columbus's arrival in the New

World. Among the papers read at the meeting, Frederick Jackson Turner's made the most lasting impression. Turner commented on the recent census, which had revealed that the United States no longer had an unbroken line of frontier. A nation that had relied on the existence of a frontier region as a "safety-valve" against social turmoil and as a font of democracy, he argued, found itself facing the dawn of a new century without such an outlet. And given the dramatic rate of urban and industrial development in the nation, the disappearance of the frontier promised to wreak havoc on democratic society and institutions.[27]

Turner's comments, which became his trademark thesis on the frontier, came at a time when Americans believed they had reason to fear for the future of their democracy and culture. Ironically, in the midst of celebrating four centuries of achievement in the New World, American historians paused to consider an uncertain future. And they were not alone. Visitors to the fair pondered the meaning of their encounters with the strange language and customs of people joining in the American experiment; a few social critics worried that the fair itself threatened to undermine American morality; and the whole nation wondered about the impact of industrial development and economic depression on bedrock American values. Though geographically and demographically the frontier in the United States was disappearing, Americans in 1893 found themselves on a new frontier of culture.

Like the pioneers of an earlier, covered-wagon era, Americans in the 1890s approached the frontier of modern culture—on which the World's Fair must be considered an early outpost—with a sense of entering the unknown, the unfamiliar. More than one fairgoer wrote of the exposition as a place never before experienced. Mary Dobel of Sedalia, Missouri, for example, referred to the fairgrounds as an "illuminated fairyland"—a place literally out of this world. The exposition represented a place she "had never expected to see on this side of the celestial shore."[28] Similarly separating the fair from ordinary experience, Carl Bowen Johnson, a correspondent for *The Independent,* reported that musically and aesthetically, the fair was "unequaled elsewhere."[29] And a correspondent for the *Chicago Tribune* reported in June that "no where else in the wide world is such a pleasure garden as that which offered its attractions to visitors yesterday at the Fair." Like Mary Dobel, he, too, referred to the fairgrounds as a "fairy land."[30]

Perceptions like these, of the extraordinariness of the fair, arose in part from the diverse assemblage of people, sights, sounds, and experiences. Where else could one quaff a German brew, listen to Dahomeyan drum music, enter a Javanese village, and observe the latest innovations in transportation all in one day? But diversity was not the sole reason for the pervasive view that the fair extended the outer limits of expectation and experience. The fair also invited people to reconsider, if not discard, an older moral code. For instance, when the fair's directors decided to experiment with Sunday opening in order to generate even larger revenues, they were perceived as escorting fairgoers dangerously close to the boundary between traditional morality and modern hedonism. Ministers, reformers, and concerned citizens flooded local papers with their fears. The Reverend John L. Withrow of the Third Presbyterian Church was among the first to voice his concerns. "Who wants the gates open?" he asked in late May. "Every saloonkeeper, every brothel-keeper, every thief, every gambler, every drunken pup, every worthless member of society." He and other critics were answered by an equally large and vehement torrent of letters reassuring readers that the "American Sunday [is] not in Danger."[31] Of course, as long as the fair was closed on Sundays, people flocked to the gates of Jackson Park anyway, where they were met by sideshows and fakers, "noisy," "blatant," and "vicious."[32]

From the exposition's inception, the juxtaposition of education and vice created the conditions for moral ambiguity. Two popular historians of Chicago remembered in the late 1920s that "the beauties of this ideal city" were accompanied by "loud carnivals, the band of fakers and 'three-shell' men, the salacious dancers, [and] the hordes of harpies." The fair represented simultaneously "an explosion of idealism" and a "circus" to the people who saw it. "Many a pious midlander secretly hoped," they continued, "that Chicago's night-life would be turned on full blast during the Fair. Then a sober villager could have fun on his trip to the exposition. Salving his conscience by resolute attendance upon the educational exhibits, he could, in the cool of the evening, look in upon the shameful glories of the wicked city."[33]

The local gossip column in the *Sedalia Democrat* confirmed the underside of the experience in Chicago for fairgoers from that Missouri city. A police officer, Frank Shackler, confessed his infatuation "with the movements of one of the muscle-dancing damsels in the Persian theater," and an unnamed married woman reportedly "saw a great deal more of some other things than she did of the World's fair," even though she told her husband otherwise. "A good many Sedalia secrets of a sensational character are temporarily buried in Chicago hotels," the columnist concluded.[34] Thus, even though the official reports and letters from people attending the fair overflowed with descriptions of the wonderful sights to be seen in the White City, small-town Americans like these Sedalians admitted that they did not go to the fair exclusively to see uplifting and edifying cultural and scientific exhibits. They went to be entertained—entertained in ways that were not yet openly permissible in their own backyards.

Of all aspects of the Columbian Exposition, sights on the Midway Plaisance surely excited the most vivid commentary, which illustrated its role in shaking up popular expectations and moral certitude. Contrasting the atmosphere there with the serious displays in the White City, the *Chicago Tribune* reported that the midway "always is more crowded," "is full of life," and attracts attention by the "gay colors, fascinating sights, and music of every description."[35] Nevertheless, the midway's denizens typically were described as "strange," "queer," or "weird." When the exhibitors and residents of the midway staged a parade in the middle of June, it was described by a local journalist as "gorgeous in color, strange in attire, weird in music—a spectacle such as it is not possible to see anywhere else on earth." Similarly, while Grace Mathews, a visitor from Missouri, admired the needlework she saw in the Turkish village, the fine horses "from the Sultan's stable," and beautiful bedsteads made of silver, she still insisted that the Midway Plaisance "looked like Bedlam, turned loose, crowded with sideshows, customs of all nations illustrated."[36] These references all suggest that previous experience had not quite prepared visitors for the sights to be seen and sounds to be heard in the White City. The fair was not like the cultural landscape they had left behind.

When Americans characterized the experience of entering the unfamiliar cultural territory of the fair, they used language that suggested both fascination and unease. They described the opening exercises, for example, in terms that conveyed awe at the size of the amassed crowd and some fear at the potential danger it posed. A reporter for the *Chicago Tribune* called the crowd "a riot of voices as well as a riot of color" that grew "wilder and wilder" as the day passed. Though impressed and heartened by the many people desiring a part in the inauguration of the exposition, the writer nevertheless described them as menacing. From Indian chieftains in a "riotous array of barbaric color" to "daring women" and "brutal men," the crowd exerted a "maddened pressure" as it became a "crowding, crushing, pushing throng."[37] Later in the summer, when the fair was in full swing and people had demonstrated their affinity for the midway, the same combination of attraction and revulsion persisted in commentaries on the exposition. Speaking of the benefits of special shows on the midway—shows that added "zest, piquancy, color and sound to the ordinary quietness of the park"—a Chicago journalist admitted that "the more bizarre and barbarian these spectacles, the better it will be."[38]

What both accounts share are references to various forms of unrestraint—"riots," "wildness," "piquancy"—and to a descent from civilization—"barbarian." That is not to say that the White City failed as an exhibition of official high culture or that it did not elevate the Western tradition above other cultural traditions. But it does suggest that the fairgoers' experience contained more than one layer of meaning. As one perceptive reporter put it, the typical visitor "soon gets tired of looking at exhibits and listening to speeches." Fairgoers wanted "amusement as well."[39] And when seeking amusement, Americans in 1893 seemed to want diversions that stood outside traditional, respectable, American Victorian culture. That desire may help account for the attraction to African American ragtime as well as to a host of other "crazes" that swept the nation in the 1890s.[40]

Joplin's experience as a child in northeastern Texas and as an itinerant in the southern heartland eloquently demonstrates that African Americans lived on the fringes of society. Respectable members of the middle class did not mix familiarly with former slaves and their descendants in Bowie County, Texas, or Miller County, Arkansas, nor did they openly support the sporting houses where Joplin entertained. But on the midway, respectable middle-class audiences could listen to ragtime. The "man of the world," the "staid and elderly of goodly face and benignant mien, the fatherly and motherly couples not often seen away from the home circle on the holy day," who made up the crowds on Sunday as well as during the week, all could respond to the melody and rhythm of ragtime without having to confront the moral question of its popularity in the cultural underworld.[41]

After the fair, composers like Joplin began experimenting with writing ragtime sheet music, thus making the music available to middle-class amateurs as well as professional performers. Moreover, representatives of official culture began to comment on the music in revealing ways. Rupert Hughes, for example, offered a "eulogy of rag-time" in April 1899, which, while supportive of the "originality" of ragtime songs written by "full-blooded negroes," described the music by turns as "an effort to translate to the piano the dance-rhythm, the banjo-accompaniment, and the almost inarticulate ululation of the negro as he expressed himself on the plantation;" "daring and irresistible;" and "dynamic and *bizarre*."[42] The evocation of the plantation is striking coming from a Yankee cultural commentator and most certainly should be understood in the context of the music's "daring" and "bizarre" qualities. Ragtime may have originated in slavery—which record numbers of northern American men had fought a war to abolish—but that did not prevent northerners from enjoying it. Ragtime's roots in slave culture allowed the listener to escape the restrictions of propriety and gentility—to take a walk on the wild side—without leaving the safety of the parlor and without having to mix socially with African Americans.

An essay that appeared in *The Metronome* a month after Hughes's eulogy of ragtime concurred that ragtime was both "of negro origin" and wildly popular. "People in every grade of society," the writer noted, "have caught the fever and are calling for this class of music. During the past winter there have been many entertainments where members of fashionable society—ladies as well as gentlemen—have taken part in cake walks and minstrel shows just simply to get an opportunity to show what they can do to imitate negro singers and dancers."[43] Once again consciousness of the music's origin—among the "negroes"—is coupled with a desire to absorb it into "fashionable society." But most telling is the author's assertion that people who like ragtime have "caught the fever." Metaphorically, ordinary conditions do not prevail. Fans of ragtime, like visitors to the fair that introduced that musical genre to a national audience, had crossed the boundary into a new cultural frontier.

Americans in 1893 and in the next few years that followed,

were drawn by that music to the new frontier of culture and in so doing danced to the music of African Americans. Whether because it was fascinatingly novel or an emblem of the forbidden "other," ragtime offered a chance to break free of the restraints imposed by a Victorian sensibility. Ragtime music countered the genteel imperative for self-control with its irresistible invitation to move to its sensuous rhythm.[44]

One important question remains, however: why did this desire to escape Victorianism find expression in the 1890s? Perhaps the answer lies in the second important event of 1893—the economic depression. For as the year unfolded, many Americans began to find that economic conditions undermined critical cultural assumptions; cultural ideals were not fulfilled by actual experience. That incongruity between expectation and achievement may have forced them to question the most important tenets of their culture and quickened their quest for authenticity.

## HARD TIMES AND AMERICAN CULTURE

While Chicagoans and fairgoers celebrated the splendor of the World's Columbian Exposition, much of the rest of the country kept a watchful and fearful eye on the nation's deteriorating economy. Early in the year, bank failures resulted in panic, business closings, and unemployment throughout the country—from the centers of industry and commerce to small interior towns and cities. The year after the World's Fair, the march of Coxey's Army of unemployed men represented the culmination of several years of hard times for American workingmen and women. As early as 1890, for example, it was nearly impossible for willing workers to find jobs in places like Topeka, Kansas; and two years later in Homestead, Pennsylvania, workers in the steel industry put up armed resistance against Andrew Carnegie's men in their fight for a living wage. Indeed, in the first half of the decade, the "Gay Nineties" were far from happy for working people.[45]

Part of the problem with the economy rested with dramatic technological advances that made possible production of goods at a pace faster than and in quantities larger than businessmen could find markets in which to sell them. In the United States, these conditions were coupled with a rapidly expanding population, swelled from a large influx of immigrants seeking new economic opportunities and asylum from oppression. These workers, poor but willing to work long hours for low wages, contributed to a deepening division within American society between the opulent lives of the "captains of industry" and the miserable poverty of residents in the urban tenement districts. Moreover, this mass of impoverished workers often made too little to purchase many of the goods they helped produce, which exacerbated the disparity between production and consumption in the economy. According to Samuel Gompers, President of the American Federation of Labor, which held its annual meeting in Chicago in 1893, "the great storehouses are glutted with the very articles required by the people, without their ability—or rather their opportunity to obtain—consume—them." He considered this part of the "abnormal conditions" of 1893.[46]

The situation in the American countryside was not much better, as the intensity of the populist movement in the early 1890s eloquently testifies. Frustrated with their dependence on railroads, distant markets, and agricultural processors, with an inflexible monetary system, and with serious inequities in their society, farmers who supported the People's party voiced their desire for political and economic change. Their plaint, like that of many other working people in the early 1890s, contained anger that the laboring classes in an industrializing economy seemed unable to reap just rewards for their hard work.[47]

These economic conditions, which culminated in the onset of depression in 1893, had important cultural consequences, for they belied a long-standing American belief that hard work and self-control produced prosperity. In countless sermons, advice books, novels, didactic works, and popular tracts, writers, speaking an essential cultural "truth," enjoined workers to diligence and industry with the promise of material and spiritual reward. People believed in the progress and social mobility that were implicit in this cultural formula. While actual conditions did not perfectly reflect this ideal, they did lend enough credence to it that—before the Civil War, at least—it was not seriously challenged. Even antebellum workingmen's groups reflected the drive for self-improvement through learning as they made reading and debate societies and political awareness essential parts of their collective vision and action.[48] Victorians, of course, hoped that individual striving in the marketplace would be men's responsibility, even as family and morality would be guarded by women in their "separate sphere" of the home. Their ideals, combined with republican notions of production and virtue, nourished a worldview in which hard work and moderation were supposed to yield comfort and success.[49]

In the 1890s, however, it appeared that this cultural world had been turned upside down. Those who worked long, tiring hours under horrendous conditions could barely make ends meet, and those who lived in luxury did so on profits from capital investment rather than on money earned from the "sweat of their brow." As early as the mid-1880s, social commentators like Washington Gladden began to remark that in spite of hard work, saving, and piety, working people failed to improve their situation. And modern industry, they discovered, was no respecter of working-class families, as children and women in factories and sweatshops clearly showed. When middle-class observers reported on these conditions, their worried tone arose from a sense that social conditions contradicted important cultural values.[50]

Perhaps of greatest concern to middle-class cultural leaders in the 1890s was the fact that their class was not immune to the economic and cultural crisis. As David Thelen showed of middle-class Wisconsinites in the 1890s, many homeowners faced the prospect of losing their property because they could not afford property taxes. Solid citizens participated in "taxpayer revolts" in order to cling to that important symbol of security and respectability—their homes. Moreover, middle-class children in some communities began to recognize that their dream of rising above the condition of their parents would not be realized. Indeed, some were slipping from the ranks of the middle class altogether. An increase in the number of college-educated women who wanted to pursue a career before or instead of settling into a marriage with children also contributed to the perception that Victorian culture was being eroded. Even the rise of nightlife in American cities, which provided an outlet for people with the means to enjoy it, also subtly moved away from an ideal of hearth, home, and family.[51]

It was in this climate of cultural confusion that novelists, artists, and musicians began to explore the world around them in new ways and to contribute images, ideas, and sounds that ran counter to Victorian imperatives. Some novelists, for example, broke with an Arnoldian notion of literature as a purveyor of "sweetness and light" to explore the ordinariness and underside of American life. In 1891, for example, Ambrose Bierce published a collection of grim, ghostly Civil War stories, *Tales of Soldiers and Civilians,* that replaced the glory and honor of battle with a sense of despair and waste in modern total war. Frank Norris's *McTeague,* completed in 1895, though not published until four years later, told of the barely contained bestiality and ultimate violence in a miner-turned-dentist in the American West. The grisly demise of McTeague in the California desert offered a striking counterpoint to celebrations of the democratic and elevating promise of that region. Similarly, Harold Frederic's *Damnation of Theron Ware* (1896) painted an un-flattering picture of small-town America, no longer the stronghold of bedrock American values. The community and the figure of Theron Ware suggested a lost innocence and the dissolution of faith in absolutes.[52]

In addition to challenging vaunted American beliefs, some writers in the 1890s elected to depict American social relations as they found them—depictions that exposed the warts and imperfections of a society in the throes of dramatic transformation. Stephen Crane's *Maggie: A Girl of the Streets* (1893) employs a journalistic style to show how a young woman is beaten down by the forces of the city, her life reduced to a brutal struggle for survival. Maggie's city is populated by fictional figures whose real-life counterparts had been captured in photographs by Jacob Riis in *How the Other Half Lives* (1890). For those who might have sought refuge from urban despair in rural America, Hamlin Garland's stories in *Main-Traveled Roads* (1891) offered little hope. The pinched, isolated lives of his characters convey a bleak view of farming in an age of industrialism. Ten years later, Frank Norris would reinforce that view in his novel, *The Octopus* (1901).

These literary images of poverty, immorality, injustice, and hy-pocrisy now challenged Victorian ideals of comfort, morality, or-der, propriety, and honesty, which had undergirded American culture for much of the nineteenth century. Artists added to the new literary images when they, too, began to choose urban and industrial subjects for their work. In some cityscapes, technology dwarfed men and women. In others, tenement neighborhoods and boxing rings replaced middle-class drawing rooms. Such pictures did not, of course, entirely crowd out older images of peaceful farmland, lighthearted city life, prosperous merchants, democratic vistas of the West, and symbols of unquestioning love of country, but their presence in the 1890s helped to contest accepted cultural wisdom. They both arose from and reinforced the questioning of cultural values. Those values were not wearing well under prevailing social and economic conditions.

If taken together, this body of art and literature implicitly suggested that the world did not always work the way people had been led to believe it should. For example, how could one exercise self-control in a world where technology overshadowed men and women, or in which social forces ground a poor but respectable girl into the depths of the underworld? Was McTeague only one man of many driven by base instincts and lusts? If America was a land of plenty, why did so many faces, worn by work and want, stare out from artists' canvases and black-and-white photographs? What was the point of restraint if it brought neither material nor spiritual reward?

In this artistic and cultural context, Americans first heard what would become ragtime music, and it spoke to them with profound power. The syncopated rhythm defied the usual order and regularity of three-quarter–time waltzes and dreamy ballads and the four-four time of marches and hymns. The steady beat of the left hand echoed the rhythm of factory, machine, and train, but the unexpected accents by the right hand, as well as the fast-paced melodies, announced a refusal to be contained by that steadiness. Ragtime's rhythmic exuberance, as performed by African American itinerants in places like Chicago and in tenderloin districts of other American cities, invited the casting off of restraint; joy, uninhibited emotion, and lively dancing seemed natural. Ragtime songs contained lyrics that told of an unfamiliar life beyond the boundaries of Victorian respectability—a world where sheer love of fun and sensuality were seductively accessible.

Ragtime was also the music of African Americans, a despised race but also one of the authentic American "folk." African Americans' position within American life was not certain, but their ragtime music literally struck a chord with the crowds in Chicago. Perhaps it spoke to the masses' inchoate, inadequately articulated frustration at the tension between stated ideals and lived experience. Perhaps its popularity at an event designed to affirm American achievement at a moment of economic trouble resulted from a desire to break free of a stifling past. As one of the early historians of ragtime saw it, the African American influence on national culture through ragtime was to loosen the grip of dominant Victorian assumptions. "The Negro is the symbol of our uninhibited expression, of our uninhibited action," wrote Isaac Goldberg in 1930.

> He is our catharsis. He is the disguise behind which we may, for a releasing moment, rejoin that part of ourselves which we have sacrificed to civilization. He helps us to a double deliverance. What we dare not say, often we freely sing. Music, too, is an absolution. And what we would not dare to sing in our own plain speech we freely sing in the Negro dialect, or in terms of the black. The popular song, like an unseen Cyrano, provides love phrases for that speechless Christian, the Public. And the Negro, a black Cyrano, adds lust to passion.

Noting the connection between Negro spirituals and the development of ragtime music, Goldberg argues that ragtime released the black from "his own addiction to holiness" and for the white "brought . . . something of that profane deliverance" as well.[53]

In the years that followed the fair, Americans' embrace of ragtime in Chicago and the economic depression combined to promote this African American music. One of the consequences of economic collapse was to drastically reduce the price of everything—including pianos and sheet music. As an editorialist in *The Etude* noted in 1899, as a result of the depression of 1893, "an instrument found its way into nearly every home in the land," and once manufacturers learned how to make good pianos inexpensively, they continued to sell them at low prices long after good economic times returned. With access to pianos, many middle-class Americans hoped to imitate some of the exciting music they had heard in Chicago, which created a demand for the publication of sheet music in "ragged time" by the end of the century.[54]

In 1893 in Chicago—the year of the exposition and the year of the depression—a cultural and economic crisis was laid bare, and a longing for new cultural expression was made known. Like the other artistic expressions alluded to above, ragtime music emerged from and seemed to address both the crisis and the longing. The turmoil and celebration of 1893 would set the stage for Joplin's breathtaking rise to fame in Sedalia, Missouri, where, by the dawn of the new century, he would be known as the King of Ragtime.

## CHAPTER 3

# JOPLIN AND SEDALIA:

## THE KING OF RAGTIME IN THE QUEEN CITY
## OF MISSOURI

When *Maple Leaf Rag* by Scott Joplin appeared in print in 1899, it captured the spirit of an emerging popular culture in the United States. Within a decade, a half-million copies of it had been sold in all parts of the United States. The form of Joplin's work eventually set the standard for other ragtime compositions, and *Maple Leaf Rag* became one of the most important pieces of ragtime music for piano.[1] It drew attention, as well, to an emerging "Missouri style" of ragtime. And publication of a composition by an African American musician marked an important moment in the incorporation of African American forms into the mainstream of American culture.

According to traditional ragtime lore, Scott Joplin, the African American King of Ragtime, and *Maple Leaf Rag* were discovered in Sedalia, Missouri, when a local music store proprietor, John Stark, happened to stroll by the Maple Leaf Club, where Joplin was playing the piano. In the legend, Stark could not resist the lilting melody, and he went inside the club and asked for the names of the pianist and the composition he was playing. So enchanted was Stark by *Maple Leaf Rag* that he offered to buy it and publish the music to sell in his music store.[2]

The Stark family remembered the moment differently. Stark family tradition has it that one day a dignified African American man named Scott Joplin entered the Starks' music store in Sedalia

An early version of *Maple Leaf Rag* that included a miniature portrait of Scott Joplin and a dedication to the Maple Leaf Club, where Joplin had found work, friends, and inspiration in Sedalia and began playing one of his compositions. A little boy, whom Joplin had brought with him, danced while the pianist played his *Maple Leaf Rag.* John Stark and his son Will watched the tiny dancer with amusement and listened to the musician in amazement. When Joplin finished, they rendered their verdict: the music, though beautiful, was far too difficult for the average Sedalia patron of their music store and was bound to be a poor investment. But Will was "so taken with the lad's dance" that he bought the music and printed ten thousand copies of it.[3] Within a few years of that decision, the Starks were advertising Scott Joplin as the "King of Ragtime Writers" on sheet music of *Maple Leaf Rag* and other Joplin compositions. Significantly, Scott Joplin left no printed recollection of the event.

*Maple Leaf Rag,* though neither Joplin's nor America's first ragtime composition, launched the African American musician's career and helped assure the popularity of ragtime music in the United States.[4] Many cultural commentators hailed ragtime as the first genuine American musical expression, and American musicians—amateur and professional alike—eagerly acquired *Maple Leaf Rag* and other compositions that followed in the next few years. Ragtime music, in general, and *Maple Leaf Rag,* in particular, were the products of African American writers and/or influences.[5] Americans who cakewalked or two-stepped to them were literally dancing to a black man's tune.

Socially and culturally, however, African Americans were still working within a white system. The anecdotes about Joplin and Stark that open this chapter suggest that while African Americans may have been important creators of ragtime music, they did not control all of its social and cultural meanings. The legend, for example, assumes that the song was irresistible—a disinterested passerby could not walk past the club unmoved. It also lionizes Stark for his ability to recognize a winning song and casts Joplin in an entirely passive role. The Stark family's version, while acknowledging Joplin's initiative, credits Will Stark's bighearted amusement, not the power of Joplin's music, for the eventual publication of *Maple Leaf Rag.* African American ragtime musicians created the music, but white businessmen, musicians, and writers mediated the presentation of African American ragtime to its audience and market.

In order to understand the nature and effect of that mediation and to begin to sort out the meanings of ragtime for black and white, it is imperative to return to Sedalia, the Queen City of Missouri, where Scott Joplin's career took off. Joplin produced his music within the rich African American community of Sedalia, and Sedalians of both races and all social positions came to enjoy it and claim it as their own. Sedalia was at once the cradle of a distinctive music and a community barely distinguishable from other communities ravaged by economic depression and cultural uncertainty in the late nineteenth century. A brief history of the Queen City will not disclose which story behind the discovery of Joplin is "true," but it will help explain why some believed the music too extraordinary for a passerby to ignore, why others thought ragtime emerged through the initiative of talented African Americans like Joplin, and how blacks and whites together forged a cultural expression that became a centerpiece of early-twentieth-century American popular culture.

## SEDALIA IN THE 1890S

When Joplin arrived in Sedalia with his friend Otis Saunders in the mid-1890s, he found himself in a growing city whose present, like its past, was influenced by railroads. In the 1850s, George Smith, a local Pettis County Whig and slaveowner, had begun buying land near the Pacific railway, which was then under construction. By 1858 he had secured a depot for Sedville, named for his daughter Sarah "Sed" Smith and later renamed Sedalia. During the Civil War, the city served as an important clearinghouse for Union men and matériel because of Smith's support for the Union cause. In 1864, Smith's election to the state senate paved the way for Sedalia's first official charter and for the location of the Pettis County seat in the city. For the next several years, the city grew and prospered because of its importance as a political and economic center. By the late 1860s, cattlemen had begun driving herds north from Texas for shipment to eastern markets, with Sedalia as one of several destinations. The first major cattle drive in the late 1860s firmly established Sedalia as an important commercial center and as the "western terminus of the railroad."[6]

The city that greeted Joplin in the 1890s had been shaped by other important social and economic factors in the previous two decades. Railroad traffic had transformed the depot of the 1850s into a thriving business center by the 1870s. By 1870 more than sixty businesses, employing nearly two hundred workers, had located in the city, and within a decade, the most important of these proved to be the Missouri, Kansas, Texas Railroad (MKT) shops. The MKT shops, housed in several massive buildings on twenty acres of land, employed workers and engineers, who serviced the forty locomotives that regularly operated on the nearby rails.[7]

The social significance of this business expansion was twofold. First, many people from around the Midwest and beyond came and went, keeping Sedalia up-to-date with regional and national trends. They came, in part, because Sedalia had grown into an important regional city, home to wholesale and retail businesses, railroads, manufacturing establishments, and government offices. Moreover, traveling people required accommodations, and the hotels and cafes that opened in response to that demand also attracted entertainers, who created a lively social atmosphere for transient businessmen and visitors. Decades later, an early ragtime pianist, Arthur Marshall, remembered Sedalia as a "live spot, a drawing card for excursions, band concerts, and a contest spot for dancing, cakewalks and bands."[8]

Second, the railroad shops employed numerous African Americans, who made up a vibrant black community within the city. Indeed, from the beginning, blacks had played an important role in the life of the city. Though a former slaveowner, Smith set aside a section of the new city he helped create for settlement by freedmen and freedwomen. The area eventually became known locally as Lincolnville in honor of the Great Emancipator. Together the rise of a service industry and the presence of a stable black community attracted African Americans to the burgeoning Missouri city.

At the time of Joplin's arrival, Sedalia was home to between fourteen and fifteen thousand people, roughly 10 percent of whom were African American. And as a fairly recently founded town, Sedalia had a young population. The vast majority of black Sedalians, for example, were between eighteen and forty-four years old—in their prime working years. Though rapidly growing and industrializing, Sedalia, in particular, and Pettis County, in general, bore few of the marks of urban life, such as crowded tenements or congested slums. With the exception of some boarders, most people lived with family members in homes they either rented or owned. In that regard, Sedalians lived like many other late-nineteenth-century midwesterners.[9]

In other respects, Sedalia was marked by its slaveholding past. Commerce, migration, railroad construction, and growth could not erase the traditional racial hierarchy or the social assumptions that went with it. The "peculiar institution" had rested on the belief that African Americans lacked the innate capacity to care and provide for themselves. After the war, the paternalism of slavery, which its defenders argued guaranteed the well-being and uplift of slaves, gave way to patronizing treatment and outright oppression of African American freedmen and freedwomen. In the twenty-odd years since the end of war, black Sedalians had had to resist this belated thinking if they had any hope of making headway economically, politically, and socially. The 1890s, often referred to as one of the lowest points of racial oppression in American history, found African Americans in Sedalia creating a community that supported black endeavor. In the midst of their struggle to advance in the Queen City, Scott Joplin arrived. Neither Joplin nor Sedalia's black community would ever be the same.

## SCOTT JOPLIN'S SEDALIA: AFRICAN AMERICANS IN A MISSOURI CITY

One of the most popular interpretations of the origins of ragtime argues that it was the music of an immoral underworld inhabited by the racial and social outcasts of urban America. "Black ragtime pianists," says one historian, writing as recently as 1992, "largely were forced to operate on the fringes of American commercial music . . . ragtime pianists were confined to performing jobs in the poorest neighborhoods, frequently on the dangerous waterfronts of riverports or in illicit gambling and prostitution districts."[10] Joplin, too, performed in the heart of Sedalia's entertainment and red-light district. According to one of his friends, G. T. Ireland, Joplin heard the Queen City Band in the Maple Leaf Club when he first arrived in Sedalia. He "thought the music was so good," Ireland insisted, "that he took his trumpet, went over and joined in."[11] Having gotten a start in one of the African American clubs in downtown Sedalia, Joplin continued playing piano in various honky tonks in the district. Arthur Marshall remembered playing piano with Joplin in brothels, "upholstered sewers," as he called them.[12]

While experiences like these would seem to justify the linkage of ragtime music and vice districts, it would be misleading to conclude that Joplin was confined to the underside of Sedalia and that his friends were pimps, prostitutes, boozers, and gamblers. In fact, Joplin's experience in the Queen City was far different. He was part of a community that participated in important ways in the social and cultural life of Sedalia. Although African Americans enjoyed the social life of their race, they nevertheless also moved fairly easily in the dominant white society. From the available evidence, it appears that African Americans in Sedalia in the 1890s were pushing against the boundaries that defined appropriate interaction between the races, and while not always successful, they found themselves actively engaged in establishing a new standard for acceptable social relations.

African Americans in Sedalia, as elsewhere, of course, did face unequal treatment. One of the clearest manifestations of discrimination was unequal sentencing in local police courts. Black defendants routinely faced a greater likelihood of serving jail time for such offenses as public drunkenness, disorderly conduct, or loitering than did their white counterparts. They often faced slightly higher fines, as well. In 1893, the editor of the *Sedalia Bazoo* noted sarcastically that "the color of the skin and the size of the winnings" determined whether an individual were found "guilty of shooting craps or not."[13] Similarly, eight years later, the editor of an African American publication, the *Sedalia Times,* wondered aloud why the African American club room had to close down while two other white clubs were allowed to stay in business. "Queer, isn't it?" was his final comment.[14]

Sedalia newspapers, like many throughout the country, routinely carried stories about notorious lynchings in other parts of the South. So even though African Americans in the community did not experience that kind of violence firsthand, they knew that some in the city considered it a legitimate way of punishing "uppity" blacks. In other, subtler, ways, racial lines were maintained in Sedalia. For example, caricatures of cakewalkers during a week-long street fair in 1899 included the usual stereotypical African American features—oversized lips, small foreheads, and carefree, uninhibited movements—which were intended, undoubtedly, to be humorous, but which, nevertheless, established a ranking for blacks below the white readers urged to laugh at their grotesque appearance. Similarly, a witty journalist for the *Sedalia Bazoo,* who regularly reported on cases in the local police court in the early 1890s, used the trial of an African American couple to take some pointed jabs at the race. He reported that a street urchin had labeled A. Emerson and Emma Smith, the two defendants, "the deuce of spades," and he ended his report with a patronizing and sarcastic poem:

> Oh! Colored children do not fight,
> And mar your lovely features.
> For you will know it is not right—
> You are God's chosen creatures.[15]

That is not to say, however, that the line between the races was never crossed. Indeed, the number of occasions on which the racial barriers broke down is rather remarkable. The ways white and black Sedalians lived together, brawled together, danced side by side, and engaged in public discussions defied the usual picture of lopsided social arrangements at the end of the century. Apart from dances where, true to long-standing tradition, African Americans performed for white dancers, members of the two races sometimes shared the dance floor. For example, in 1897, one of the physicians at the MKT hospital sponsored a cakewalk for hospital staff and railroad employees. Both blacks and whites sashayed along the "beautiful grade . . . in front of the hospital" in hopes of winning a cake made by a local caterer. Two winners were named: J. K. LaDuke was white, and Harvey Williams was black.[16]

People of both races not only mixed at social events, they also occasionally ended up in court together. Fox Beatty and Charles Wasson, for instance, black and white, respectively, faced charges of disturbing the peace after they were arrested for participating in a fight in which several "youths of various ages and colors [were] also mixed up."[17]

This kind of racial interaction arose in part because the races were not completely segregated in Sedalia. Apart from Lincolnville, which did have a heavy concentration of African American residents, most neighborhoods in Sedalia included people of both races. Indeed, by 1900, Scott Joplin and Belle Jones, who soon would become his wife, lived in a house owned by German immigrants, Michael Seethaler and his family. Others in the neighborhood included German- and Irish-born whites, white migrants from other parts of the South, and working- and middle-class African Americans, a number of whom owned their homes.[18]

It should come as no surprise then, that African American and white Sedalians influenced one another musically. One of the most celebrated collaborations, of course, was between Joplin and John Stark, the white music store owner who published his compositions. The generous terms of the contract Stark gave Joplin have often been cited as evidence of Stark's warm regard for the black musician. Moreover, Stark's willingness to publish Joplin's music gave his work a wider hearing than he otherwise would have gotten. But there were other examples besides the influence of Stark and Joplin on one another. In the early 1890s, Otto Juhl left Barnum's Circus when it came to Sedalia, and he decided to settle in the city. He was not permitted to join the Second Regiment Band, a white organization, so he joined instead the African American Queen City Band. According to one of the band's members, G. T. Ireland, Juhl was a "wonderful musician," who eventually "went to live among the colored people. . . . The band furnished him a suit and under his direction the Queen City Band became the best Negro band in the State of Missouri."[19] Though the Second Regiment Band rejected Juhl in 1892, they did adopt Fletcher Dandy, an African American Alabaman, whom they had met while preparing for war against Spain in 1898. He played with the group for about six months in 1898, and after a brief stay in his Courtland, Alabama, home, Dandy traveled to Sedalia to rejoin the white military band.[20]

In very important respects, however, African Americans drew strength from one another and worked to alter their treatment at the hands of whites, who held power locally and nationally. What Joplin found in Sedalia was a richly talented, articulate, and strong African American community of which he eagerly became an integral part. Months before he arrived, for example, the black community had organized a public meeting to discuss the race question in the state and nation. They elected a delegate to attend an "Afro-American convention in Cincinnati, the principal object of which is to secure the passage of laws for the better protection of negroes."[21] Two years later, certainly after Joplin had come to town, black Sedalians created an organization called the Grand United Brothers of Equal Rights and Justice, which was devoted to the prevention of the "hanging (lynching) of negroes, suspicioned or accused of crime, without trial, according to law." The group met twice a week and reputedly was "obtaining a large membership." Their presence and convictions demonstrate a purposeful and principled desire for equal treatment.[22]

Given this roused consciousness, it is not surprising that when the local school board threatened to close the only school in town that African American children were permitted to attend, leaders in the black community organized a protest. A public letter, signed by M. A. Eilonth, Hiram Hughes, and Richard Brown, argued for the school to remain open on the grounds that it would be a "means of bettering the city and fostering the condition of our people."[23] Just a day earlier hundreds of African Americans had turned out for a rally to support Sedalia's bid to become the new state capital of Missouri. Those in attendance vowed to "cooperate with their white brethren" to lobby for this outcome.[24] In both cases, the language of their participation shows clearly an identification with the interests of both the entire community and a particular racial agenda. It also provides evidence of an engaged minority in the city.

The people Joplin knew best, of course, were those who worked at least part-time as entertainers, and unlike the usual accounts of early ragtime, they were among the leaders of the African American community. Three members of the Queen City Band—G. T. Ireland, Dailey Steele, and W. H. Carter—for example, served as vice-presidents on the community's committee to push for the removal of the state capital from Jefferson City to Sedalia. All undoubtedly were selected for the honor because of their prominence in the city and their reputations as responsible citizens. Ireland had published *The Western World,* a local newspaper, for three years, chaired the Queen City Republican Club, and worked at various times for the *Sedalia Gazette, Sedalia Democrat,* and *Sedalia Capital.* Carter worked as a newspaperman, editing and publishing the *Sedalia Times.* Steele owned a barbershop as well as a farm near Sedalia.[25]

By all accounts, Joplin became part of a well-established African American entertainment community when he arrived in 1894.

According to S. Brunson Campbell, the African American's "piano services were so much in demand to play for white and Negro parties and dances, that he surrounded himself with the crack Negro pianists of Sedalia and placed them on party and dance jobs." He performed for dances on West Second Street and in a dance hall on the corner of Main Street and Ohio Avenue. As one of his appreciative fans recalled in the 1940s, Joplin came to Sedalia "about the time the cake walk came out," and Joplin and his friends "really made music."[26]

Joplin's early association with the Queen City Band also did much to spread his fame in the community, and it brought him in contact with talented musicians and entertainers. The band performed in a wide variety of settings—from parades to private dances and just about everything in between. They provided music for Emancipation Day celebrations in nearby communities like Fayette and Warrensburg, Missouri, and they accompanied the activities of black societies in the city. And once Joplin began to publish his musical compositions, the Queen City Band often gave the first performance of a new tune.[27] So the band's tour through the Midwest in 1901 likely acquainted midwesterners with music Joplin was beginning to publish.

In addition to the Queen City Band, which provided music for myriad public entertainments, a number of African American musicians in Sedalia deserve special mention for the influence they had on Joplin. According to the Ragtime Kid, S. Brunson Campbell, who made a pilgrimage to Sedalia in 1899 to learn ragtime from Joplin, such pianists as Otis Saunders, Melford Alexander, Tony Williams, and Jim and Ida Hastings "helped Joplin make ragtime history."[28]

Tony Williams appears to have been an extraordinary figure. Joplin eventually achieved great national acclaim, but judging from local newspaper reports, Tony Williams was in higher demand as an entertainer in Sedalia. He provided music for dances held by whites and blacks, and he hosted local cakewalk competitions. In March 1899, for example, Williams organized an evening of entertainment at the Woods Opera House, which attracted a racially mixed audience that included "some of the young society people" of white Sedalia. The *Sedalia Capital* promoted the show as one that "promises to be full of fun" and one in which "every member of the company resides in Sedalia."[29] Such coverage of Williams's

The Queen City Band of Sedalia, Missouri
*Front Row* (left to right): A. H. Hickman, R. O. Henderson, H.
Martin, W. H. Carter, A. Wheeler, J. Stewart; *Second Row:* W.
Travis, J. Chisholm, J. Scott; *Third Row:* G. T. Ireland, N. Diggs, E.
Gravitt; *Back Row:* C. W. Gravitt, E. Cook; photo courtesy Fisk
University Library, Special Collections

activities suggests more than patronizing interest in a local black
entertainer. It implies pride in local talent and a sharing in the
emergence of a new kind of entertainment.

In addition to his talent as an entertainer, Williams also provided Joplin with an example of entrepreneurial ability necessary to promote African American forms of entertainment. Tony
Williams ran the Maple Leaf Club when Joplin arrived in 1894,
and he later opened a second African American dance spot, the
Black 400 Club. When these clubs began to flounder in the late
1890s, Williams turned his attention to railroad excursions. He
would book a train for a short trip, sell the tickets to interested
passengers, then provide musical entertainment to and from the
appointed destination. His activities took him to other Missouri

cities, where he often stayed for a time to promote cakewalks, vaudeville programs, and dance contests. In all of these activities, Williams not only established the precedent for entertaining white audiences as well as black, but he also provided an example of the entrepreneurial spirit necessary to promote African American entertainment in turn-of-the-century Sedalia.[30]

Williams and other African American Sedalians also gained regional attention after local performances brought them into contact with booking agents interested in organizing tours. G. T. Ireland recalled that during a week-long fair held in 1901, "the Queen City Band played the 'Hoochy-Coochy' music, that the commissioners particularly liked." At the end of the week, Dekro Brothers Amusements arranged to take the Queen City Band to Kansas City, Missouri, and Des Moines, Iowa, where they played their Sedalia-style music to appreciative audiences.[31] According to the *Sedalia Times,* "It was acknowledged in every town that they stopped that [the Queen City Band] was the best Negro band that had ever been heard in those sections."[32] Tony Williams and his company also were booked for shows in Marshall and Jefferson City, Missouri, as a result of their performance at a Sedalia fair held in 1899.[33]

Unlike most members of this talented African American community, however, Scott Joplin made a lasting impression on musical trends beyond Sedalia and its immediate surroundings, a difference that must be explained. First, in contrast with the local African American celebrities who held jobs in addition to their work in the entertainment business, Joplin consistently called himself a "musician" or "composer" and probably supplemented the income from his performances with money from teaching.[34] Second, in spite of fewer years in the community, Joplin quickly emerged as one of its musical leaders. Perhaps his early training in Texarkana distinguished him from the majority of black Sedalia musicians who made their way as improvisers. Likewise, his years as an itinerant musician had forced him to learn how to make his own arrangements for the music groups he formed and afforded him greater contact with a wider range of musical styles and genres, which allowed him to experiment with different sounds and combinations of instruments.

Most important, however, Joplin emphasized a written record of his musical compositions, which he achieved with greater alacrity after enrolling in an advanced composition course at the George R. Smith College for Negroes in the mid-1890s. Friends—especially Otis Saunders and Tony Williams—had encouraged him to attend the recently founded college, because they believed he had a solid base of musical knowledge on which to build.[35] The music department at the college would have provided instruction in the fundamentals of harmony and composition, and his early compositions, comparatively undistinguished, bore the marks of this conventional training. The instruction itself was invaluable. His friends in Sedalia eagerly gave him ideas for new pieces that reflected the jagged rhythms and more complicated melodies that marked the work that brought him fame. His mastery of the principles of harmony and composition permitted Joplin to record and refine the improvisational works of his friends and no doubt contributed to his aspirations to write serious music.

Joplin not only learned about music, but he also passed his knowledge on to the younger musicians in the community. Although S. Brunson Campbell journeyed to Sedalia to learn ragtime from a masterful African American, Joplin's most important protégés were Scott Hayden and Arthur Marshall. Marshall, like other adult black musicians in Sedalia, earned his keep primarily from manual labor, but both he and Hayden were still in high school when they first hooked up with Joplin. Indeed, Hayden did not strike out on his own until June 1900, after Joplin's *Maple Leaf Rag* had begun to attract attention and after he and Joplin had begun working on their first compositions together.[36]

For a time, Joplin lived in Arthur Marshall's home at 135 West Henry Street and regularly visited in the Hayden home at 133 North Osage, where he and Scott Hayden composed ragtime pieces. One of Hayden's young nephews, Alonzo Hayden, remembered Joplin as a "very kind person, quiet and civil," who would play with him until his uncle Scott was ready to settle down to work with Joplin.[37] The two musicians went into a music room, he recalled, "where they were not to be disturbed." Years later Marshall remembered Joplin as "a quiet person with perfect manners who loved music and liked to talk about it." Moreover, Joplin helped Marshall with his compositions, offering advice on melody, bass, and harmony and putting the music in manuscript form. Joplin was "a brother in kindness to all," Marshall remembered.[38] *Sunflower Slow Drag* (1901) was the first collaboration between Joplin and Hayden. They later produced *Something Doing* (1903), *Felicity Rag* (1911), and *Kismet Rag* (1913). Marshall and Joplin wrote *Swipesy Cake Walk* (1900) and *Lily Queen—A Ragtime Two-Step* (1907). Both Marshall and Hayden, under Joplin's tutelage, went on to enjoy musical careers that took them beyond the confines of central Missouri.[39]

In the African American community of Sedalia, Joplin became both a student and a teacher of music. He was surrounded by talented, inventive, and race-conscious black Sedalians, who nurtured the talent that promised such brilliance and who set their sights beyond 1890s Sedalia. As Joplin's friend W. H. Carter put it, "Every Negro should have race pride enough to enable him to forget personal prejudices. Any man who tries to live above his race will never amount to much. With his race, he must rise or fall . . . Above all, love your race."[40] The black musicians of Sedalia encouraged, prodded, and taught one another in the art of ragtime and African American entertainment. They loved their race and their music.

White Sedalians might not have loved their African American neighbors, but they could not get enough of their music. As Campbell remembered it, the publication of Joplin's *Maple Leaf Rag* in 1899 "blew the lid off the musical world and set it into the greatest musical craze that the world has ever known."[41] That "musical revolution" would not have been possible without the support of the white community in Sedalia and in the nation. A look at African Americans in the Queen City showed how the various strands of music, culture, and aspiration came together for Joplin and were woven into a particular racial community; a look at white Sedalia will help explain how ragtime became a popular musical form for many Americans at the turn of the century, regardless of race. Sedalians, like other Americans in the 1890s, faced economic and cultural challenges that predisposed them to the daring new African American music that offered emotional and cultural release to a beleaguered majority. Their experience of those challenges helped them make Scott Joplin the King of Ragtime.

## THE WHITE COMMUNITY IN 1890S SEDALIA

In the 1890s, Sedalians found themselves at an economic crossroads that had important cultural ramifications. Like other Americans in 1893, Sedalians survived the panic and ensuing depression with little of their Victorian cultural faith intact. While initially they learned only new economic truths, Sedalians eventually began to question other dimensions of their culture as well. Just as the changing financial picture required different kinds of business practices and underlying assumptions, the emerging cultural climate permitted behavior once proscribed by Victorian restraint. That openness to new sights, sounds, dances, and experience redounded to the benefit of African American entertainers like Scott Joplin. The economic conditions of the early 1890s paved the way for the embrace of ragtime and African American entertainment by white Sedalians later in the decade.

Sedalians, like other Americans in 1894 when Joplin first came to town, were trying to recover from recent economic difficulties. Economic woes of the previous year had taken a serious toll on the commercial life of the city. In spite of a New Year's Day prediction that "the year 1893 offers opportunity to lay the foundation for a prosperity greater than even the Queen City has known," depression conditions appeared early.[42] In January, newspapermen announced that Charles, Pearl, and Joseph Minter, whose store "carried one of the largest and finest stocks of dry goods in Central Missouri" had gone out of business. The *Sedalia Bazoo* characterized the Minters as some of "the most enterprising and progressive citizens of Sedalia," but on January 9, 1893, they closed the doors to their business, unable to continue in a consolidating economy. Their diligence and self-control had not yielded success.[43] About a month later, Will and Sam Osborn, two more of "Sedalia's progressive grocers," quit the business because of hard times.[44]

Within months, other businesses followed the Minters' and the Osborns' into bankruptcy. Indeed, the *Sedalia Bazoo,* which had been reporting the mounting crisis through spring and summer, reduced its size on August 10, and two days later suspended publication. On the last day of publication, the paper reported, "Hard times seem to have struck railroad work in earnest, judging from cuts being made in wages and employees." The *Sedalia Bazoo,* like other local businesses that depended on a large patronage, folded. It did not reappear until late November.[45] The effects of cuts in wages rippled through Sedalia's depressed economy. In the summer, the St. Louis Clothing Company announced an unprecedented "Mid-Summer Clearing Out Sale." In June, Frank B. Meyer sold stock he had purchased at forty cents on the dollar at J. B. Murphy's bankruptcy sale, but by mid-July, he too was advertising a sale—"Our Great Mid Summer Sale"—in an effort to liquidate his oversupply of goods. Another store, in hopes of generating some reliable liquid assets offered a 25 percent discount to anyone who paid for goods in cash.[46]

Sedalians thus either witnessed or experienced firsthand the cold reality of the 1890s: sometimes people suffered financial disaster even though they worked diligently and lived modestly. Enormous sales throughout summer did not seem to jump-start the sluggish economy. "Vagrants" became a common sight, as they looked unsuccessfully for work or at least for some way to survive. While the city policemen in past years typically had arrested loiterers "who they thought had no visible means of support," by 1893 the problem was getting out of hand. No work was to be had; the men had few alternatives; and the city had fewer resources to keep vagrants in jail. No one wanted to ignore the growing number of unemployed men whose desperation might lead to robbery "and various other depredations," but the city simply could not afford to house and feed an army of inmates. As in so many other areas, the depression of 1893 upset Sedalians' sense of order, economic justice, and cultural truth.[47]

Other social and cultural expectations were shifting in Sedalia as well. In early 1894, a new publication called *Rosa Pearle's Paper,* appeared. Its stated purpose was "to keep up with the age in which we live."[48] Though devoted primarily to society events and local gossip, *Rosa Pearle's Paper* contained cultural commentary that provides insight into the values governing respectable white Sedalians in those changing times. In one of the first editions of the newspaper, a column on "The Woman of To-Day" character- ized her as intelligent, independent, conscious of style, and no longer bound to traditions of the past.[49] The same issue also ex- plored what it meant to be "up-to-date" in Sedalia in 1894. The article contained two lists of questions, one that might have been asked in the past and one that must be asked "today." While the "out-of-date" reader was asked, "What does your wife say to your going to the theatres?" and "Does your wife approve of your smoking?" The "up-to-date" reader had to consider, "What do you say to your daughters going to the theatre?" and "Do you approve of your wife smoking?" The list of questions supported the char- acterization of "The Woman of To-day." Opportunities and education were open to women, and they were taking a more prominent place in life outside the family. Both men and women were wriggling free of Victorian constraints.[50]

Changing social relations and ideals forced Sedalians in the 1890s to consider what they believed to be the boundary between acceptable and unacceptable behavior. Traditional morality, it seemed, was no longer embraced without question. Local reporting of Sedalians who went to visit the World's Columbian Exposition in Chicago in 1893, for example, suggested that some people in the community were making somewhat questionable moral choices. Some took in more than the educational exhibits of the fair, it was implied, and some spent money they did not have to enjoy the sights of the exposition even though they owed money to local creditors. "It is disgraceful for a man to stand on the street and tell of the sights he saw at the great show while an army of collectors are vainly trying to induce him to pay last month's bills," the *Sedalia Democrat* insisted in the summer of 1893.[51] Even in Sedalia, some citizens seemed to flaunt their disregard for traditional values. It was reported that a "certain high-flying wife" who flirted "with every stranger she meets" would cause a "sensation" if she did not soon shape up. Similarly, two unmarried couples brought before Judge Fisher in 1893 for adultery provided an opportunity for disquieted commentary from local editors. The *Sedalia Bazoo* reported that the prosecuting attorney Hoffman asked Sam Bass incredulously, "Don't you know that such conduct is wrong?" And when Bass answered, "Yes, but it couldn't be holpen," he was fined $50 and put in jail.[52] Likewise, when John Ruby and Sarah Venable were jailed and fined for "lewd conduct," the editor of the *Sedalia Democrat* lamented, "The judge is at a loss to know what to do with such characters. They openly and repeatedly violate the law and yet stand in no fear of prosecution."[53] The reported incredulity of these court officials is evidence of Sedalians' sense of the changing times.

By the time Joplin arrived in the city, the depression of 1893 had loosened Sedalians' attachment to Victorian prescriptions, and the people's inchoate dissatisfaction with self-control and repression was finding expression in new social relations and cultural interests. Local journalists, for example, defended theater going against attacks made by visiting revivalists, and they reported on and reviewed numerous productions put on by traveling troupes in the city's theaters. A theatrical production like "The Spider and the Fly," which had been roundly condemned as immoral in 1892, by 1899 was advertised as a "gorgeous spectacular extravaganza," complete with a "beautiful array of forty pretty girls . . . [opera], comedy, and vaudeville," and was scheduled to perform on a *Sunday* afternoon and evening.[54] At the height of the depression, the *Sedalia Bazoo* announced ironically that the business district was "the only quiet place for peaceful repose in the Queen City," because outdoor opera attracted crowds to Forest Park; Chautauqua programs were the main event at Association Park; Negro dance halls in Lincolnville drew masses of high-stepping dancers; and for the religious, there were camp meetings in East Sedalia.[55] Indeed, one editor noted that old-time amusements no longer satisfied Sedalians—they were too well informed to be interested in lectures, and ease of travel made panoramas and dioramas seem pathetically unconvincing.[56]

One senses in the newspaper commentary of the 1890s a restlessness in Sedalia that reflected an urge for new kinds of entertainment and release from Victorian imperatives. Dances and theaters had become important venues for expressing emotions and independence from tradition. Later in the decade, it became the local vogue to sit out dances so the couples could embrace without having to "gallop a mile or two for a hug or two."[57] Moreover, such vices as gambling and prostitution and such institutions as saloons and dance halls were increasingly visible in the city. While some madames like Mrs. Ingram in 1892 publically insisted that they merely ran women's boarding houses, others unabashedly told census takers that their "boarders" were prostitutes.[58] By the late 1890s, respectable Sedalians of both races were clucking disapprovingly at the range of racy entertainments in Sedalia's downtown. But by then, their own appetite for the exotic was being satisfied in other, more socially acceptable ways. Sedalia's cultural leaders in the 1890s, though too fastidious to go to clubs and saloons in the raucous part of town near the railroad tracks, eagerly brought ragtime music, cakewalk dances, and African American musicians into their parlors, cotillions, and social entertainments.

The popularity of ragtime among Sedalia's cultural elite is unquestionable judging from the many references to it in newspapers of the period. Whites attended and participated in cakewalks,

organized private dances that featured Joplin's music, and promoted local black vaudeville performers at the community's opera
house. In 1897, for example, the women of the local Methodist
Episcopal Church, South, organized a watermelon social in the
home of the Danforth family, who lived in one of the exclusive
white neighborhoods of Sedalia. The guests were white, but "a
colored quartette furnished both vocal and instrumental music"
which "greatly amused the crowd." The unnamed quartette may
have been one Joplin organized—the Texas Medley Quartette—
but there were many other such African American entertainers
who were also gaining popularity among whites. Tony Williams,
for instance, in addition to his other activities as an entertainer,
had become the director of a mandolin club that furnished the
music for "one of the most delightful social events" of 1899 hosted
by the Reeves family.[59]

Similarly, varieties of African American music and dancing
became popular forms of entertainment among white Sedalians
in the 1890s. Guests in the homes of society families concluded
evenings of cardplaying with cakewalks; dance classes featured
cakewalks in their recitals; and charity organizers often used a
cakewalk as the grand finale for a benefit program.[60] In 1900, a
"number of society young ladies" gave a minstrel entertainment
in the city. A year earlier, the Methodist church became deeply
divided when the Reverend S. H. Swearinger denounced the plan
by some members "to give a cake-walk and minstrel show."
Though the congregation weathered the storm, many feared that
the minister's attack would "result in a split in the church."[61] Even
the Sedalia Military band included numerous African American
songs, such as "The Black Four Hundred," "I Don't Love Nobody,"
and "Pickaninnies on Parade," in a program that included more
traditional waltzes, marches, polkas, and overtures.[62]

Unmistakably African American–styled entertainment, cakewalks and ragtime took white Sedalia by storm in the years
following the depression of 1893. But it is equally clear that whites
delimited the social meaning of this cultural embrace by the way
they reported their activities and their treatment of the black
entertainers. For example, when Scott Joplin composed a waltz
in honor of an exclusive white men's social organization called
the Augustan Club, the society's leader acknowledged the honor
in a local newspaper, but he hired a local white band to play it

at the club's first major social event.[63] When African Americans performed for white dances, newspaper accounts often deleted the name of the band. Such entertainers as Tony and Charles Williams, proprietors of the Black 400 Club, Robert Henderson, member of the Queen City Band and a traveling vaudevillian, Dailey Steele, who performed at Wood's Opera House and ran a dance studio, and Arthur Marshall, musician and collaborator with Joplin, all performed on numerous occasions for public dances, parades, street fairs, vaudeville shows and made extended midwestern tours as musical entertainers. Nevertheless, compilers of business and city directories insisted on listing their occupations as "porters," "laborer," "barber," and "worker," respectively, rather than acknowledge their status in the entertainment industry.[64] Taken together these examples suggest that white Sedalians embraced the liberating possibilities of the music as a cultural form though they limited the radical social implications of their choice.

Sedalia in the 1890s was a city experiencing enormous social, economic, and cultural change. The city's growth, fueled by investment by traditional white leaders, attracted a diverse population, who helped create the conditions for change. African Americans played a vital role both in the city's economic life and in the popular culture that had emerged by the end of the nineteenth century—that fed the pervasive desire on the part of many white Sedalians for something different. The experience of Sedalians—black and white—in the 1890s, reinforces our perception of a community at work establishing new ground rules for social interaction, cultural expression, and communal order. In that context it was possible for an African American musician and a white music store proprietor to take some chances—to write and to publish music that gave vent to the music of an impressive subcommunity and for which a market potentially existed. Scott Joplin and John Stark, representatives of their racial communities in Sedalia, found or made sufficient cultural space in the Queen City to engender a cultural revolution.

## JOHN STARK: PROMOTING BUSINESS AND CULTURE IN SEDALIA

Let us consider the Stark family's version of the meeting of publisher and musician. In a sense, John Stark had nothing to lose the day that Scott Joplin wandered into his music shop clasping a sheaf of manuscript pages in one hand and the hand of a small boy in the other. At fifty-eight, Stark was more comfortably fixed than at many other times during his professional life. He could afford to publish the piece—difficult though it clearly was—and not run the risk of losing his business. His main interest lay in selling and tuning pianos, so to indulge his son's fancy and publish the piece was a small side interest. He decided it was worth the investment. He recognized that he did not have to print a huge run to satisfy either the eager African American musician or himself. So when Stark agreed to publish Joplin's *Maple Leaf Rag* in 1899, he probably did so unaware that this was a momentous decision.

If viewed from Joplin's perspective, the meeting represented a great deal. Both a Kansas City publisher and a local rival of Stark's—A. W. Perry—had already refused *Maple Leaf Rag*. To put his musical future in the hands of John Stark, Joplin must have realized, was to entrust it to an aging white businessman who might not have been aware of recent popular musical trends. Joplin probably did not know that Stark had started out in the music business as an itinerant peddler. Indeed, if he knew of Stark at all it likely would have been either as a piano dealer or as the father of a locally acclaimed pianist, Miss Nellie Stark. Neither role would have made Stark seem likely to be an effective promoter of African American music. So it must have been with some dismay that Joplin took his composition to the shop of John Stark & Son.

As it turned out, each man completely altered the life of the other. As a consequence of their venture in 1899, Stark's business attracted national attention, and Joplin's music was heard and played from one end of the country to the other. The two men, of different generations and from vastly different backgrounds, worked together to promote ragtime. Within a few years of their meeting—whether that meeting was in Stark's shop or in the Maple Leaf Club—both men had left Sedalia for greener pastures, bigger markets, and greater exposure. But their experiences leading up to that first encounter deepen our understanding of the importance of their collaboration.

John Stark had come to Sedalia in 1885 to establish a music house with his son Will. John Stark & Son moved frequently from one location to another in Sedalia, perhaps to take advantage of a better marketing position, to obtain lower lease payments, or to reflect the family's changing status and success. Stark had come to Sedalia from Chillicothe, Missouri, where he had been selling ice cream and reed organs, an unlikely combination of wares, to farm families in that community and its vicinity. So for Stark, the new business, while perhaps unstable initially, represented an important step upward. For the next decade and a half, John Stark & Son supported the proprietor, his wife, and their three children: Etilmon, William, and Eleanor.

John Stark was no stranger to either striving or adversity. Born in 1841 in Shelby County, Kentucky, the eleventh of twelve children, Stark had learned early about the rigors of making one's way in the world. His mother died when John was three, and three years after that an older brother, Etilmon Justus Stark, took the child to his homestead in Gosport, Indiana. When the Civil War was in its fourth year in 1864, twenty-three-year-old John Stark enlisted, fought with the First Regiment of Indiana, and eventually wound up in New Orleans, where he met Sarah Ann Casey, whom he married after the war. After a short time in Indiana, Stark, his wife, and newborn son, Etilmon Justus, moved to a farmstead near Maysville, Missouri, and by 1872, the Stark family had grown to five.

For the next decade, Stark continued to farm, but for unknown reasons, he began looking for a new way to make a living sometime in the early 1880s. He left the farm for Cameron, Missouri, where he began making ice cream, a new business at the time, and peddled his wares in town as well as in the countryside. Within a couple of years, he had moved to Chillicothe, a larger town, to ply his trade. And he branched out. John Stark began carrying reed organs in his covered wagon in hopes of convincing farming families to lease or buy the instruments as a source of family entertainment that would help break up the monotony of rural isolation. Though successful in his new venture, Stark was by then in his mid-forties, and he may well have longed for a less strenuous and more sedentary existence. He discovered that Sedalia had only one music store, so in 1885, he traded bumpy wagon rides for the proprietorship of his own music store in the Queen City of Missouri.[65]

At this point, two observations about Stark should be noted.

First and foremost, John Stark was an entrepreneur. Cut from the typical mid-nineteenth-century pattern, Stark entered more than one business in pursuit of the main chance. Without much apparent support from other family members, Stark made his way by his own imagination and effort. His main goal was to make enough money to support his family. He was willing to take chances—as his ice-cream-making venture suggests—but he also wanted a stable income for his family's comfort and security and for investment. He undoubtedly shared the cultural views held by many Sedalia businessmen before the depression of 1893.

Second, Stark was something of a hybrid. Born a Southerner, he eventually sympathized with Northerners in the Civil War, and then married a southern woman. Raised in Indiana, which was no safe haven for African Americans despite the state's support for the Union cause, Stark nevertheless had an affinity for black culture. Family members recalled hearing him play black folk songs on the guitar when they lived on the Maysville farm— songs he remembered from his childhood in Kentucky. In this respect, he may have differed somewhat from many of his white neighbors in the Queen City who caricatured, ridiculed, and tried to hold back African Americans in the community, and who held strong views about regional divisions and loyalties in the United States.

A third characteristic of Stark, not readily apparent in a brief sketch of his life, must also be noted. Stark fancied himself an arbiter of musical taste. In the mid-1890s, Stark began to stage musical programs at his store and invited local musicians to take part. A typical program included chamber music, vocal solos, and piano duets—all the selections drawn from classical, serious sources. In 1895, the *Sedalia Gazette* noted that Stark's musicales had become "extremely popular," featured a "high-class" program, and involved "the leading musicians of the city."[66] One of the participants, Richard Johnson, for example, studied music in New York in the 1890s, and when he returned to Sedalia in 1899, he opened a studio in Stark's store, where he gave voice lessons.[67]

Stark also provided musical education for two of his children. While Will joined in the family business, Etilmon studied the violin and performed on numerous occasions in Sedalia. In 1893, he joined the faculty of the Marmaduke Military Academy as director of music, but he continued to participate in his father's musicales and was fondly remembered as "one of Sedalia's finest musicians."[68] Eleanor Stark, Nellie as she was known locally, became a great favorite as a pianist and performer of classical pieces. By 1895, after many years of playing the piano in local musical programs, Nellie had earned the honor of being "Sedalia's favorite musician." Miss Stark gave a farewell concert at the Woods Opera House in late August of 1895 right before leaving Sedalia to study piano in Europe. After two years of working with two masters—Schulze and Moszkowski—in Berlin, Nellie Stark returned to rave reviews in the local newspapers. "From a dashing player she has developed into an intellectual pianiste," the *Sedalia Democrat* reported in 1897. "Her technique has become more brilliant, her scale even, her power immense, and yet her touch is like velvet."[69] When the family moved to St. Louis in 1900, the talented Nellie Stark accompanied them and opened her own studio.[70]

The father of two accomplished musicians and the sponsor of tasteful musical programs, John Stark projected an image of musical cultivation. Even though he sold and tuned pianos and stocked popular sheet music to make his living, in some ways, his ambitions transcended mere moneymaking. He was an important purveyor of culture in the Queen City.

Stark, then, served as perhaps the ideal intermediary between the African American composer and the piano-playing, sheet music–buying public. For he could lend an air of legitimacy to the acquisition of and enthusiasm for compositions by a black musician. He could help satisfy the desire of customers in Sedalia and elsewhere for exotic entertainment in the guise of refinement and good taste, and in the safety of their parlor or music room. His affection for African American folk songs may have predisposed him to the compositional efforts of Joplin; and the structure, complexity, and beauty of *Maple Leaf Rag* probably appealed to his notions of worthwhile and challenging music. And as important as all these factors put together, the originality and appeal of Joplin's music may have sparked somewhere in the back of Stark's mind the hope that this composer could add to his wealth. As his daughter-in-law later recalled, "Over the years, both [Will and John Stark] came to love [*Maple Leaf Rag*] which launched them on a new career." Soon after the rag took off, the Starks established the Stark Music Company in St. Louis and got into the music publishing business fulltime.[71]

Looked at from that angle, Joplin's choice of Stark was perhaps less desperate and more calculated than it at first appears. Stark's publication of Joplin's compositions not only improved the composer's financial condition, it also helped Joplin accomplish an important goal: the preservation of the music of his race and generation. Moreover, the endorsement of a white cultural leader permitted him to claim with some confidence that he was contributing to an American school of music, which was still in the making. Stark's reputation would have rescued Joplin's work from unthinking relegation to the rubbish heap of faddish popular music. And to the African American community that had embraced and nurtured him, taught and emulated him, Joplin's publishing with John Stark may well have given other members hope that their struggle for better treatment, for a fair hearing of their music, and for a place in American life was beginning to bear fruit. African Americans in Sedalia knew what barriers they had faced in the past, but they knew not what lay ahead. For a time, at least, in the late 1890s, the alliance of Scott Joplin and John Stark promised the respect and prosperity for which they had been striving in postwar Missouri.

## POSTSCRIPT TO SEDALIA:
## THE QUEEN CITY AFTER JOPLIN

Even though the Starks moved their business to St. Louis shortly after they began selling copies of Joplin's *Maple Leaf Rag,* Joplin himself remained in Sedalia. The African American had become a local celebrity and had earned the respect of many in the community. Indeed, he cultivated the support of well-placed cultural leaders by composing special songs in their honor—the best example of this was the waltz he wrote for the Augustan Club. "Scott Joplin, well known as a composer," reported the *Sedalia Democrat* in 1900, "is at work on a piece of music to be dedicated to the Augustain [sic] club. It will be a waltz and will make a 'hit' in this city."[72] But he also remained at the heart of the African American musical community, as his collaborations with Hayden and Marshall eloquently attest. Moreover, he continued to supply the Queen City Band with new material for local dances and concerts. In the immediate aftermath of his first publishing success, Joplin composed and taught music in Sedalia, where he had friends and followers among both blacks and whites.

It is not surprising, therefore, that, when he followed the Starks to St. Louis sometime in late 1900 or early 1901, in order to fulfill his contractual obligation to publish all his work with them, people in the Queen City continued to follow his career with interest.[73] In June 1903, for instance, Monroe H. Rosenfeld published a feature on Scott Joplin in the *St. Louis Globe-Democrat* that touted him as both "The King of Rag-Time Composers" and "A Colored St. Louisan." About a week later the *Sedalia Times* reprinted the article under the title, "Scott Joplin a King." While the *Times* editor wanted to underscore the importance of Joplin's being featured by a big-city newspaper and reviewed by a famous music critic, he could not resist trying to set the record straight. "Was Raised in Sedalia," read the first subtitle, and the first paragraph concluded: "Sunday's Globe Democrat will be read with interest here for the reason that it refers to a composer hailing from Sedalia, whose publisher is also a Sedalian." After presenting Rosenfeld's commentary in full, the editor reminded Sedalians that his newspaper "was the first Sedalia paper to begin giving Mr. Joplin a public boom as a Negro music writer and composer of the catchy music known as 'Rag Time.'"[74] A week after the *Times* column, the *Sedalia Weekly Conservator* reported on Joplin's latest compositions, which by 1903 included *Cleopha* (1902), *The Entertainer* (1902), *Elite Syncopations* (1902), and *Weeping Willow* (1903), and noted that they "can be heard in the evening on almost any avenue."[75]

Local newspapers also followed Joplin's venture into opera with interest and enthusiasm. Earlier in 1903, the *Sedalia Times* had reported on Scott Hayden's return from St. Louis to Sedalia to visit his family and friends. He had signed a contract with the Scott Joplin Drama Company in St. Louis and was scheduled to perform alongside Latisha Howell and Arthur Marshall in an upcoming performance of *A Guest of Honor*. In August the *Sedalia Weekly Conservator* announced that the cast of Joplin's opera had begun daily rehearsals at Crawford's Theatre in East St. Louis, where they were scheduled to open on August 30, 1903. The book had been published; Joplin had secured the backing of a "strong capitalist" for the production; and the composer had finished all of the songs and drills. The promise that the opera would be staged in Sedalia must have excited considerable interest in the Queen City.[76]

When local black leaders traveled to St. Louis, as W. H. Carter did in 1902, they made a point of looking up Scott Joplin and other former Sedalians. On that particular visit, Carter reported that Joplin was "gaining a world's reputation as the Rag Time King" and spent all his time "writing, composing, and collecting his money from the different music houses in St. Louis, Chicago, New York, and a number of other cities." He further noted that Joplin's recent works—*Easy Winners* (1901), *The Ragtime Dance* (1902), and *Peacherine Rag* (1901)—were "used by the leading piano players and orchestras."[77]

The remaining observations made by Carter in St. Louis reveal an important result of Joplin's departure from Sedalia. Encouraged perhaps by Joplin's growing fame and fortune, others of the dynamic African American musical community in Sedalia apparently also tried to make their way in St. Louis. Carter met up with R. O. Henderson, who accompanied him on a visit to see Lee Marshall, Hense Watson, Frank Kelly, and George Parker, all of whom he knew as "old friends." Perhaps least surprising of all, Tony Williams and his brother, Charles, also spent time with their friend from the Queen City. After conquering Sedalia and the surrounding area, it was natural for the talented entertainer to take a crack at opportunities in one of Missouri's most important cultural centers.[78]

The presence of entertainers like R. O. Henderson and Tony Williams in St. Louis alerts us to an important development in the African American community in Sedalia. At the dawn of the new century, many of these gifted musicians left the Queen City, lured toward opportunities in a rapidly growing entertainment industry. R. O. Henderson and his wife, Lagretta, had moved away from Sedalia in September 1901, when they signed a contract with the Harrison Brothers Minstrel Company.[79] Similarly, Tony Williams had gone first to Joplin, Missouri, in 1900, where he opened a club and sponsored dances, before he tried his luck in St. Louis.[80] And, of course, Scott Hayden and Arthur Marshall followed their teacher, Scott Joplin, to St. Louis in hopes of advancing their own careers as entertainers.

At the same time, the abundance of opportunities in communities large and small for ragtime entertainers meant that the music was readily available in a wide range of forms. Amateur performers could acquire sheet music and play their favorite compositions in their own homes. Audiences could attend concerts and dances in respectable neighborhoods where black or white bands might offer renditions of rags. In other words, the musical products of a vibrant African American community and generation were steadily being incorporated into the mainstream of American popular culture.

Ironically, however, the widespread dissemination and acceptance of ragtime music had a peculiar and deleterious effect on Sedalia's entertainment district. As the publication of *Maple Leaf Rag* made possible the formal reproduction of African American music by trained musicians, anyone who craved a good hearing no longer had to go to the district around the railroad tracks to get satisfaction. Moreover, the drain of talent out of Sedalia into markets perceived as more promising and lucrative meant that fewer of the great performers remained in Sedalia as entertainers. As a consequence, places like the Maple Leaf Club and the Black 400 Club, where Joplin and others had offered premium entertainment, attracted few respectable citizens and became the scene of notorious and drunken brawls.

Instead of stories about prominent African Americans like G. T. Ireland, Dailey Steele, W. H. Carter, Tony Williams, or R. O. Henderson, newspapers carried stories from Main Street about heretofore unknown people like Will and Dora Hubbard and Lizzie Jennings, given to intoxication and violence. In January 1900—before Joplin left town—Dora Hubbard was accidentally shot by her husband in a fracas on Main Street and arrested for disorderly conduct. Hubbard had been aiming at Jennings, but had missed. Two months later, the two women were involved in another brawl that the *Sedalia Sentinel* called "almost a riot" that lasted throughout the night.[81]

Such goings-on made Main Street a dangerous and unsavory place to visit, and since other Sedalians—both black and white—could hear good music in other venues, there was widespread support for the closing of the Maple Leaf and Black 400 clubs. African American ministers had taken the initiative to urge city officials to close the clubs because the "carryings on within were alleged to be disgraceful in the extreme." More than a year later, the clubs were still going when older black musicians who remembered the glory days but a few years past formed a "Colored Orchestra" in order to distinguish themselves from the rough element in town. W. H. Carter, G. T. Ireland, and Mr. and Mrs.

Dailey Steele formed the core of the group. Although at one time they had played in the Maple Leaf Club, they supported the efforts of city officials to close the trouble spots. "We are informed that orders have been issued to shut down the piano 'thumping' on Main street," they noted approvingly. "Why is it not stopped? Someone answer the question."[82] In time the clubs were shut for good, and the buildings eventually were razed. A marble monument in a city parking lot marks the spot where Joplin's style of ragtime first was heard.

Joplin and black Sedalia had a profound impact on one another that illustrates the complex and ambiguous legacy of the ragtimer's life in the Queen City of Missouri. Each nurtured and shaped the other; each was engaged in a long-term struggle for success, acceptance, and dignity in American life. The successful achievements of one helped open doors for the other. But in the end, the story of Joplin is not one of undiluted triumph. Joplin's rise coincided with (and perhaps instigated) the diaspora of a remarkable African American community in central Missouri. Unfortunately, the role they played in the advancement of their music has been obscured by their difficulties in overcoming social barriers outside Sedalia, where they were not as well known and respected. Moreover, the dependence of ragtime's success on white approval, backing, and promotion meant that the subsequent embrace of ragtime by Americans of both races across the nation was only partly on African American terms. Missouri-style ragtime, which took shape in Sedalia in the 1890s, started a cultural revolution. But as Joplin and black Sedalians learned the hard way, cultural revolution often has unclear social consequences.

## CHAPTER 4

# The Incorporation of Ragtime

Shortly before they moved their business from Sedalia to St. Louis in 1900, John and Will Stark placed an advertisement in one of the local newspapers, the *Sedalia Evening Sentinel*. At the center of the advertisement, the Starks had placed a drawing of a cozy family scene: a woman plays the piano observed closely by her daughter and appreciated by her husband who relaxes in a nearby chair. From the clothes to the furnishings, every detail indicates a middle-class, white family. This evocation of bourgeois family entertainment perpetuated a nineteenth-century association between pianos, women, refinement, and effort. In a sense it reinforced Victorian ideals of domesticity and industry. Piano playing encouraged families to seek amusement and wholesome leisure in their parlors instead of in the outside world, and it required study, perseverance, development of skills, and diligence. It was a form of leisure that could build good character and a happy home life.[1]

The text of the advertisement went on to plug the "excellent makes" of pianos and organs as well as a full line of stringed instruments and sheet music available in the Starks' store. These items represented the bread and butter of their enterprise. Perhaps a bit surprising, the Starks made absolutely no mention of Joplin's *Maple Leaf Rag*, released a few months earlier in 1899 and rapidly gaining in popularity and sales. Having "discovered" Joplin, the Starks could not have been faulted for announcing their exclusive rights to his compositions as a way to attract new business. Oddly, they chose to ignore Joplin's hit—the chief reason they would be

Advertisement for John Stark & Son that appeared in the *Sedalia Evening Sentinel* on February 3, 1900, photo courtesy State Historical Society of Missouri, Columbia

moving their operation to St. Louis—in favor of a more conventional approach to musical sales—the piano as a source of sweetness and light and family harmony.

That 1900 advertisement embodies a number of fascinating tensions that accompanied the rising popularity of ragtime— tensions between nineteenth-century middle-class imperatives and twentieth-century economic incorporation. Joplin and Stark depended for their success in part on the widespread dissemination of pianos in American households. After all, in order to justify the publication of new compositions, musical entrepreneurs had to assume that large numbers of customers would buy their wares. The more families with pianos in their parlors, the greater the demand for sheet music. At the same time, however, the large-scale production of pianos and sheet music, on which that assumption relied, was made possible by a changing economy and society that, in turn, upset familiar notions about the place of pianos, leisure, and popular entertainment in American life. If the early, savage commentary on ragtime is to be believed, many critics saw it as the musical accompaniment to a cultural experience qualitatively different than that which prevailed in Victorian homes. So while the Stark advertisement continued to appeal to amateur pianists (indeed, *had* to appeal to that clientele), the economic conditions that underlay Stark's production and the social changes resulting from the popularity of ragtime pointed to the emergence of an entertainment industry that would have a dramatic impact on domestic amusements.

It is worth our while to pause for a moment in the story of Scott Joplin's life to consider the business of producing and promoting his music, which was essential for his rise to fame. For not only does it shed light on Joplin's transition from popular entertainer to serious composer, but it also promises some insights into a question that has long bedeviled scholars of popular culture. Ever since Theodor Adorno's pathbreaking essays on popular culture, one of the critical debates on music history has centered on the extent to which the industry has limited, degraded, and commodified musical expression. Recognizing the marketing imperatives of the music business in a mass society, Adorno and his followers have argued that musical products are standardized and banal as a result of industrialization. Moreover, as part of a critique of advanced capitalism, this interpretation identifies the mode of production as decisive in the creation of a debased mass culture.[2]

Not all scholars are persuaded by this critical interpretation—especially those who have studied the music of racial and ethnic minorities. Viewing them as mouthpieces for authentic experience or grassroots beliefs, values, and desires, these scholars see the genuineness, the potential for political insurgency, and the crude but powerful artistry of these popular musicians.[3]

While offering vastly different views of the artistic merit of popular music, the two interpretive traditions agree on one point—contact with the marketplace sullies the purity and originality of music. Adorno and company see the flaw inherent in the popular music of a mass culture, and celebrants of grassroots ethnic or racial music view commercialization as a watering-down of the essential music and its message. Like so many other articles mass-produced in an industrial economy, they argue, music created for and disseminated in a mass society has to strive for banality and appeal to a homogeneous audience so as not to offend potential consumers.

While these insights are useful to an extent—they force scholars of a particular kind of music to examine it against a wider backdrop of popular music—they flatten out an enormously complex relationship between music and the industries that produce and disseminate it. They overlook how linkages between industries can affect the perception of the music. Both perceptions about and marketing of the music shape the way people initially think about a composition. And these ideas about music, I would argue, add to its "meaning." In the case of Joplin's ragtime music, it is essential to examine the linkages between the manufacture of pianos and the production of sheet music, for example, because the success of the latter depended on the easy availability of the former. Moreover, ragtime's reputation as a new and racy—though immensely appealing—form of entertainment affected both the reception of Joplin's compositions and the way people thought about pianos in the parlor. Advertising proved to be an essential factor in the way people were urged to think about both Joplin and his music.

An examination of the business of music thus promises to shed light on the "incorporation" of ragtime, by which I intend to imply two meanings. The emergence of ragtime music coincided with the emergence of incorporation in the American economy—that is, the domination of American economic life by large-scale, highly organized producers. As a form of African American expression, ragtime also was "incorporated" into the mainstream of popular entertainment that was largely dominated by white actors and sensibilities. Both these definitions of incorporation had a profound impact on ragtime, Scott Joplin, and American culture. Joplin and Stark, for example, initially rode the crest of incorporation in the music business, but they could not control the direction various musical enterprises eventually would take in the early twentieth century. Moreover, their promotion of ragtime encouraged or reinforced attitudes toward leisure and amusement that in many ways contradicted their business interests. Similarly, incorporation of the music of African American outsiders into popular commercial entertainment provided opportunities to men and women of color to contribute to the construction of an American style of music. But their works did not necessarily alter the place of racial minorities in the larger society, and they certainly could not control all the uses to which their art could be put.

John Stark and Scott Joplin were minor but revealing actors in the incorporation of ragtime. They participated in the emergence of some aspects of the developing entertainment industry, and they were important advocates for including African American music in the main body of American music. Their experiences help explain the complicated transition American families made from home-based amusements to popular entertainment outside the home that was under way in the last half of the nineteenth century and that involved a shift away from participation in musical entertainment and in the direction of a more passive reception of music. Stark and Joplin also sought to legitimize ragtime as a serious American musical form even as they tried to capitalize on its popularity—both at a time when ragtime as a genre was widely perceived as a racy alternative to stuffy, but respectable, Victorian parlor music.

Two important discussions about America's emerging entertainment industry arise in an examination of Stark and Joplin. One involves the linkages between various aspects of the music industry. The evolution, mass production, and marketing of pianos constituted an important dimension of an evolving entertainment industry. In Stark's previous career as a piano salesman, he advertised pianos in such a way as to permit a combination of Victorian striving and modern attention to national trends and crazes. But the entertainment industry itself rested on a concept of amusement that was more thoroughly consumer oriented and passive. Although perhaps out of step with certain branches of public entertainment, John Stark's business enterprise must be seen as a critical link between private, participatory musical entertainment and public, consumer-oriented endeavors. They must also be seen as a reminder that at the turn of the century, the nation did not move in lockstep from one cultural world to another. Stark's experience defies such an analysis.

The second dimension of business activity to be scrutinized involves Stark's advertisement of Joplin's music. The method, content, and nature of his advertising offer insights into the cultural, racial, and class-based messages conveyed by purveyors of African American music in American markets. Through visual images and advertising copy, these messages were deployed to convince amateur musicians to buy their music, and in the process they affirmed critical ideals, values, and attitudes that contributed to and drew from popular thought. Thus the business of ragtime helped shape the emerging culture of which ragtime music was a key component.

An examination of the promotion of ragtime forces us to consider the interplay between two forms of incorporation—economic and cultural. Although by no means the same thing and probably not perfectly reflexive, the two historical phenomena produced important changes in the way people related to one another and the way they conceived of their world in the early twentieth century.[4] Stark's and Joplin's experiences provide a window into a society and a culture in flux, where economic incorporation permitted and promoted cultural incorporation. But as we shall see, the evolution of the ragtime business had social consequences no one anticipated.

## EBONY AND IVORY: PIANOS AND AFRICAN AMERICAN MUSIC

Scholars of the twentieth-century African American experience have noted the central place of the piano to black culture in the

United States. As substantial pieces of furniture, pianos represented respectability and a degree of comfort that reflected the fruit of upward mobility, but at the same time, under the real conditions of early-twentieth-century urban life, piano-owning black families came to rely on the instrument for the musical accompaniment to "rent parties" by which they avoided eviction during lean times. As noted above, piano music by African Americans in the first few decades of this century conveyed key tensions in black life—tensions between industrial rhythms and spontaneous, unpredictable emotional response, captured respectively in the steady beat of the left hand and the syncopated melodies of the right. And finally, any consideration of African American contributions to American culture in the twentieth century must recognize the artistry of great black pianists like Jelly Roll Morton, Duke Ellington, and Count Basie. They are important representatives of African American musical achievement.[5]

As important as these associations between the piano and African American experience are, they represent relatively recent developments. They are products of the post-Reconstruction era—the historical moment that coincides with the rise to fame of freeborn musicians like Scott Joplin. Indeed, former slaves, commenting on their musical experience on southern plantations, remembered hearing, dancing to, or playing fiddles, guitars, banjos, and other stringed instruments, but as one former slave put it, they "didn't know nothin' 'bout no piano."[6] Even for many white Americans in the mid-nineteenth century, a piano was a badge of middle-class comfort still unattained, and in recently settled areas, pianos were especially scarce. In order to understand the connection between African Americans and pianos and the meaning of that connection, we must briefly survey the history of the piano in the United States.

From the late eighteenth century until well into the nineteenth, pianos in America were generally the property of wealthy white Americans. In the 1770s, when prominent people like Thomas Jefferson and Colonel Carter in Virginia began ordering pianofortes from England, the instrument had been in existence for only a few decades. The product of a desire to refine the harpsichord to permit modulation between soft and loud tones—hence, the pianoforte—this eighteenth-century instrument was still "a rudimentary affair, a mongrel," according to H. E. Krehbiel, an early-twentieth-century music scholar, "neither a harpsichord nor a pianoforte in the modern sense."[7] Because they were handcrafted from fine woods, these musical "mongrels" were scarce in the United States and expensive. But because they rapidly were gaining a reputation for producing beautiful tones in public performances, demand for pianos grew sufficiently in the late eighteenth century to warrant their production and distribution in North America. All of these factors conspired to keep pianos out of the reach of ordinary Americans until decades after their introduction to this continent.[8]

Technological developments in the early nineteenth century eventually made piano making a thriving American business, which resulted in greater availability of the instruments and changes in the kind of performances possible. In 1800, John Isaac Hawkins, a civil engineer from Philadelphia, invented an upright piano in which metal was used for part of the frame. Though the upright style did not catch on at the dawn of the new century, the use of metal in piano making inspired new ideas. In 1825 Alpheus Babcock took out a patent for a cast-iron sounding board support, which set the trend for American piano construction. Similarly, after 1820, companies like Chickering & Mackay replaced wooden frames with metal to support metal strings with greater strength, rigidity, and durability. Beautiful wooden square piano cabinets in the United States covered metal frames that could produce lovely, pure tones and that could sustain good pitch through extended performances. In addition to preserving good tone without frequent tuning, the metal-framed American pianos could also withstand more vigorous piano-playing techniques, which were used to express deeper emotion and intensified energy. The florid Romantic style of the nineteenth century and these various technological innovations served to reinforce one another, and the rise of the middle class created a market for less-expensive, less-troublesome instruments.[9]

Although American-made pianos allowed pianists to stage more elaborate, emotional performances, by far the most popular compositions played in American homes were hymns.[10] Hymn-playing provided wholesome, moral entertainment that sustained Victorian notions about the home as a haven from a heartless, immoral world, and the steady meter and relatively uncomplicated melodies and harmonies made hymns easily accessible to inexperienced, frequently self-taught players.[11] Though perhaps eager to learn new hymns, typical nineteenth-century pianists probably did not view such music in the same way that later generations viewed sheet music—such compositions were neither "sensations" nor the latest "hit" of a particular writer. As Arthur Loesser has observed, "ordinary song consumers of 1820, and long after, were inclined to assume vaguely that music was generated anonymously by a kind of spontaneous combustion."[12] The emphasis among amateur pianists in the United States was on mastering the instrument rather than on keeping up-to-date with the latest hits by popular composers.

By 1860, more than two hundred establishments in the United States were devoted to the manufacture of musical instruments, and most of these were located in large cities like New York, Baltimore, and Boston.[13] Of these, Chickering & Sons, established in 1823, and William Knabe & Co., established in 1837, had been joined more recently by firms like Harris Brothers and Marshall & Mendell founded in the 1850s. These firms took advantage of technological innovations that had occurred since the 1820s to produce good pianos at increasingly affordable prices. Following the Civil War, the popularity of the American square piano gave way to a new penchant for upright pianos; the old squares—like the one acquired by Jiles Joplin in Texarkana for his son—became affordable to less-well-off families as wealthier Americans discarded their older, used instruments for newer, better, upright models. By the end of the century, four hundred firms were producing nearly one hundred fifty thousand pianos each year.[14]

By the time John Stark got into the business of selling pianos, another trend was beginning to alter the landscape of the music business in the United States: the incorporation of several smaller companies into single, large-scale operations. Firms like the American Piano Company, which integrated the operations of Chickering & Sons, William Knabe & Co., and the Foster-Armstrong Company, were highly capitalized and produced thousands of pianos a year in a range of styles and prices, of varying quality.[15] The effect of this development was to lower prices and to make the growing field of musical instrument sales extremely competitive.

As an itinerant peddler of reed organs and pianos, John Stark in the 1880s could still take advantage of the relative isolation of rural Missouri to avoid the increasingly rough-and-tumble competition in the business. After he moved to Sedalia, however, Stark faced sharp competition from other music store proprietors in the community in the 1890s. Sharp's Central Missouri Music House, for example, sold Kimball pianos in 1894, marketing them as "the purest toned, the most artistic finish, the cheapest in the long run." Within three years, the store advertised a much wider range of pianos, from grands to square pianos and with prices ranging from twenty-five dollars to five hundred dollars. "We are willing to close them out at factory prices and on easy payments— if desired," they boasted, and the claim suggests that music store owners were obliged by the late 1890s to compete aggressively for a share of the trade.[16] While F. C. Billings, a former piano tuner for the Starks, could not boast of having Kimball pianos in 1895, he claimed to be the "only music house in the city that carries in stock standard pianos and organs" made by the Decker, Estey, and Camp companies—less expensive brands.[17]

Stark countered these advertisements with big promises of his own. In 1894, for example, he proclaimed, "We keep more makes of Pianos and Organs and other Music Goods than any one in Sedalia, and we sell closer to cost and give easier terms." In addition to instruments, he offered an "immense stock" of sheet music and a "complete ten-cent catalogue," which must have been attractive to Sedalians in the aftermath of the depression of 1893.[18] By the end of the decade—indeed, just before Christmas 1899— Stark advertised a piano sale in language that reeked of hyperbole and nineteenth-century hucksterism. The sale would "dwarf into insignificance all previous attempts in this line," he insisted immodestly.

> All future sales will be but the echo of a past event. Our reason is, we will turn our attention more exclusively to our own piano, "The Stark & Son." We have new and good grade pianos that will be sold at prices so far below goods of equal grade elsewhere as to astonish you. We have shop worn pianos at sacrifice prices. We have pianos that were sold on installments and $25 to $100 paid. This and further discount is yours if you want it. We have second-hand pianos and organs that have been taken in exchange at any price. Or will trade them for a good pocket knife.[19]

The stores owned by John Stark, F. C. Billings, the Sharps, and others in Sedalia served primarily as the distributors and clearing-houses of mass-produced new and used pianos in a single Missouri city in the 1890s. Their fortunes depended on low prices, high turnover, and some additional interest to supplement trade in musical instruments—piano tuning, publishing and selling sheet music, or furniture-moving services. An 1892 article in the *Sedalia Bazoo* on the care of the piano attests both to the success of their enterprise and to the relative recentness of the widespread ownership of this "beloved instrument."[20] And their experiences and advertisements underscore an important change that had taken place in Americans' perception of pianos. Robert Braine called it a "quiet revolution" in an 1899 article for *The Etude*—a revolution that would "result in doubling and trebling the number of piano pupils in the United States, inasmuch as pianos are becoming so cheap that literally everybody can afford to own one."[21] Moreover, "literally everyone" was rapidly coming to include African Americans as well as their white neighbors. J. Hillary Taylor, a writer for *The Negro Music Journal* in 1903, for example, contemplated the "enormity of the piano industry" by recounting the "prodigious number" of instruments made each year and "the astonishing number of pianos sold yearly to homes situated in all parts of the United States." Pianos were available to most people, almost anywhere in the United States.[22]

By and large, the business of making and selling pianos fell to those with money to invest, and, with a few exceptions, most, like the Starks, Billings, and Sharps, were white and middle-class. They controlled and profited from the marketing of an item that provided wholesome, potentially uplifting, diversion to Americans—black and white—with the means necessary to buy the instrument. Judging from his sponsoring of musicales and his daughter's European training, Stark probably made fairly traditional Victorian assumptions about the uplifting uses to which pianos should be put. But he was also participating in a dimension of the budding music business that was forcing a reconsideration of those assumptions—publishing popular sheet music.

An early suggestion that the new sheet music altered the meaning and place of the piano of the twentieth century appeared in an article written by Charles M. Skinner in 1900 for the *Saturday Evening Post*. "There are more pianos in America in proportion to the population, than in any other land," he began, "and in no country are the poor things more cruelly tortured." Piano playing, he went on to argue, had become "our national vice" comparable to "the chewing of tobacco," which resulted in "the tweaking and pounding and ignorant misuse of an instrument that was made for comfort and joy." This last phrase posits a "before" and "after" dichotomy. Pianos once had contributed to "comfort and joy" in the home, but by 1900, they had become contemptible. The contrast lay in the music played. Before, amateurs would have offered "a nice, peaceful rendition of a Chopin nocturne," but now they insisted on playing "'The Tra-la-loo Polka,' or 'Hullo, Mah Rag-Time Gal,' or the march from 'The Blind Cow.'" He credited the desire for "new music" and "the search for novelty" for having created such a din in America's parlors.[23]

Whether Skinner's analysis is correct is debatable, but his identification of a new trend is important to an understanding of the musical world occupied by John Stark and Scott Joplin. Mass production of sheet music *did* alter attitudes toward home music and entertainment in both blatant and subtle ways. Obviously, different sounds were emanating from American parlors in the late 1890s and early 1900s, and similarly, the justification of choosing one piece over another had less to do with tradition and familiarity than with its composer and recent popularity. As Arthur Weld put it in 1899, "Pass along the streets of any large city of a summer evening when the windows are open and take note of what music you hear being played. It is no longer the great masters, or the lesser classicists—nor even the 'Salon-componisten' that used to be prime favorites with the boarding-school misses. Not a bit of it! It is 'rag-time'—'coon' songs, skirt dances, and all the rest of the tawdry crew."[24] These sounds must have been particularly jarring if they replaced the comforting sound of beloved hymns, and that shift—from sacred to secular music—may help account for early vitriolic attacks on ragtime as a degenerate form of music.

Less obviously, however, the nature of "popularity" was becoming tied to other institutions of entertainment—the vaudeville stage, concerts by celebrities, musical accompaniment to films, and before long, phonographic recordings. Music publishers, who eventually gravitated to "Tin-Pan Alley," an area in New York City between Fourteenth and Twenty-Eighth Streets, quickly learned to hire "pluggers" and to convince popular "stars" to use their newest pieces in successful shows.[25] More than one piece of sheet music carried a portrait of the famous person who had endorsed it or used it in a hit show. As Isaac Goldberg, a magazine and newspaper editor and aficionado of popular music in the first third of the twentieth century, put it, the "hard-boiled ladies and gentlemen" in the music industry were "not in business for their health. . . . Staff notes into bank notes might be their motto," he argued. And, as early as 1899, those staff notes had translated into three and a half million dollars worth of serious music and three and a quarter million dollars worth of popular music each year.[26]

At the same time that consolidation in the piano-making industry permitted most Americans to own instruments once considered luxuries, the social conditions that accompanied this incorporation fostered urban growth, changes in social relations, the expansion of alternatives to domestic amusement, and a booming sheet music–publishing business, all of which altered what it meant to own a piano. Although owning a piano no longer represented merely middle-class Victorian "comfort and joy," many Americans acquiring or selling pianos still operated on that assumption. But the music they could buy at their local music store reflected the important influences of African American music, commercial entertainments, and awareness of popular trends that compromised Victorian notions of piano ownership and piano music in the home. By the late nineteenth century, the piano business in which Stark engaged—and the image of pianos in American culture—were in the midst of change. An examination of Stark's other interest—sheet music publishing—helps explain the nature of those changes.

## "TRY THIS ON YOUR PIANO"

Like most sheet music publishers, John Stark used each piece of sheet music itself as a miniature billboard on which to advertise other numbers on his list. In all the advertisements placed in Sedalia newspapers, Stark never tried to trade on the popularity of Scott Joplin, and he rarely even mentioned that he sold sheet music. But people who purchased the sheet music he published were urged, somewhere on the jacket, to "Try this on your Piano," under which the first few lines of another Stark song appeared.[27] These kinds of advertisements on sheet music offered a sure way of promoting compositions with people likely to buy them; they were designed to tantalize the prospective buyer and to provide a reason to return to the publisher for a new piece.

Stark's ads for Joplin's compositions did much more than lure repeat customers, however; they gave buyers a way of thinking about the African American composer as an artist, a person, a source of exotic (but safe) amusement, and as a serious composer whose status lent legitimacy to their craving for the latest musical fad. Moreover, the ads eased the incorporation of African American music into the mainstream by simultaneously praising the African American dimension to ragtime and "whitening" it as much as possible.

Perhaps the most important way Stark presented Joplin was as the premier composer of ragtime music in the country. After the initial, short run of *Maple Leaf Rag,* Stark began to illustrate the jacket of the music with a simple, elegant maple leaf and dubbed Joplin the "King of Ragtime Writers." The title carried more weight as an advertising ploy than anything else. It cost Stark nothing, and while it was undoubtedly inspired by confidence in Joplin's talent, it was based on no identifiable criteria. But it boldly asserted that to buy a Joplin rag was to buy the best. As more compositions followed in 1901 and 1902, Stark supplemented the regal appellation with a reminder of what the King of Ragtime had already produced. A later printing of *Maple Leaf Rag,* for example, identified Joplin as the "composer of The Cascades, Sunflower Slow Drag, Elite Syncopations" as well as the King of Ragtime Writers.[28] Eventually Stark could write, "It is needless to say anything of the writer of 'Maple Leaf,' 'Cascades,' 'Sunflower' or 'Entertainer.' You know him."[29] By 1903 the reputation had stuck sufficiently for Monroe Rosenfeld to write of Joplin in the *St. Louis Globe-Democrat,* "He is better known as 'the King of Rag-Time Writers,' because of the many famous works in syncopated melodies which he has written."[30] Rosenfeld's praise underscored Stark's initial construction of Joplin as a celebrity.

The identification of Joplin as the King of Ragtime Writers had two important consequences. The first was that Stark (and presumably Joplin) self-consciously called their music ragtime, which, at the turn of the century, was tantamount to inviting the scorn of serious musicians. True enough, ragtime in the early twentieth century was extremely popular. As more than one commentator noted, ragtime had become the premier choice of piano players, a popular favorite at dances, the accompaniment to marching soldiers, and a stock part of theatre and vaudeville productions.[31] It was the latest craze, and it offered sensuality, unrestraint, and entertainment heretofore off-limits to respectable middle-class Victorians. But from the time Stark first started publishing and promoting Joplin's compositions, ragtime was also subject to severe criticism. A year before *Maple Leaf Rag* appeared in print, for example, *The Etude* had answered a reader's question about ragtime by asserting that "'Rag time' is a term applied to the peculiar, broken, rhythmic features of the popular 'coon song.'" Ragtime, the editor continued, contained the same aesthetic elements "as that in the monotonous recurring rhythmic chant of barbarous races," and he concluded that its popularity in 1898 "is somewhat to be deplored."[32] For the next several years, musical commentators used "disease" metaphors to describe the popular taste for ragtime, calling it by turns an "epidemic," "a rapidly increasing mania," musical "pimples," and the source of "mental ailments."[33] Even in Sedalia, the home of Missouri-style ragtime, a local newspaper editor reprinted an article from the *Philadelphia Enquirer* at about the same time that Stark published *Maple Leaf Rag.* The writer insisted that "'Rag time' is doomed" because of its simplistic and irritating character. "It is the easiest form of musical expression to write," he argued, "and when all things are considered it really expresses nothing."[34] Stark must have counted on the immense popularity of the genre to make money before he linked his name with ragtime music. For despite continued criticism, Stark doggedly maintained the identification of Joplin's music with ragtime throughout the early years of the new century.

The second consequence of Stark's crowning Joplin the King of Ragtime was his elevation of the composer to the status of a celebrity. In a sense, Stark became an impresario and agent for Joplin the star, which made Stark's enterprise something besides mere sheet music publishing. When Scott Joplin died in 1917, for example, Stark reminded a reporter for the *Ragtime Review* that he had "quickly discerned [the] quality" of Joplin's works in the late 1890s, "bought them and made a five-year contract with Joplin to write only for his firm, which firm has all of his great compositions." In 1917 Stark wanted prospective buyers to think that he was the principal caretaker of Joplin's work.[35] Just a couple of years earlier, the Winn School of Popular Music in New York had reported in an advertisement that "SCOTT JOPLIN, world's greatest composer of ragtime, writer of the celebrated 'Maple Leaf Rag,'" endorsed the Winn Method for learning how to play ragtime. "I commend your system as being wonderfully simple, easy and comprehensive," Joplin supposedly had written, clearly contradicting his own method in *School of Ragtime* (1908) that demanded careful attention to the music, diligence, and long hours of practice. Thus, one could debate the genuineness of this endorsement, but real or not, it represents a perception that Joplin was a celebrity whose support for a ragtime school would add to its appeal.[36]

As the years passed, Stark used Joplin's celebrity status to make an emotional appeal to prospective buyers. In an ad for *Sunflower Slow Drag*, for instance, Stark told readers that the piece had been written when Joplin was in love and "touching the ground only in the highest places." "Hold your ear to the ground while someone plays it," he urged, "and you can hear Scott Joplin's heart beat." This kind of personal appeal suggests that Stark hoped to trade on a growing desire by ordinary Americans to get close to "stars" in the emerging field of popular entertainment. In another advertisement for *Sunflower Slow Drag*, Stark told of a careless woman who had tripped her way through a number of Joplin rags until she had become bored with them and laid them aside. "But it chanced that she incidentally dropped into a store one day," Stark reported, "where Joplin was playing the 'Sunflower Slow Drag.' She was instantly struck with its unique and soulful story, and— what do you think! She asked someone what it was! She had played over it and around it for twelve months and had never touched it. She went home and began to practice it, as though she had never seen it before." Contact with the famed composer gave the music new power; it "breathed new life and spoke a new language."[37]

One of the reasons Americans desired such intimacy, however contrived it may have been, was to gain insights into the lives of successful people in an age when people increasingly looked to others for social cues.[38] In that regard, Stark packaged Joplin's rags in the trappings of middle-class respectability. He avoided vulgar, demeaning illustrations on the covers of Joplin compositions in favor of straightforward, sometimes elegant designs. He used

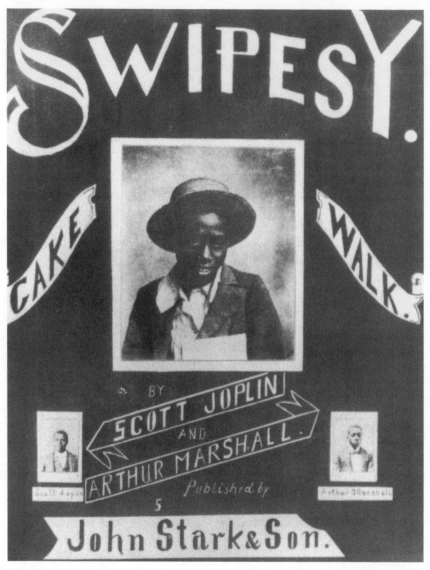

Covers for *Swipesy Cake Walk* and *The Cascades* published by Stark and Son that feature portraits of African Americans

graphic flourishes to good effect for the original title pages of *Augustan Club Waltz* (1901) and *The Cascades* (1904), and he illustrated *Sunflower Slow Drag* (1901), *The Chrysanthemum* (1904), and *Heliotrope Bouquet* (1907) with stylized versions of the appropriate flowers. A stylishly dressed white couple adorns the cover of *Elite*

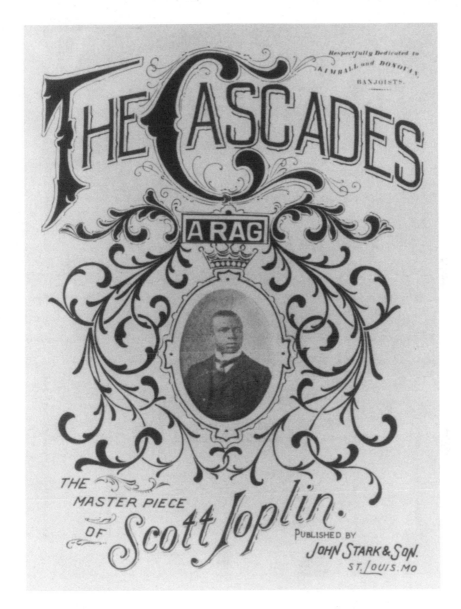

*Syncopations* (1902). Joplin employed the same artistic strategies when he published his own pieces, as the design of *The Easy Winners* (1901) attests. Each of the cameos on the cover features white competitors engaged in sports like football, baseball, horse racing, and sailing, which were then associated with the middle and upper classes. In these ways, Stark and Joplin hoped to con-

*Elite Syncopations, The Easy Winners,* and *Euphonic Sounds* all display scenes of respectable, white middle-class experience on their covers.

vince consumers that Joplin's style of ragtime was respectable and accessible to the white middle class and that it had little in common with the "flood of Rags, Drags and Jags on the market."[39]

That is not to say, however, that they avoided the issue of race in their presentation of Joplin's compositions. Some covers included cameo photographs of the composer or other African

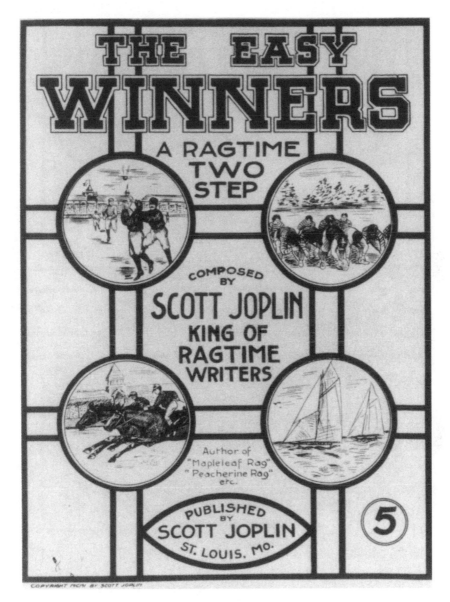

Americans, like his collaborator Arthur Marshall, or people to whom a piece was dedicated, like P. G. Lowery, touted as the "World's Challenging Colored Cornetist and Band Master." *The Chrysanthemum* was identified as an "Afro-Intermezzo," and the original covers of *Maple Leaf Rag* (1899), *The Entertainer* (1902), and *Felicity Rag* (1911) featured drawings of African American

figures. Although all the drawings included some physical features that were stereotypical and exaggerated, the people depicted were handsomely clad and seemingly well-to-do. Even the entertainer, with his overlarge mouth and shoes, is presented on stage above a white audience that looks up to him appreciatively and admiringly. Unlike the cover by Carl Hoffman for *Original Rags* (1899), which pictured a decrepit old African American, picking rags off the ground, and his grizzly-looking dog in front of a rundown shack, none of the Stark illustrations for Joplin's music contained blatantly insulting images of African Americans.

Race and class were both seemingly less troublesome issues for Stark and Joplin than knowing whether to pitch to a clientele with popular or classical interests. From what is known about Joplin's rise to fame in Sedalia, it is clear that he had become a popular entertainer. His music accompanied festive days, dances, parties, and exclusive balls, and he himself had entertained in the lively establishments along Main Street. By calling his music ragtime and striving to learn appropriate musical notation for the syncopated melodies that he and his friends had been improvising for years, Joplin seems to have purposefully aimed to penetrate the field of popular entertainment.

Joplin's ample success in the field of popular music, however, did not deter him from writing serious music, and Stark's interest in Joplin seems to have been divided between his enthusiastic support for the African American's popular, highly sought-after rags and his more fitful and at times reluctant underwriting of more ambitious, serious forays into ballet and opera. Stark's advertisements made claims for the novelty and originality of their publications, which would suggest an interest in setting and keeping current with popular trends. But the Starks also insisted on the durability of the compositions on their list. These were the "classic rags," which to many music critics must have sounded like a contradiction in terms.

"Our Rag Time Is Different," Stark proclaimed on an early-twentieth-century printing of *Maple Leaf Rag,* emphasizing its popular appeal and implying that it was superior to ordinary popular music. He blended popular and serious forms of entertainment in promoting his list. "If played by request or as an encore at a concert," he wrote of any rag on the Stark list, "it smashes the programme and must be repeated to the end of the show. . . . Seriously, [rags published by Stark & Son] are both classic and popular, profound and simple. They please at once the untutored and the cultured." Later in the same advertisement, Stark appealed simultaneously to "the country fiddler" and the "greatest bands and orchestras." Regardless of the players or the

The original covers for two Joplin compositions that feature sketches of African Americans. Compare the presentation of both Joplin and his race in *The Ragtime Dance* and *Felicity Rag,* both published by John Stark, with *Original Rags* published by Carl Hoffman

audience, "everybody likes them the first time they hear them played, and they like them still better when they have heard them one hundred times or more."[40]

These marketing strategies betray Joplin's and Stark's position as transitional figures between parlor entertainment and the bud-

ding industries of music. They needed to make a pitch to large numbers of buyers in order to stay in business, but they wanted to leave a lasting impression on the field of serious American music. To buy a composition of Joplin's was not a momentary impulse and waste of money. Rather, it was an investment in art that would nevertheless be popular. Joplin, they argued, blended the most appealing aspects of popular entertainment with classical

music—or as Stark put it, "the skill of a Beethoven with the sentiment of the Black Mamma's croon." The Starks predicted that Joplin's rags "will not go out of style or fashion as long as Chopin lasts; they are as permanent as the everlasting hills, at least as far as this generation is concerned."[41] At least in the early part of the century, Stark and Joplin believed they could aim for both popular and serious markets.

By the 1910s, however, it was becoming apparent that Joplin's music was getting caught between "highbrow" and "lowbrow" impulses.[42] That is, the identification with ragtime led to its dismissal by those with musical pretensions, but the difficulty of the compositions frustrated many average amateur players trying their hand at popular pieces.[43] In 1914, Stark included the following humorous vignette entitled "A FIERCE TRAGEDY—IN ONE ACT" in one of his advertisements to illustrate the hypocrisy of an aspiring cultural elite:

> Scene—a Fashionable Theater. Enter Mrs. Van Clausenberg and party—late, of course.
>
> Mrs. Van C.—What is the orchestra playing; it is the grandest thing I have ever heard. It is positively inspiring.
>
> Young America (in the seat behind)—Why that is the Cascades by Joplin.
>
> Mrs. Van C.—Well, that is one on me. I thought I had heard all of the great music, but that is the most thrilling piece that I have ever heard. I suppose Joplin is a Pole who has been educated in Paris.
>
> Young America—Not so you could notice it. He's a young Negro from Texarkana, and the piece they are playing is a rag.
>
> (Sensation—Perturbation—Trepidation—and Seven Other Kinds of Emotion.)
>
> (Mrs. Van C. fumbling for smelling salts.)
>
> Young man of the Van Clausenberg party rising—Is Dr. Pillsbury in the house?
>
> Mrs. Van C.—There. Never mind; I am better now. The idea. The very word ragtime rasps any finer sensibilities. (Rising)—I'm going home and I'll never come to this theater again. I just can't stand trashy music.[44]

In early 1915 Stark placed an ad in *Christensen's Ragtime Review* (itself the advertising mouthpiece of Axel Christensen's national network of ragtime-method schools) in which he described his publishing house as "the storm center of high-class instrumental rags." He argued that *Maple Leaf Rag, Sunflower Slow Drag, Cascades, The Entertainer,* and *Frog Legs* (by James Scott) had set the tone for the ragtime craze of the turn of the century. These "classic rags" had "lifted ragtime from its low estate and lined it up with Beethoven and Bach." The ad concluded with a letter from a satisfied customer endorsing the ragtime music published by Stark as "an oasis in a dreary desert of piffle."[45] This ad illuminates Stark's continued insistence on Joplin's music as ragtime as well

WE HAVE THE

# LARGEST AND FINEST MUSIC HOUSE

In Central Missouri. We keep more makes of Pianos and Organs and other Music Goods than any one in Sedalia, and we sell closer to cost and give easier terms. We are continually publishing new pieces of music and keep an immense stock on hand, including the complete ten-cent catalogue. Our store is the recognized headquarters of the musical people of Sedalia. Call and see us.

## JOHN -:- STARK -:- & -:- SON.

514 OHIO STREET, SEDALIA, MO.

Compare the advertisement for John Stark & Son, which appeared in *Rosa Pearle's Paper* in 1894, with the one placed in *Ragtime Review* in the 1910s. The Sedalia ad focuses on instruments and sheet music as commodities, while the national ad that appeared twenty years later emphasizes specific "hit" compositions and the company's reputation for publishing good music. Photo of advertisement in *Rosa Pearle's Paper* courtesy State Historical Society of Missouri, Columbia

as his ambivalence about that designation. For while Stark continued to associate Joplin's music with the popular style of ragtime, he also equated Joplin with widely accepted musical giants and consented to a view of popular ragtime as both "low" and "piffle."

As Edward Berlin has demonstrated convincingly, ragtime music by this time—roundly condemned in serious musical circles—had earned its reputation as a low form of music because of songs with vulgar lyrics and inane melodies cranked out by the tunesmiths of Tin Pan Alley. Music publishers kept hack writers on hand to write one song after another in hopes of making a hit. Some of the writers eventually went into business for themselves. Rayner Dalheim & Co. in Chicago, for example, promised to "write words to your music or set music to your words" to anyone wishing to engage their services. Similarly, J. Forrest Thompson wrote parodies on the latest popular songs at the amazingly low price of one dollar per song.[46] Indeed, the presence of such professional hacks lends some credence to the thesis advanced by critics of mass culture like Theodore Adorno that the commercialization of popular forms of entertainment resulted in a standardized, degraded, and uninspired product.[47]

Stark and Joplin, however, make this critical analysis problematic. Joplin's compositions showed his talent and genius—he was no mere tunesmith. Moreover, while Stark resisted some of Joplin's loftier ambitions in favor of more popular music, he would have been the last to claim that he dictated the form and content of the African American's work. Joplin was hardly contained and controlled by John Stark & Son. Having said that, however, one must recognize that Joplin did have to contend with the enormous volume of popular music being turned out each year by the music publishers of the nation. The sensations of one year quickly gave way to the hits of the next and, in the process, helped establish the boundaries between appealing and unappealing musical styles. Anyone hoping to make a living by writing popular sheet music had to produce material that was familiar enough not to challenge popular expectations but original enough—"catchy," as they said—to attract a following. As long as Joplin published short compositions, he was in some ways at the mercy of those business and cultural imperatives.

The presentation of Joplin's music by Stark provides some interesting insights into the turn-of-the-century world of music publishing. We can be fairly certain that the business flourished, because the tremendous availability of pianos had helped create a demand for sheet music. Much of the earlier Stark advertisement copy—such as that with which this chapter opens—traded on middle-class, genteel notions of what a piano represented. Consequently, Stark's desire to create beautiful, inoffensive cover art, his soft pedaling of potentially inflammatory race and class issues, and his efforts to equate Joplin with recognized musical giants all make sense as part of a larger business strategy to gain loyal patrons from among the ranks of respectable, middle-class families.

But at the same time, Stark's unwillingness to obscure Joplin's race and the racial origin of his music did much to advance the incorporation of African American music into American popular entertainment. Thanks to efforts like his, by 1910 serious musical commentators could assert without hesitation that "America owes much to the negro in the creation and development of its popular music, for a large part of such music is due either directly or indirectly to negro sources."[48] However implicitly, Stark participated in a national conversation about the acceptable boundaries of American culture. His own boundaries, it seems, extended far enough to include African American contributions like those of Scott Joplin, Scott Hayden, Arthur Marshall, and James Scott in his definition of American music.

Moreover, Stark's identification of Joplin's compositions as ragtime music—an alluring but slightly naughty form of entertainment—suggested that the piano in the parlor could become a safe vehicle for the wilder, more exotic forms of entertainment that were becoming increasingly available in the early twentieth century. Thus Stark invited respectable Americans to experience the emotion and unrestraint of ragtime in the security of their own parlors. In that way Stark and Joplin served as a bridge between the staid, moral standards of piano playing of Victorian America and the more wide-open entertainment options of the early twentieth century.

Ironically, however, their incidental encouragement of these public forms of entertainment helped to shape a cultural world in which their view of private piano playing eventually would figure less prominently. While learning how to play the piano required either natural talent or dedicated practice, much less was required of the patron of a vaudeville show, musical theater, or dance hall. This passive reception of popular entertainment underlay the rapid demand for phonographic reproduction of musical performances. Hearing a recording of a popular ragtime piece might have added to its popularity, but it might not have prompted either additional sales of sheet music or increased at-home piano playing. Moreover, since Joplin and Stark had no way of anticipating the immense market for piano rolls and phonographic recordings, they were unable to secure the appropriate copyrights and lost out on a tremendous source of wealth. And those new ways of reproducing popular music helped diminish the importance of piano playing to domestic amusement.

As their stories make clear, Joplin and Stark played very small parts in the drama of an emerging, many-faceted industry. But even their limited involvement shows that the incorporation of ragtime—into big business and into the mainstream of popular culture—is impossible to reduce to some simplistic interpretation.

While it was shaped by cultural assumptions and business decisions, it was determined by neither. It was African American in origin but became an American tradition. And Joplin's music displayed a genius that, despite his drive, was limited in some ways by popular demand. This brief foray into Stark's marketing of Joplin's music helps explain how the white Sedalian capitalized on the African American's compositions and how the incorporation of ragtime into popular culture encouraged Americans to dance to the black man's tunes.

## CHAPTER 5

# LOST IN URBAN AMERICA

Scott Joplin arrived in St. Louis late in 1900. His move from Sedalia was the next logical step in a career that had begun rather inauspiciously in the 1880s when he first set out as an itinerant entertainer. His wandering and performing in the southern heartland had culminated in a visit to the great cultural spectacle of 1893—the World's Columbian Exposition. Following the fair, he had eventually landed in the thriving community of Sedalia, Missouri. There he had made many friends among the warm and talented African American musical community, and he had gained confidence in his abilities as a composer, performer, and teacher. Almost overnight, the publication of *Maple Leaf Rag* had propelled him into the national spotlight, and at the dawn of the new century, he was making his way to St. Louis, where he hoped to lay claim to and capitalize on this imminent stardom. If he reflected at all on the move he was making, it may well have been to wonder at the distances—geographical and cultural—he had traveled since his boyhood days in northeastern Texas. From sharecropping to composing, from fearing white vigilantes to making an alliance with a white publisher, from accompanying country dances to instigating a musical revolution—Scott Joplin had come a long way, indeed.

The urban world of which Joplin was soon to become a part, however, differed enormously from the small communities out of which he had come. Although he came to the attention of musicians in the city and across the nation through the publication of numerous two-steps, rags, and ragtime waltzes, he was less easily distinguished as a leader in the African American community of St. Louis, and later of New York. Indeed, like many of the immigrants to American cities from overseas and from rural America, Joplin—though a celebrity—became lost in urban America. The subcommunity of musicians within the African American community in St. Louis and New York undoubtedly sustained him, and Joplin did write prolifically during those years. But except for a few instances when he was featured prominently, the King of Ragtime faded from public chronicles of the urban communities in which he lived.

The seeming contradiction between Joplin's great fame and his increasing invisibility in St. Louis and New York is important for understanding the African American musician's place in American culture—then and now. For his eventual obscurity was never portended by his early career in St. Louis. So one must begin to understand how the gap between popular cultural acceptance and social ostracism of African Americans widened in the early twentieth century. Moreover, Joplin's experience in Harlem, the emerging capital of African American culture in the United States, illustrates regional differences and tensions within the African American community. The difficulties Joplin faced in penetrating the inner circle of popular black entertainers in Harlem belies any interpretation of African American experience in American cities as monolithic and undifferentiated. Finally, Joplin's seventeen years in urban America provide an opportunity to explore the relationship between community and culture at a time when communities of all kinds were challenged by dramatic social change. In that context being lost, despite celebrity, perhaps will begin to make more sense.

At the turn of the century, Scott Joplin ventured away from the Queen City of Missouri to seek his fortune in St. Louis. As he made his way in that cultural capital of Missouri and eventually to the burgeoning cultural capital of the nation, Scott Joplin came to learn a great deal about the crosscurrents in social and artistic life in the United States. His creative mind and deft hands helped shape the popular music of a land eagerly seeking a national musical identity. As we shall see, the nation eventually embraced African American ragtime as its quintessential music, but this triumph could not prevent the King of Ragtime from getting lost in the shuffle.

## "MEET ME IN ST. LOUIS": SCOTT JOPLIN AT THE GATEWAY OF STARDOM

In 1900, isolation and obscurity were far from Joplin's mind. Indeed, the emerging world of popular music beckoned to him, promising both fame and fortune. By the end of 1901, Joplin had published six new compositions—*Swipesy Cake Walk* (1900) with Arthur Marshall, *Sunflower Slow Drag* (1901) with Scott Hayden, *Peacherine Rag* (1901), *Augustan Club Waltz* (1901), *I am Thinking of My Pickaninny Days* (1901), and *The Easy Winners—A Ragtime Two Step* (1901). The first four were published by the Starks, the fifth by Thiebes-Stierlin Music Company, a piano and music house in St. Louis, and the last by Joplin himself. The Starks set out immediately to create a star and to capitalize on his budding fame. The original cover of *Peacherine Rag* proudly proclaimed its author the King of Ragtime Writers and the composer of the other rags published that year as well as *Maple Leaf Rag*. The covers of the other compositions also touted Joplin as an accomplished composer—the man responsible for the new songs on the Stark list.[1] Each new composition attracted attention by building on the success of earlier pieces.

In 1901, Joplin came to the attention of Alfred Ernst, then director of the St. Louis Choral Symphony, who called the musician "an extraordinary genius as a composer of ragtime music." Speaking to a journalist for the *St. Louis Post-Dispatch* in February, Ernst declared his intention of introducing Joplin's music to the "dignified disciples of Wagner, Liszt, Mendelssohn and other European masters of music" when he traveled to Germany later in the year, and he hinted that he might ask the African American to accompany him on the trip. "I am deeply interested in this man," Ernst continued. "He is young and undoubtedly has a fine future. With proper cultivation, I believe, his talent will develop into positive genius. Being of African blood himself, Joplin has a keener insight into that peculiar branch of melody than white composers. His ear is particularly acute."[2]Alfred Ernst was the second arbiter of serious music to offer Joplin encouragement. Within months of arriving in St. Louis, Joplin stood poised on the brink of national and international fame.[3]

Joplin's fame promised to work to the advantage of his two protégés, Arthur Marshall and Scott Hayden, who had followed him to St. Louis. As their teacher, Joplin must have been pleased that collaborations with his students advanced their musical careers even as they enhanced his own reputation as an up-and-coming composer. Hayden signed with Joplin's opera company, and Marshall was also scheduled to perform in *A Guest of Honor,* Joplin's first opera. Marshall's fame, however, extended beyond his association with the King of Ragtime. He played for two years with Dan McCabe's Minstrel Show, one of the more famous companies at the turn of the century, and he later became part of a vaudeville act called the Lyle Miller Ebony Five. Marshall remembered with pride that he enjoyed sufficient acclaim to play on the midway at the 1904 Louisiana Purchase Exposition in St. Louis.[4]

These two students from Sedalia were not alone in following the King of Ragtime to St. Louis. According to S. Brunson Campbell, St. Louis in the early 1900s "became the mecca for . . . Negro Ragtime pianists."[5] St. Louis offered plenty of opportunities to play the music in pool halls, saloons, and restaurants, and many believed a peculiar Missouri style of ragtime was being worked out in places like Tom Turpin's Rosebud Cafe.[6] To some extent— difficult to measure precisely—Joplin's presence in the city added to its fame as a ragtime center.

After W. S. B. Mathews's report on St. Louis in *The Etude* in 1905, the city also enjoyed a budding reputation as a center for "art music." The city, "as a whole," he reported, "is quite musical and probably has a good average of teachers and pupils who appreciate the better class of music." According to St. Louisans, on whom Mathews relied for such information, the city was home to about eight hundred music teachers—one for every eight hundred people in the community. Although Mathews attributed St. Louis's reputation to the presence of Germans and French, it was also clear, according to the census, that African American teachers like Joplin added to the musical consciousness of the city in the early twentieth century.[7]

On a personal level, Joplin's life was also on an upswing in 1900. He had married Belle Jones shortly before leaving the Queen City and settled into a new home with her in St. Louis with hopes of starting a family.[8] Although his busy itinerancy had seldom left him in isolation—surrounded by the members of his Texas Medley Quartette, the Queen City Band, and others in the

The Scott Joplin House in St. Louis, photo by Charles R. Cutter

musical community in Sedalia, Joplin did not take to the road alone—it had meant that he lacked the rootedness of his childhood home in Texas or of some of his friends in Sedalia. The fact that his name appears in more than one St. Louis city directory in the early 1900s, and that he listed his occupation as musician, indicates greater stability and settledness than he had known in the Queen City.[9] In 1900 Joplin was surrounded by a new family, friends, and business associates, and he looked forward to creating and to taking advantage of opportunities in the music business.

Joplin must have seen all of these accomplishments, acclaim, and conditions, as indications of success. People—white and black—liked his music. He could create opportunities for students and friends because of his growing fame, and chances to promote his music opened up before him. By every indication, Joplin forged ahead to advance the music for which he was becoming famous. At the same time, Joplin began to focus his attention on the composition of serious music. Given his effort to incorporate African American elements into classical forms, Joplin seemed to believe that he had as much right as any other American composer to participate in the development of an American school of music.

It was precisely Joplin's serious ambitions that exposed the limits placed on the aspirations of African American musicians in early-twentieth-century American society. Even Alfred Ernst's enthusiastic endorsement of Joplin in 1901 contained hints of the obstacles the African American composer would have to overcome. While acknowledging the "original" and "distinctly individual" character of Joplin's work to that time, Ernst identified what he called "a certain crudeness" in his work, which he chalked up to "his lack of musical education." If "set free by knowledge of technique," Ernst believed, Joplin was capable of doing "something fine in compositions of a higher class."[10] Implicitly, Ernst argued that Joplin's genius had to be harnessed to European forms and musical assumptions. Left alone, Joplin's African American sensibility would remain "crude" and "lacking."

Monroe Rosenfeld's assessment of Joplin as a composer in 1903 contains similar prejudices against the prospects of greatness for an African American composer. Most obviously, the famous music critic failed to bother with obtaining accurate details of his subject's life—"Scott Joplin," he asserted inaccurately, "was reared and educated in St. Louis." Rosenfeld, even more blatantly than Ernst, seemed to find it hard to believe that an African American could produce music of the caliber Joplin was publishing in the early 1900s. This St. Louisan was an acclaimed composer of music, he wrote, "despite the ebony hugh [*sic*] of his features." Moreover, "although his appearance would not indicate it, he is attractive socially, because of the refinement of his speech and demeanor," Rosenfeld wrote of Joplin with a left-handed compliment that came at the expense of the composer's race. Similarly, Rosenfeld contrasted Joplin's "syncopated music" (only a "pastime" for him) with serious composition, which he considered "more arduous work." Although this article served to secure Joplin's reputation as a noteworthy composer—indeed, the "King of Rag-Time Composers"—it made of Joplin an anomalous African American musician, whose greatness would be realized fully when he turned from African American–style popular music to opera.[11]

This praise mingled with doubt may not have dampened Joplin's hope immediately. For even as he granted Rosenfeld an interview, the African American already was at work on his first opera. But he had already gotten a taste of the frustration that he would have to cope with throughout the following decade. As early as 1899, Joplin had completed a ragtime ballet called *The*

*Ragtime Dance,* a daring composition and performance concept that featured current African American dance steps choreographed to vocal and piano accompaniment. It offered a fascinating blend of country square dance, urban setting and sensibility, and modern stage performance. The opening lyric immediately identified the urban setting—"a ball" held among "the dark town swells" and a "hall . . . illuminated by electric lights"—but the song eventually employed the old-time technique of calling out instructions to the dancers—to "do the ragtime dance," "the clean up dance," "the cake walk prance," and "the Jennie Cooler dance," among many others—but the dancers were, of course, performing on stage.[12]

To Joplin's great disappointment, the Starks showed no interest in publishing the lengthy and innovative piece. He had rented the Woods Opera House in Sedalia for a single performance to present it to an audience of which the Stark family were the most important members. John Stark did not reject the piece; he just did not offer to publish it. Three years later, after Joplin had written numerous successful compositions for the Starks, he staged a private showing of *The Ragtime Dance,* and this time, at the urging of Nellie Stark, John Stark agreed to publish it in 1902. In spite of the *Sedalia Times*'s proud assertion that *The Ragtime Dance* was "largely in demand" in St. Louis, Chicago, and New York, the piece failed to attract much attention. Its poor sales probably confirmed John Stark's original reservations about issuing it and suggested the rather limited expectations Joplin's fans had for his compositions.[13]

Joplin's struggle to find backing for *A Guest of Honor* also tarnished the bright years of his early fame. John Stark's reluctance to publish anything but short, popular piano compositions stiffened into resistance after the disappointing sales of *The Ragtime Dance.* In preparation for ultimate publication, Joplin applied for a copyright for *A Guest of Honor* in February 1903. Moreover, he organized the Scott Joplin Drama Company, which by August reportedly was "rehearsing daily at Crawford's theatre" in East St. Louis. Although the *Sedalia Weekly Conservator* reported that "Joplin is backed by a strong capitalist who for many years has been manager and proprietor of several well known high class operas (white)," Joplin's chief problem lay in his inability to secure substantial backing for his venture. Years later, Stark family members confessed that *A Guest of Honor* was the subject of much heated debate in their family. There was some support for the opera initially, but they wanted Joplin to write a stronger book, something he refused to do. As a result, the Starks offered no support for the enterprise. According to Arthur Marshall, *A Guest of Honor* was performed only once in St. Louis as "a dress rehearsal to get the idea of the public sentiment." Although Marshall claimed years later that Joplin was on the verge of being backed by Haviland or Majestic Producers, Marshall actually left St. Louis after the first performance and never learned "just how far it got."[14] Moreover, though Sedalians were promised at least one peformance of the opera in late August 1903, no source indicates that the promise was kept. One of the sad consequences of Joplin's inability to secure backing for *A Guest of Honor* was its disappearance as a coherent operatic work.[15]

Joplin's experiences with *The Ragtime Dance* and *A Guest of Honor* contrasted sharply with his efforts to publish shorter, popular pieces. At the same time that he could find no one to bankroll the staging of ragtime ballet or opera, publishers eagerly issued two-steps, ragtime waltzes, and slow drags. *Cleopha, A Breeze from Alabama, Elite Syncopations, The Entertainer, March Majestic,* and *The Strenuous Life,* all appeared in 1902; and *Weeping Willow, Palm Leaf Rag, Little Black Baby, Maple Leaf Rag—Song,* and *Something Doing* with Scott Hayden came out the following year. In addition to John Stark, S. Simon and Val A. Reis of St. Louis and Victor Kremer and the Success Music Company of Chicago published Joplin pieces in those years. So while music commentators were beginning to advocate the appropriation of popular, African American sounds for serious American music, Joplin found little encouragement for his efforts in that direction, but he had no trouble convincing publishers to issue work aimed at a popular, amateur audience.

As Joplin worked feverishly on the ballet, the opera, and popular rags in the early twentieth century, the city of St. Louis was hard at work planning a world's fair to commemorate the one hundredth anniversary of the Louisiana Purchase. Like world's fairs in the past, the Louisiana Purchase Exposition promised to celebrate American achievement in the arts, sciences, and industry. Planners envisioned exhibits from states and nations that would be both informative and accessible to the ordinary Americans they urged to visit the fair. In keeping with the tradition of having an amusement center and ethnological exhibit begun in 1893 with the Midway Plaisance in Chicago, fair organizers planned to have a district—the Pike—given over to entertainment, spectacle, and frivolous pleasure. When the Louisiana Purchase Exposition eventually opened in 1904—a year later than originally planned—the fair's exhibit halls, cascading fountain, tower of progress, and Pike offered myriad attractions for education and amusement to the thousands of people who flocked to St. Louis. Not surprisingly, the coming of the fair was a great boon to musicians and entertainers in the city.

Actually fair planners in St. Louis, at the urging of prominent musical commentators, hoped to avoid the problems that had confronted music directors of expositions in the past. The fair board announced in 1902 its intention to surpass the musical offerings of past fairs. "No world's fair in this country has up to this time possessed a really successful musical department," they asserted, quoting a lengthy passage from the *Musical Courier*. "Chicago made frantic efforts to . . . educate the public, and the public fled to the Midway. Omaha scored . . . a failure. . . . Buffalo was more successful in that it attempted to do little and did it. The field is open to St. Louis," the article concluded, "to bring forth a musical department which shall exhibit the musical resources and achievements of the whole world."[16] So when Ernest R. Kroeger was named Director of Programmes by the Music Bureau a few months later, it was "with the distinct understanding that he shall have authority to arrange a broader and more comprehensive scheme of musical features" than the bureau first had envisioned. "There will be music for all at the World's Fair in 1904," the directors announced, "the music of the present as well as 'the music of the future'—music for the multitude as well as for the most exclusive sort of virtuosos." Indeed, the board promised "brass bands and rag-time for the many."[17]

Joplin's experience of the Louisiana Purchase Exposition illustrates the persistent incongruity between his early fame and his social invisibility. For in spite of the stated intention of the board to include ragtime music in the program of the fair, the King of Ragtime, whose home was in St. Louis, was offered no official place on the program. That omission would not be as egregious but for the fact that Alfred Ernst, Joplin's erstwhile champion, became the official conductor of the orchestra and chorus but did

nothing to promote Joplin or his music.[18] Likewise, programs
indicate that official musicians showed a preference for popular
compositions by John Philip Sousa, Victor Herbert, and Stephen
Foster. None of the popular bands at the fair featured the King of
Ragtime or his music. Moreover, three compositions were com-
missioned by the Louisiana Purchase Exposition—*Louisiana March*
by Frank Van der Stucken, *Along the Plaza* by Henry K. Hadley, and
*Hymn of the West* by John Knowles Paine—and in May 1904, the
Music Bureau announced on the editorial pages of the *St. Louis
Globe-Democrat* that "the music officially recognized by the Louis-
iana Purchase Exposition" were the works by Van der Stucken,
Hadley, and Paine, and that "no other musical composition is
endorsed or recognized by the Exposition Company as official
music." None of the official compositions, however, achieved the
popularity of Kerry Mills's *Meet Me in St. Louis, Louis* or Scott
Joplin's *The Cascades*.[19]

Although excluded from the official program of the Louisiana
Purchase Exposition, Joplin did play ragtime on the Pike and may
well have shared the view held initially by many in the black community that the fair would be an important showcase for African
American achievement. As early as 1901, fair planners had indicated
their commitment to include African Americans in the exposition.
"The Negro has been so important a factor in the development and
cultivation of the Louisiana Purchase," the *World's Fair Bulletin* reported in 1901, "and is now an element of such great importance
in the industrial, political and social life of the Union that he cannot
be omitted from the great exposition of 1903."[20] The National Afro-
American Council endorsed the exposition, urged its members to
work for it, and planned to hold its annual meeting in St. Louis
during the fair.[21] As the opening of the fair approached, leaders
in St. Louis's sizeable black community heralded the celebration
as "a momentous event in the history of St. Louis." Their school-
aged children had begun working on fair exhibits, and newspapers
like the *St. Louis Palladium* had been invited to prepare entries for
the display of journalism in Missouri. Voluntary associations like
the Egyptian Club made provisions for the entertainment of "colored visitors." They opened a cafe, reading rooms, barber shop,
bowling alley, billiard rooms, music pavilion, and theater, as well
as facilities for bathing.[22]

But perhaps most cheering of all, they learned that African

Scott Joplin around 1904, photo courtesy Music Division, New York Public Library for the Performing Arts, Astor, Lenox and Tilden Foundations

Americans were not to be kept separate from the other visitors and displays. As the *St. Louis Palladium* put it, "[Negroes] will be represented only as American citizens. No discrimination will be made."[23] Indeed, after the fair had been open for about one month, the same newspaper defended it against accusations of discrimination. "Rumors are abroad that the color line is shown at the fair. One rumor heard recently was that the Colored people had to enter through separate gates," they reported. "All such tales need to be eradicated. All privileges are given anyone who has the money."[24]

Within a few months of the opening of the fair, however, it became clear to African Americans across the nation that the promise of equal treatment was not being kept. Very few exhibits contained African American contributions. Many black visitors to the exposition were denied admission to cafes and concessions on the grounds, and St. Louis itself had become increasingly segregated. In June, the managers of the exposition tried to distance themselves from the reports of discrimination by issuing an official statement that they did not approve of concessioners' mistreatment of African American visitors. They did nothing, however, to stop the practices. By July, the situation had become so deplorable that the National Association of Colored Women decided not to hold their annual meeting in St. Louis. A month later, W. S. Scarborough, writing in *The Voice of the Negro,* reported that "the Negro will receive no consideration from any hotel not managed by some member of the race, and . . . he will be denied many of the privileges and advantages of the Exposition because of his color—because he is a Negro." Indeed, in October the *St. Louis Palladium* encouraged "Afro-Americans with any pride" to stay away from the fair.[25]

In one way, Joplin's performing on the Pike exemplified the desire of the managers of the exposition to include African Americans in the world's fair. But in another way, the Pike itself compromised the meaning of that inclusion and participation. From the outset, fair organizers wanted the Pike to provide diversion and spectacle as a counterpoint to the serious exhibits devoted to charting a century's progress in the Trans-Mississippi West. "The Exposition's management is not boasting of the 'Pike,'" reported a local newspaper at the end of the first week of the fair. "They wish the visiting public to remember the fair by what might be termed its legitimate portion, its wealth of educational exhibits."[26] Even the fair planners themselves contrasted the "high motive of the Exposition" with the "lighter vein" of the Pike.[27] The implication, it would seem, was that the acts on the Pike were not to be taken all that seriously. It was a "spectacular attraction" filled with "flare," "noise," "sound," and "color"—a "pulsation of mad merriment." Or as the *World's Fair Bulletin* put it at the end of the exposition's first month, "Whatever of the serious the Exposition teaches, the Pike will impress upon the public the necessity for pleasure in a life too full of tragedies."[28]

Embedded in the frivolous fun of the Pike, however, lay a serious matter, indeed. For though this entertainment district was designed to amuse, thrill, and divert, the Pike also contained concessions and historical reenactments that featured races from around the world, their state of development, and a comparison with the typical American way of life. As the director of the Department of Admissions and Concessions put it, "Through the guise of amusement, . . . lives and manners of peoples may be contrasted with our own, thus establishing by the most striking comparison, true ethnological values." And given that the educational halls and grounds of the fair proper contained one of the largest ethnological exhibits ever presented at an American exposition, which ordered and ranked the races of the world, the lessons of the Pike were not hard to discern. Reenactments of the Boer War, for example, pitted white British troops against their Boer enemies before a backdrop of Zulu, Swazi, and South African tribal villages, offering a graphic reminder of the European conquest and domination of Africa.[29] Similarly, at the Oriental theatre, a "barbaric picture of the East" was contrasted by the "richly dressed Americans" who came to witness the "bizarre shows."[30] Photographs, cartoons, and public commentary on these kinds of displays along the Pike made it clear that inclusion of a multitude of races and peoples was never meant to imply their equality.

Joplin's presence on the Pike undoubtedly contributed to the gaiety of the exposition—the variety, excitement, and the captivating rhythms of the fair's atmosphere. A visitor from Rochester, Minnesota, reported that in his three-day visit to St. Louis, "the electric illumination absorbed and thrilled" him, and he "heard the best music" when he visited the Pike.[31] By midsummer, local journalists were describing the Pike as the source for "a merry time for . . . sightseers," full of "'hip, hip, hurrah' and 'siz-boom, ah'" and "enough fun to please everybody."[32] Music by Joplin, Marshall, and other ragtime pianists would have added sounds that by 1904 Americans had come to love. But being on the Pike meant that Joplin was cast as a popular entertainer rather than a serious artist in the protean American school of music. Moreover, given the subtle and not-so-subtle racial lessons of the fair, Joplin's relegation to the Pike encouraged visitors to draw the conclusion that African American music—though immensely popular—represented a "lower" form of art. Thus, the Louisiana Purchase Exposition sent mixed messages to and about the King of Ragtime.

In the years following the world's fair, the contradictions in Joplin's life, illuminated by the bright lights of the exposition, became even more pronounced. As the emerging "capital of ragtime," St. Louis attracted ragtime artists from around the country who displayed their talents at the dozens of night spots in the city. Unlike Joplin, however, who had become committed to the task of composing works that accurately conveyed the rhythms and accents of his performances, most musicians who came to St. Louis were intent on showing off their speed and technical brilliance. They were performers rather than composers, and Joplin self-consciously distanced himself from them. As Arthur Marshall remembered those early days, "Everything was dance music." And though Joplin certainly had played at his share of dances in Texas, as an itinerant, and in Sedalia, his serious compositions in the early 1900s suggest that he was eager to move away from dance halls and toward the serious stage.[33]

Joplin increasingly was drawn to men like Tom Turpin, who in 1897 had published *Harlem Rag,* considered by some to be the first African American ragtime composition in print, and who continued to publish musical compositions of that order. In 1905, Joplin published *Rosebud Two-Step,* which he "respectfully dedicated" to his friend, Tom Turpin. But even Turpin promoted performance artists at the Rosebud Cafe. Just months before the Louisiana Purchase Exposition opened, Turpin sponsored a great piano contest among the performers who had come to St. Louis in anticipation of that event. Scott Joplin's friend Louis Chauvin won the gold medal, and Joe Jordan and Charles Warfield tied for second place. The *St. Louis Palladium*'s account of the affair noted that "a great many of the best people in town were present," and it mentioned many musicians by name. Scott Joplin's was not among them.[34]

Although not a participant in piano contests—at least not a successful or noteworthy contestant—Joplin published numerous compositions during and in the aftermath of the world's fair. In addition to *The Cascades,* which offered a musical tribute to that popular attraction of the fair, Joplin published *The Sycamore, The Chrysanthemum—An Afro-Intermezzo,* and *The Favorite* in 1904. In the following year, he published *Bethena, Leola, Binks' Waltz, Eugenia,* and *Sarah Dear,* as well as the rag dedicated to Turpin. Of these only *The Cascades, The Chrysanthemum,* and *Rosebud Two-Step* were issued by Stark. Joplin's independence from Stark has been interpreted by some scholars as evidence of his ongoing frustration with the limits placed on him by his early benefactor. After the commercial failure of *The Ragtime Dance* and *A Guest of Honor,* the Starks—though still very interested in Joplin's work—apparently quailed at the prospect of underwriting anything but his shorter pieces, for which they perceived a steady, profitable market. But beyond this interpretation of the Starks' actions, Joplin's publishing with a variety of companies should also be seen as evidence of the popularity of his music, his positive reputation on the national music scene, and his initiative to make a living as a composer and teacher rather than as a performer.

In 1905 Joplin helped launch the career of a young African American man who had made a pilgrimage from Joplin, Missouri, to St. Louis to meet the King of Ragtime. After asking for directions at the Rosebud Cafe, James Scott met Joplin at his home on Lucas Avenue and began playing some of his own work. Scott's work was patterned after the model established in *Maple Leaf Rag,* and it appealed to the older man. Joplin introduced the nineteen-year-old to John Stark, who bought a composition called *Frog Legs* and published it in 1906. The Starks later endorsed it as "away and beyond the best of all 1906 copyrights"—a piece that "touches all sides of American appreciation."[35] Scott's work over the next several years earned him a place among the classic ragtime writers.[36]

This particularly bright episode punctuated an otherwise difficult year for Joplin. In addition to professional disappointments, Joplin endured troubling changes in his private life. Perhaps the disparity between his musical reputation and his exclusion from certain social circles had a sufficient impact on the family finances to embitter Belle Joplin. Perhaps Joplin's need to invest money in publishing and staging his more ambitious efforts, when others refused to back them, cut into the household budget. Perhaps the unrealized dream of a traditional home and family in St. Louis—the Joplins had begun running a boardinghouse in order to make ends meet—took its toll on the couple's relationship. Whatever the private reasons, Joplin's "composing and teaching of ragtime music was greatly disturbed" by domestic difficulties, according to Arthur Marshall. It is known that Mrs. Joplin had delivered a baby girl and that the child had lived only a few months. That tragedy may well have been only the most dramatic event in a marriage that was in trouble for other reasons. Arthur Marshall remembered Mrs. Joplin as uninterested in music, and Joplin's efforts to initiate her into his world—he gave her violin lessons—ended in "perfect failure." Eventually the Joplins separated, and within a couple of years, Belle Joplin died.[37]

Within a short time of these events, Joplin's days in St. Louis came to an end. In all of 1906 Joplin produced only one new number, *Antoinette,* and a shortened version of *The Ragtime Dance,* which was released in hopes of recouping some of the losses on the longer piece.[38] Friends who had sustained Joplin began to disperse, cutting him adrift from the community of musicians out of which he had risen. Arthur Marshall, who bought the Joplins' boardinghouse after they separated, operated it for only a short time before he left for Chicago. Scott Hayden, whose wife had died in childbirth, also moved to Chicago. Another of Joplin's friends, Louis Chauvin, had never been able to give up the sporting life, and he too, lived in Chicago, mired in a profligate's existence in the tenderloin district. By 1906, the thirty-seven-year-old composer had lost his hold on family, students, friends, and that elusive hope for acclaim that had drawn him to St. Louis.

The music-loving public had met Joplin in St. Louis—in the newspapers, at the Rosebud Cafe, at the fair, and through his published compositions. His popular music sold well, making his title, the King of Ragtime, something much more than a mere advertising gimmick. Musicians like James Scott eagerly sought his advice and endorsement, and he made new friends among the musical leaders of the black community. But at the end of more than five years, Joplin found himself curiously at odds with the ragtime world he had helped create and cut off from traditional sources of inspiration, support, and validation. Racial and social barriers had proved to be stubborn obstacles to stardom, and perhaps they made him realize the tension inherent in the desire to write African American music and contribute to an American school of music.

Joplin spent the last decade of his life in New York City amid the cultural leaders of his race. He focused anew on his work and became obsessed with leaving a lasting mark on American music and on the culture of his people. His experience in that great cultural center highlights the complex demands placed on writers of popular music, the divisions within the African American community, and ultimately, the dissonance between community life and mass culture.

## SCOTT JOPLIN IN NEW YORK— "CENTER OF GLORY, WEALTH, FREEDOM"

Scott Joplin did not travel to New York directly from St. Louis. For several months his life was filled with a kind of restlessness characteristic of one searching for a place and personal direction. In early 1906, Joplin went to Chicago for a reunion of sorts with three people who represented both his ties to the past and his hopes for the future. He stayed for three weeks with Arthur Marshall and visited Scott Hayden, rekindling their collaborative efforts. Marshall and Hayden, two loyal students, friends, and collaborators, embodied the creative spirit of the ragtime era for Joplin and undoubtedly reminded him of the importance of teaching and guiding a younger generation of race artists. Joplin also spent time with Louis Chauvin, who by 1906 was beginning to show the terminal symptoms of syphilis. According to Sam Patterson, one of Joplin's piano-playing contemporaries, in the bawdy house parlor where Chauvin resided, the two men worked out complementary themes for a piece that Rudi Blesh has called "one of the masterpieces of ragtime literature," *Heliotrope Bouquet*.[39] Chauvin's deteriorating health may well have shocked and troubled Joplin at a time when he himself was groping for purpose and direction. Surely Chauvin's wastrel ways were not the answer to the older man's quest for meaning and purpose.

While in Chicago, Joplin "went downtown to see some publishers," and he told Arthur Marshall that "they received him cordially and asked further contact with him." He also began receiving "many letters from Von Tilzer and others" in New York, which ultimately persuaded him to try his luck in that city. Apparently, however, Joplin was encountering the familiar problems of the past few years—interest in his popular pieces and reluctance to sponsor anything more ambitious—for he did not go to New York immediately, and Marshall reported that Joplin did not really say anything more about his contacts in Chicago. At last, he moved on. "This was the last time I ever saw him," Marshall reported.[40]

It is doubtful that Joplin was turning away from his friends in Chicago. Throughout the last years of his marriage to Belle Jones Joplin, he had often asked Marshall and Hayden to talk to her on his behalf. In fact, they were the only ones then aware of the deepening domestic crisis in the Joplin home.[41] But the separation, the loss of his child, Belle's death, and the continuing professional frustrations simply took their toll on Joplin. In 1907, after several months' stay with the Tom Turpins in St. Louis, Joplin set out to regain his personal, musical, and professional bearings. Although little is known of the circumstances surrounding the trip, Joplin did travel to Texarkana for a short visit in 1907. That visit may well have served as a sharp reminder of a social world better left behind, but it may also have jolted Joplin's creativity. In any case, the Muses began to speak to Joplin once again in the aftermath of his homecoming. And though he remained rootless for the next couple of years, his peripatetic ways were designed to promote himself and his music and reflected his restored sense of purpose. Joplin must have begun to realize that only as a known quantity could he hope to advance his serious musical and educational vision.

The two important ways Joplin pursued this necessary notice both involved public performance in a national arena. First, he went on the vaudeville circuit, working for Percy G. Williams as "King of Ragtime Composers—Author of *Maple Leaf Rag.*" Still uncomfortable with the speed pianists' technique of thrilling their audiences with feats of unusual dexterity and musical execution, Joplin played in his trademark legato style, a performance style that must have added a touch of refinement and quiet elegance to the programs on which he appeared. By booking his act with a company that had national visibility, Joplin maximized his exposure in the hope of increasing public interest in his work.[42]

Joplin's vaudeville tours, however, must be viewed from the perspective of the early twentieth century to be appreciated fully. He did not have the luxury of later African American performers, who could choose from a wide variety of performance venues. Lester A. Walton, writing in 1903 for *The Colored American Magazine,* noted that African American performers had not enjoyed many opportunities in prominent theaters until recently. Most were forced to play in theaters "of minor importance" until the noted comedy team of (Bert) Williams and (George) Walker appeared at "first-class New York show houses" in the spring of 1903. This "big event in stagedom," he remarked with irony and pride, had earned a headline that read: "The First Coon Show on Broadway." In 1903, Walton hoped that more black performers would soon be booked in "high-class," popular, and respectable theaters in the city and across the nation, because he believed that blacks' portrayals of their own lives on stage would result "in the future upbuilding of the race and in the effacement of race prejudice."[43] By the time Joplin joined the Percy G. Williams Circuit, Walton could announce that "the public seems to be developing a taste for colored shows more and more," and as a consequence, theaters for black performers had opened in places like New Orleans, Memphis, Atlanta, and Chicago.[44]

In addition to touring and performing, Joplin also cut piano rolls of his own compositions, including *Maple Leaf Rag, Original Rags, Weeping Willows Rag,* and *Gladiolus Rag* for such companies as Connorized, Uni-Record Melody, and Metro Art. Pianolas and player pianos were, in the early 1900s, relatively recent inventions, but successive improvements in the technology in the first few years of the twentieth century made it possible to replicate fairly accurately the style and technique of the recording artist. Advertising themselves as offering virtuoso performances in the privacy of your parlor—Welte-Mignon, for example, used the slogan "The Master's Fingers On Your Piano"—player piano companies enlisted the services of internationally acclaimed artists to promote their particular machines by cutting piano rolls of famous, serious works. Such virtuosi as Artur Rubinstein, Leopold Godowsky, Ignacy Paderewski, and Claude Debussy cut piano rolls in the early twentieth century.[45] Joplin thus joined elite company and prompted an association between his work and the work of famous musicians to substantiate his claim to serious critical consideration.

Despite these two demanding enterprises, in 1907 Joplin began once more to produce beautiful compositions, many of which evince, according to Rudi Blesh, an evolving maturity. In addition to *Heliotrope Bouquet,* which appeared in print in 1907, Joplin published another collaborative work, *Lily Queen* with Arthur Marshall, *Gladiolus Rag, Nonpareil,* and *When Your Hair is Like the Snow* in that year. In 1908, he published *Sugar Cane, Pine Apple Rag,* and *School of Ragtime—Six Exercises for Piano.* Joseph W. Stern and Company, who had offices in Chicago, New York, and London, published *Gladiolus Rag;* Seminary Music Company of New York published *Sugar Cane* and *Pine Apple Rag;* and W. W. Stuart of New York published *Lily Queen.* These compositions mark Joplin's penetration of the cultural capital of the nation.

While New York had been his home base during the years of vaudeville touring, Joplin finally made it more permanently his settled home when he married Lottie Stokes.[46] They traveled together for a time but eventually moved into a house at 252 West Forty-Seventh Street, where the composer taught and worked on his own music while his wife ran a boardinghouse. At that location he was within easy walking distance of the Starks' New York office at 127 East Twenty-Third Street and of other great music publishing houses located in Tin Pan Alley.

Joplin also was in the heart of the cultural capital of African Americans. Since the end of the nineteenth century, African American artists, writers, and entertainers had been moving into the tenderloin district of New York City. In his novel about black life in New York in the 1890s, *The Sport of the Gods* (1902), Paul Laurence Dunbar had written about African Americans drawn to the city because "it seemed to them the center of all the glory, all the wealth, and all the freedom of the world."[47] By the time he wrote that passage in the early 1900s, blacks from all parts of the country, rich and poor, refined and shady, had flocked into neighborhoods between the Twenties and the Fifties west of Sixth Avenue, extending north as far as Sixty-Fourth Street west of Broadway. Because of racial prejudice, blacks usually paid higher rents and had fewer opportunities to differentiate themselves by class and social position. As Mary White Ovington, a white social worker among and advocate for African Americans, put it in 1905, "Their difficulty in procuring a place to live compels the colored people to dwell good and bad together." They came for business and pleasure, for legitimate as well as immoral purposes, and to write the music and books that would form the foundation of the Harlem Renaissance.[48]

Music was a critical part of this world. It served as a backdrop to the goings on in the tenderloin, as entertainment, and as an opportunity for work and promotion of black culture. Places like Barron Wilkins's Cafe and Ike Hines's place attracted talented musicians and earned reputations as the premier meeting grounds for aspiring black entertainers and appreciative white audiences. According to one black musician, Wilkins's place on West Thirty-Fifth Street was "the most important spot where Negro musicians got acquainted with the wealthy New York clientele, who became the first patrons of their music."[49]It was at Hines's resort on West Twenty-Seventh Street, however, that ragtime piano music reportedly first was heard. James Weldon Johnson included the following passage in *The Autobiography of an Ex-Colored Man* (1912) to describe the first time his protagonist heard ragtime music:

> The stout man at the piano began to run his fingers up and down the keyboard. This he did in a manner which indicated that he was master of a good deal of technique. Then he began to play; and such playing! I stopped talking to listen. It was music of a kind I had never heard before. It was music that demanded physical response, patting of the feet, drumming of the fingers, or nodding of the head in time with the beat. The barbaric harmonies, the audacious resolutions, often consisting of an abrupt jump from one key to another, the intricate rhythms in which the accents fell in the most unexpected places, but in which the beat was never lost, produced a most curious effect. And, too, the player— the dexterity of his left hand in making rapid octave runs and jumps was little short of marvellous; and with his right hand he frequently swept half the keyboard with clean-cut chromatics which he fitted in so nicely as never to fail to arouse in his listeners a sort of pleasant surprise at the accomplishment of the feat.[50]

Ragtime music had blown into town from the South and West, and it took New Yorkers—black and white—by storm. More than likely, the ragtime Johnson described in his novel was of the amazing performance variety. But its immediate and immense popularity undoubtedly predisposed musical circles in the city to the more difficult, complex, and sophisticated compositions Joplin began to produce and publish. Indeed, in 1910, when a dance was organized by the Colored Vaudeville Benevolent Association and featured music by African American composers only, five of Scott Joplin's numbers were included on the dance program.[51] Moreover, in 1909 and 1910, Joplin published eight new works— *Wall Street Rag, Solace, Pleasant Moments, Country Club, Euphonic Sounds, Paragon Rag, Stoptime Rag,* and *Pine Apple Rag—Song—* with a number of New York publishers. A notice in the *New York Age* in 1910 promoted *Euphonic Sounds* as "another 'Maple Leaf Rag,'" indicating both Joplin's stature in the music world and the continued appeal of his new work. "Although the instrumental piece has been out only a short time," the article continued, "many of the leading musicians and orchestras throughout the country are using this late syncopated number, which can be heard nightly in the cafes on the 'Gay White Way.'"[52]

While in New York, Joplin attracted another aspiring musician into his circle of students and admirers. Sometime in 1907, Joseph Francis Lamb, an eager white composer, entered the Stark offices in order to select some rags. He especially wanted any new compositions by Scott Joplin. He did not pay much attention to the African American man with a bandaged foot seated in the corner until he mentioned on his way out the door that someday he sure wanted to meet the King of Ragtime. Mrs. Stark introduced the African American as Scott Joplin and mentioned that Lamb had sent some compositions to the office. After the two composers left the office and talked about music for a while, Joplin invited Lamb to bring his music to his home. "I went to his boarding house a few evenings later," Lamb later recalled, "and he asked me to play my pieces on the piano in the parlor. A lot of colored people were sitting around talking. I played my *Sensation* first and they began to crowd around and watch me. When I finished, Joplin said, 'That's a good rag—a regular Negro rag.'" With Joplin's assistance and endorsement, Lamb began publishing his work with the Starks, and he, too, eventually earned a place among the ranks of classic ragtime composers.[53]

Joplin's affinity for and influence on composers of both races interested in writing serious music in syncopated rhythm attests to the role he wanted to play in the formulation of an American school of composition. His evident surprise at hearing excellent ragtime composed by a white man like Lamb testifies to his perception of that music as a product of black culture. At the same time, his love of music and his generosity meant that he did all he could to advance the career of Lamb without regard for his race. Perhaps the atmosphere of New York itself enhanced both dimensions of his musical aspiration. Americans from all parts of the country looked to New York as the center of cultural production, and the city rapidly was becoming a haven for talented African American artists, writers, musicians, and entrepreneurs. Here, if anywhere, an African American could speak to the wider American public with a message about and for the people of his race.

As is evident from his prolific composing and his visibility in the *New York Age* for the first few years in the city, Joplin immersed himself in the cultural scene of black New York. He placed compositions with publishers and collaborated with younger writers. He also let it be known that he had begun work on an opera, which occasioned an editorial endorsement from the *New York Age* that "the time is not far off when America will produce several S. Coleridge Taylors who will prove to the public that the black man can compose other than ragtime music."[54] He attended parties, dances, benefits, and other social meetings. Joplin undoubtedly noted with interest the opening of black theaters in New York and elsewhere, which offered opportunities to people of color. Likewise, he may well have been cheered by the founding of the Clef Club in 1910, which brought together "well-known musicians and singers of Greater New York," though he was not listed as a member. And he might have shared the excitement of the *New York Age* writer who waxed enthusiastic about the popularity of ragtime. "There seems to be at this time" the editor wrote in 1910, "a craze for songs with the word 'rag' as the title." He went on to urge African American performers to include ragtime music in all their productions. And given his interest in education, Joplin may have attended some of the many meetings in the African American community devoted to education.[55]

It is certain that Joplin became involved in a social organization that brought him into contact with many of the prominent entertainers in the African American community of New York and that may account for his being featured in the *New York Age*. In May 1909, twenty-five black entertainers formed the Colored

Vaudeville Benevolent Association (C.V.B.A.), which they hoped would "play an important part in the elevation and advancement of vaudeville" and serve as an advocate for better bookings for African American performers. Among the members of the board of trustees were Lester A. Walton, the theater and drama editor for *New York Age,* and Bob Slater, one of Joplin's friends. Although he was not listed as a charter member, Joplin undoubtedly was drawn by the C.V.B.A.'s motto:

> C.V.B.A.
> Stands for Colored Vaudeville Benevolent Association
> We hope some day
> To spread our name and fame all over the whole creation
> Onward we march with our banner flying gay.
> Be loyal to each other, always love and help a brother,
> Is the motto of the C.V.B.A.[56]

Joplin became an active participant in C.V.B.A. activities after he joined sometime in the first year of the organization's existence. He served on the arrangements committee in February 1910 for a dance held by the group, and a year later, he agreed to perform in a musical benefit at the Crescent Theatre. When his friend Bob Slater "tastefully prepared" a Creole dinner for the C.V.B.A. members, Joplin was listed as one of the members who "enjoyed one of the most pleasant evenings that has been spent at the club."[57] Indeed, when he published *Paragon Rag* in 1909 with Seminary Music Company, Joplin "Respectfully Dedicated" the composition to the C.V.B.A.

Changes in the C.V.B.A. in the next few years, however, mirrored a transforming African American entertainment community and sensibility in New York in the early twentieth century. About three years after its founding, the C.V.B.A. underwent a reorganization designed to make it a "stronger and more influential body." The association named new leaders and made arrangements to make a five-city tour in July 1912. In the newly organized C.V.B.A., Scott Joplin figured prominently. He was installed as one of the members of the Executive Committee headed by Lester A. Walton and was usually named as one of the organizers or participants in the association's parties and benefits. Club headquarters were located in Joplin's neighborhood, and he was part of this community.

But just months after this reorganization, C.V.B.A. members

decided to move to Harlem—to move themselves closer to where, culturally speaking, all the action was. From its founding in 1909 to its reorganization, the club's headquarters had been inching its way from the African American neighborhoods in the Twenties and Thirties north toward West Fifty-Ninth Street. After debating the "Moving to Harlem" question for several months, the members decided "to become Harlemites" and found new quarters at 109 West One Hundred Thirty-Third Street.[58] Although keeping in step with the fashionable move uptown, the association made it much more difficult for members like Joplin, still living on West Forty-Seventh Street, to remain actively involved in the organization. Indeed, Scott Joplin's name no longer appeared regularly in reports of the association's activities after this move.[59]

The musical figures who did appear frequently and prominently on the pages of the *New York Age* and who have come to be most intimately associated with the flowering of black culture in New York were people like Bob Cole, J. Rosamond Johnson, George Walker, Bert Williams, Will Marion Cook, Harry T. Burleigh, and James Reese Europe, whose popular songs and musical productions amused millions in New York and on successful national tours. Lester Walton tracked their tours and accomplishments with great regularity, and he cited their work as evidence of a coming African American culture. For some reason, however, Walton did not include Joplin among the leaders of the black musical community. For example, even though Joplin had succeeded in publishing *Treemonisha* and had received a rave review in *The American Musician*, Lester Walton never offered any critical comment on this achievement. Instead, he congratulated Cook and Burleigh for organizing a Negro Choral Society, because their efforts showed that African Americans were capable of much more than insubstantial popular music.[60] Similarly, when all-black programs were organized and publicized in Harlem and performed by the Clef Club, Joplin's compositions were conspicuous by their absence.

Perhaps Joplin's growing invisibility resulted from his deepening commitment of time and energy to *Treemonisha,* his second opera. Set in rural Arkansas on a plantation just outside Texarkana, *Treemonisha* chronicled the efforts of a young black woman to lead her people out of the darkness of ignorance and superstition and toward the liberating possibilities of literacy. It offered a musical and dramatic tribute to learning and diligence, things Joplin believed were essential to African Americans intent upon taking their rightful place in American society. Joplin's opera addressed two dimensions of his race's struggle for advancement and equality—the need for education and the importance of courageous leaders.

Since 1908 the *New York Age* had been heralding Joplin's serious composition, and in May 1911 it announced, "'Treemonisha,' an opera in three acts, is the latest contribution to the musical world by a colored composer." Joplin characterized his work, the article continued, as "strictly Negro." About a month later, the *New York Age* reported that Miss Christie Hawkins had held a reception for Scott Joplin "in honor of his success in writing and publishing an opera entitled 'Treemonisha.'" Of the guests in attendance, Black Carl, W. N. Spiller, Tom Crow, Sam Cook, and Bob Slater were the only friends from the C.V.B.A. mentioned by name.[61] Even at the pinnacle of his artistic achievement, Joplin seemed unable to interest the most prominent and influential African Americans in his vision and work.

Like many African Americans, Joplin had come to New York in the early 1900s with great expectations and focused ambitions. He composed. He met prominent publishers, composers, and entertainers in the music business. And he found a new cluster of friends, who sustained his drive to produce music that could speak to Americans black and white. But Joplin ultimately found it difficult to penetrate the inner circle of African American cultural leadership, and his work failed to excite the interest he desired. In the last years of his life, Joplin's musical efforts did not diminish— though, as a result of the creeping effects of syphilis, clearly his skills and focus did.[62] Joplin was part of a musical culture that was in the midst of transition, and though his work in the early twentieth century had shaped that culture, it was incompatible with its new focus and direction. An examination of the last few years of Joplin's life reveals the widening gap between his music and popular trends and the divisions within the African American cultural community that cut adrift people who, like Joplin, lived on its fringes.

## OUT OF STEP, OUT OF TIME

Years after Joplin's death in 1917, his wife, Lottie Stokes Joplin, granted an interview to Kay C. Thompson for the *Record Changer.*

"You might say he died of disappointments, his health broken mentally and physically," she argued.

> But he was a great man, a great man! He wanted to be a real leader. He wanted to free his people from poverty and ignorance, and superstition, just like the heroine of his ragtime opera, 'Treemonisha.' That's why he was so ambitious; that's why he tackled major projects. In fact, that's why he was so far ahead of his time . . . You know, he would often say that he'd never be appreciated until after he was dead.[63]

The open disappointment and feeling of rejection reported by Lottie Joplin in this interview are at once perplexing and revealing. One wonders at the rejection of a willing leader by an African American community that continued to cry for cultural leadership. In another sense one is forced to conclude that the inability of Joplin to satisfy the need for leadership in his community arose from the fact that he was not exactly in step with the trends and values of that community in New York.

That is not to say that Joplin was completely ignored. Soon after he published *Treemonisha* in 1911, a review of his work appeared in *The American Musician* that said, in part, "Scott Joplin has proved himself a teacher as well as a scholar and an optimist with a mission which has been splendidly performed. Moreover, he has created an entirely new phase of musical art and has produced a thoroughly American opera, dealing with a typical American subject, yet free from all extraneous influence. He has discovered something new because he had confidence in himself and in his mission." The reviewer likened Joplin's use of African American motifs to Antonin Dvorak's appropriation of them in *New World Symphony,* and he saw Joplin as the musical counterpart to literature's Booker T. Washington and Paul Laurence Dunbar. In the end, he saw Joplin's opera as "an interesting and potent achievement."[64] But the review was written by a white reviewer and appeared in a chiefly white publication; members of Joplin's own race did not comment on the opera. Moreover, in spite of this rousing endorsement, within a year, writers addressing the subject of higher music and African Americans continued to assert that "colored musicians" remained in the "music hall" and were "ashamed of their best heritage—the folk music of the plantations." Consequently, they implied, African Americans were not rising to the challenge of writing serious art music. It was as if Joplin had written nothing at all.[65]

Writing opera was one thing, but producing it was another matter. It took Joplin two years to find a backer for his opera. In 1913, the *New York Age* announced that Benjamin Nibur, manager of the Lafayette Theatre, had agreed to stage the show sometime in the fall.[66] The Lafayette Theatre was still in the process of redeeming itself in the African American community for its segregated seating policies. In January, Lester Walton had blasted it in the *New York Age,* writing, "Self-respecting colored people refuse to patronize the place."[67] By late February, the Lafayette had dropped its policy of segregating its patrons and shortly thereafter begun producing shows that featured such popular African American entertainers as Will Marion Cook, Henry S. Creamer, and Jesse Shipp.[68] In the summer, the Lafayette Theatre agreed to feature the Negro Players, a company organized to bring to the stage "our young people with talent—those who have aspired but have had no opportunity" and who used exclusively African American compositions.[69] And sometime in 1913, Leubrie Hill produced "Darktown Follies," which prompted the white critic of black culture, Carl Van Vechten, to proclaim a "renaissance of the Negro theatre."[70]

Joplin's selection of this reforming and race-conscious theater is consistent with his desire to become a leader and a teacher in the black community. He undoubtedly lauded the integration of the Lafayette Theatre and its support of organizations like the Negro Players. To have his work presented on the same stage as a production by Will Marion Cook may well have pleased him, too. But in the end, *Treemonisha* did not open in the Lafayette Theatre in the autumn of 1913. In spite of a frantic call for performers—"Singers Wanted at Once, call or write Scott Joplin, 252 W. 47th Street, New York City"—and undoubted efforts to prepare for an imminent opening, the show did not premier at the up-and-coming theater. According to James Haskins, the Lafayette Theatre changed management, and the "Coleman brothers, who took over that fall, preferred musical comedy offerings," like the one that opened instead of *Treemonisha.*[71]

The change in management undoubtedly hurt Joplin's chances of producing *Treemonisha,* but it probably is not the only or even the most important reason for his failure to present his opera to

Harlemites. More and more, Joplin was falling out of step with his times. His vision for African American advancement, for example, differed markedly from other cultural spokesmen of the community. In 1913, Lester Walton had declared that "better times are coming by and by for the colored performer" at least for "those of ability and possessing modern ideas." Those with "modern ideas," he argued, chose ragtime songs as a medium for their style and expression in American culture.[72] By contrast, Joplin openly distanced himself from this "modern" sensibility by denouncing ragtime songs. "I have often sat in theatres and listened to beautiful ragtime melodies set to almost vulgar words as a song, and I have wondered why some composers will continue to make the public hate ragtime melodies because the melodies are set to such bad words," he told Walton.[73] This kind of open disagreement probably did little to endear Joplin to Walton, who could have done a great deal to promote the King of Ragtime in the black community.

Joplin was out of step with the black community in other ways as well. He differed most apparently in musical style. When the *New York Age* described the "new type of Negro musician" that was emerging in 1915, for instance, it applauded his "spontaneous enthusiasm," "superior sense of rhythm," and his "art of playing modern syncopated music."[74] The writer lauded the speed pianists and dazzling performers and uttered not a word about composition or an American school of music. Joplin, of course, since writing the six exercises that made up *School of Ragtime* (1908), had been preaching to anyone who would listen to "play slowly until you catch the swing, and never play ragtime fast at any time." Many of his later compositions advised performers to avoid speeding up the tempo. As he put it on the opening page of *Pine Apple Rag* (1908), "NOTE: Do not play this piece fast. *Composer.*" As a performer, Joplin always followed his own advice, with the result that his music was less flashy than the performances of prize-winning improvisers.[75]

Similarly, Joplin was moving toward serious, dramatic art at a time when such promoters of popular entertainment as *Christensen's Ragtime Review* were reporting "the desertions from the drama, by men and women of talent, who find variety, an easy method of making a good living. Some of the brightest stars that have illuminated the dramatic stage have found favor in the 'two-a-day,' and some of them have not rebelled at four-a-day in times of competition."[76] At the end of his career, Joplin diverted his attention away from performing and from the C.V.B.A. in order to concentrate on his opera, a musical comedy, and a symphony.[77] In 1914, Joplin also published an orchestral version of *Magnetic Rag*, which pointed to his desire to write serious scores rather than to compose for or perform as a dance-hall musician.[78]

When Carl Van Vechten looked back on the black theater in Harlem in the 1910s, he praised *My Friend from Kentucky* as an effort "to present the Negro as he really is and not as he wants to be on the stage." Set on a Virginia plantation, the show "diffused a general atmosphere of black joy. How the darkies danced, sang, and cavorted," wrote Van Vechten. "Real nigger stuff, this, done with spontaneity and joy in the doing." By contrast, Joplin's *Treemonisha,* set on an Arkansas plantation, presented rural life for blacks as socially isolated, intellectually stifling, and physically demanding. While a number of scenes featured lighthearted dancing, the upshot of the opera was serious. Likewise, Van Vechten celebrated Ridgely Torrence's *Granny Maumee,* which opened in March 1914, as "the first serious attempt to depict the Negro, from his own point of view." In *Granny Maumee,* a "proud Negro grandmother" uses voodoo and magic to assert her racial pride. "By burning in effigy the white man who has seduced her granddaughter and lynched her son she hopes to expiate the crime of the one and revenge the other," noted Van Vechten. Unlike Joplin's *Treemonisha,* which sees superstition and folk magic as hindrances to the advancement of the race, Torrence's drama received critical acclaim for affirming magic as part of African American culture. Significantly, Van Vechten did not include Joplin's efforts as part of the renaissance of black theater in the 1910s.[79]

In a sense, Joplin's message against superstition and in favor of education—a message draped in the setting of *Treemonisha*'s rural Arkansas—fell on the ears of cultural leaders who simply could not identify with that experience. Will Marion Cook had studied music at the Oberlin Conservatory, the National Conservatory of Music, and with Josef Joachim in Berlin. Bob Cole was a graduate of Atlanta University, and J. Rosamond Johnson had studied at the New England Conservatory. Even James Reese Europe, founder of the Clef Club, who had been born in Mobile, Alabama, had grown up principally in Washington, D. C., and studied the violin with

Harry T. Burleigh, another graduate of the National Conservatory of Music. Europe refused to perform compositions with rag in the title. In short, these musical leaders had obtained excellent formal education and knew very little firsthand of oppressive plantation life.[80] They projected an urban style that left little room for the folksy opera Scott Joplin offered in *Treemonisha*. While Joplin's work may well have spoken profoundly to African Americans outside of Harlem in regions where rural hierarchy and culture presented enormous obstacles to social advancement—African Americans who shared Joplin's experience—it did not have the desired effect on the arbiters of culture in the Harlem musical community. Indeed, years later, J. Rosamond Johnson remembered Scott Joplin as a representative of "dance-hall musicians," not as a composer of serious operatic works.[81]

From 1911 until the end of his life, Joplin put most of his energy into the opera. He published *Scott Joplin's New Rag* in 1912 and *Magnetic Rag* in 1914, and Stark issued a couple of collaborations between Joplin and Hayden—*Felicity Rag* (1911) and *Kismet Rag* (1913). After the disappointment in 1913, Joplin continued to struggle to find a producer and a stage for his opera. In 1915, he had to settle for a performance at the Lincoln Theatre in Harlem.[82] Instead of the forty-piece orchestra he had lined up in 1913, Joplin himself played the accompaniment on the piano. Instead of the costumes and sets for which the Lafayette was becoming known in 1913, Joplin staged the opera with virtually no props or costumes in 1915. And in spite of his hours of rehearsal—Sam Patterson remembered that Joplin "worked like a dog" with the cast—the singers' performances lacked the force and polish that might have drawn attention away from the opera's other deficiencies. The single performance of *Treemonisha* at the Lincoln Theatre was a complete disaster, and it was followed by utter critical silence.

In late 1914, the Joplins had moved to 133 West 138th Street, nearer the heart of Harlem. He made a living principally by teaching violin and piano.[83] Probably less than a year after *Treemonisha*, the Joplins moved again—to 163 West 131st Street—where Lottie rented rooms and took in boarders, some of whom may have been prostitutes. Joplin rented a room a few blocks away for his teaching and composing, but he engaged in both these activities erratically at best. Like his friend Louis Chauvin before him, Joplin began to display symptoms associated with the advanced stages of syphilis, and as a result, his work in 1916 took place in short frenzied bursts, usually not sustained enough for him to complete a project or to maintain interest in or the loyalty of his students. In February 1917, Joplin was hospitalized for dementia, and on April 1, 1917, he died.[84]

Contrary to apocryphal stories that circulated afterward, Joplin's death did not result in a grand Harlem-style funeral with a parade, music, and flower-covered wagons bearing the names of Joplin's most popular works.[85] Quiet services were held at the "undertaking establishment of G. O. Paris, 116 West One Hundred Thirty-First Street," and Lottie Joplin refused to permit the playing of *Maple Leaf Rag,* a decision she later regretted. The King of Ragtime left the world almost as quietly and obscurely as he had entered it.

## CHAPTER 6

# THE LEGACY OF SCOTT JOPLIN

If Scott Joplin's birth and death were unremarkable, the years between were anything but. He lived in an era of dramatic social and cultural change, and he helped define a musical style and sound that became associated with American culture. Like others in the era, Joplin experienced the tumultuous decades of Reconstruction, industrial and urban development, and budding cultural modernism and struggled to derive meaning from those events and to give tangible form to those meanings. In that way, he participated in the making of American culture.

At the same time, the events and condition of Joplin's life eloquently testify to continuing barriers to social equality for African American people in the United States. Music critics found it impossible to comment on Joplin's music without also commenting on his race. Champions—like John Stark and Alfred Ernst—established limits to their promotion of the King of Ragtime, whose fame they helped create. The "musical revolution" he helped engender did not—perhaps could not—spark social changes that would advance the material, economic, political, and physical well-being of other members of his race. So in spite of his success at penetrating the dominant white popular culture, Joplin's achievements did not immediately contribute to the bettering of social conditions for his people.

Social progress for African Americans, however, is not the only issue involved in assessing Scott Joplin's legacy, and the lack of social equality for blacks in America should not obscure the important contributions the King of Ragtime made in early-twentieth-century

America. His music won popular national attention as a hybrid of African American and European elements, and it occasioned an important debate about the meaning of America—a debate that was carried on with great vigor in the early twentieth century and continues unabated almost a century later. Ragtime, as an exuberant musical style often associated with sensually suggestive lyrics, contributed to a loosening of attachment to nineteenth century Victorian values. Moreover, ragtime complicated discussions of Americanness because of its roots in African American experience. Thus ragtime forced Americans to consider the race question in discussions of national character and culture.

Joplin also participated in important debates within the African American community. His decision to conjoin African American musical elements with European forms was not uncontested by fellow African American musicians, some of whom preferred to offer something less formal in their music or refused to commit their work to the printed page. In his opera, Joplin joined a timely discussion of the best road to advancement for African Americans in the early twentieth century. His ideas on education, as encapsulated in *Treemonisha,* for example, added his voice to a conversation in African American intellectual circles about the role and nature of education in the advancement of the race. And his use of African American dialect in popular songs and in the opera placed him at the center of a controversy in the community over the best ways to present the experience of black Americans to white Americans without sacrificing either accuracy or dignity.

In all of these ways, Joplin permits a reconsideration of critical cultural debates by offering an angle of vision from outside the circle of dominant cultural arbiters. His experience and his art allow us to understand the complexities of the making of culture and to appreciate the personal and social implications of cultural formation in a diverse society like turn-of-the-century America. By exploring these issues with some care, we can begin to measure the legacy of this great Missourian.

## RAGTIME, NATIONAL CHARACTER, AND RACE

The single greatest legacy of Scott Joplin is the body of music he created. From short piano compositions to extended efforts like ragtime ballet and grand opera, Joplin's music represents the meeting of two musical traditions—the structures of Western serious music and the melodies and rhythms of nineteenth-century African American communities. African American contemporaries recognized the ways that Joplin incorporated songs from his race into his compositions and noted the ways his music evolved from his Texarkana days to his years in the national spotlight. He borrowed liberally from the traditions of his people by using "ring shouts" and "juba patting," which had developed in the antebellum South as part of a distinct slave culture and which he rendered in complex piano compositions. That white Americans heard only the "novelty" of his work demonstrates how separately the races had lived. But what white Americans heard was, of course, only partly African American, for it took its form from established musical traditions with which they were familiar—forms like the waltz, the march, and the schottische. So through his music, Joplin infused life and vigor into the music of *both* African Americans and their white neighbors.

In 1913, Natalie Curtis authored an essay on "The Negro's Contribution to the Music of America" for *The Craftsman.* "Our children dance, our people sing, even our soldiers march to 'ragtime,' which is fast becoming a national 'Pied Piper' to whose rhythm the whole country moves," she began. "This bizarre and fascinating music with its hide-and-seek of accent has not only swept over the United States, but it has also captured Europe, where it is rightly known as 'American Music,' and is taken quite seriously as typical of this country." As she explored the nature and origin of ragtime music, Curtis identified two important elements—syncopated rhythm and Negro melodies—that gave this national music its distinctiveness. Ragtime was "original," compelling, and typically American—but it also "received its first impulse from Negro songs."[1] The quintessential American music, she argued, had come from African American sources.

Curtis was not the only one to see ragtime as America's national music. A flurry of letters appeared in *The New Republic* in 1915 in response to Hiram K. Moderwell's assertion that ragtime might "form the basis of an 'American school of composition.'" A. Walter Kramer, for example, wrote emphatically, "Ragtime is American and no one can prove that it is not. It expresses something that we feel." And when James Cloyd Bowman condemned ragtime and Moderwell's defense of it as "inferior" and "perverted," respectively, Moderwell responded, "Ragtime is American exactly as skyscrapers are American—having been invented, developed, and chiefly used in America." Whether good or bad, ragtime, he argued "is original with Americans."[2] Writers in *Christensen's Ragtime Review*, not surprisingly, also defended ragtime as typically American. Bessie Hanson, head of one of Axel Christensen's Schools of Ragtime in Milwaukee, asked rhetorically in 1915, "What so typifies genuine Americanism as real ragtime?" Only ragtime compositions, she believed, "breathe the spirit of the country" and could "form the foundation" of national music. Likewise, Peter Frank Meyer wrote a few months later that "ragtime is unquestionably in the spirit of Americanism, both from a musical and psychological viewpoint." And the magazine happily quoted Josef Stransky, conductor of the New York Philharmonic, who thought that ragtime "may contain the germ of a national music," because it "has a characteristic American lilt."[3]

In the early 1900s, it was also recognized that ragtime as a distinctive national music had arisen from the experience and creative impulse of African Americans. The respected and learned music scholar, H. E. Krehbiel, for example, had argued as early as 1906 that popular music, derived from African American sources, appealed to the tastes of many Americans. "I have no hesitation in confessing," he wrote, "that were I anywhere in the world, far from home and thoughts of home, I would not be able to keep down a swelling of the heart were the strains of 'The Old Folks at Home' or 'At a Georgia Campmeeting' to fall into my unsuspecting ear. No other popular music would affect me in such a manner. For me, then, there is something American about it."[4] More than a decade later, Olin Downes asserted that "our most prevalent popular idiom . . . is 'rag-time,' the contribution of the Negro."[5] Likewise, various musical encyclopedias of the era clearly identified the African American roots of ragtime music.[6]

Thus, ragtime, though commercialized and appropriated by white composers in the early twentieth century and an important American expression, had not lost its distinctive African American character. Pioneers like Scott Joplin had blended African American rhythms and melodies with certain European conventions and forms to produce an irresistible kind of music—music that Americans of both races could claim as their own. Indeed, *The American Musician* called Joplin's *Treemonisha* "an opening wedge" for the development of "a typical American opera," because "it is in every respect indigenous" and "has sprung from our soil practically of its own accord."[7] Although less successful at writing popular ragtime songs with catchy lyrics and unforgettable melody, Joplin did compose instrumental works that established an accepted form for what came to be known as classic ragtime. He experimented with syncopation in waltzes, though he was not the first to compose a "ragtime waltz." He used marches, cakewalks, and two-steps as forms for conveying complex rhythms and melodies borrowed unabashedly from African American sources. Through the music of Scott Joplin, Americans became acquainted with a hybrid music—African American and European—that was at once familiar and novel.

One important legacy of the King of Ragtime, then, is his contribution to the development of a distinctive American music in the early twentieth century; he was one of the architects of an American school of music. He, like other American composers of the era, captured something about the American experience— something of the national character—that distinguished the nation from others, especially European rivals. As Daniel Gregory Mason put it, ragtime captured "a certain aspect of American character— our restlessness, our insatiable nervous activity, our thoughtless superficial 'optimism,' our fondness for hustling, our carelessness of whither, how, or why we are moving if only we can 'keep on the move.'"[8] Moreover, ragtime captured the spirit and expressed it in a musical style that melded the traditions of two races.

In the end, however, the full significance of Joplin's accomplishment has been obscured by the context in which it occurred and the debate that it helped foster. The idea of an American school of music resting on African American foundations was not easily or immediately embraced by a nation that, at the turn of the century, devoted numerous volumes and journal pages to the "race question." Indeed, Joplin's great contribution to American ragtime fueled a difficult and intense discussion about the nature of American identity. For both the establishment of an American school of music and a solution to the race question involved a definition of national character big enough to include all of the diverse elements that comprised American society. And as the commentary on distinctive American music indicates, race consciousness and a desire to maintain a racial hierarchy informed many opinions about the place of African American musical influences in an emerging national music.

When W. S. B. Mathews prepared an essay on "The Great American Composer: The Where, the Why, and the When" for *The Etude* in 1906, for example, it did not take him long to introduce the subject of race. Ostensibly, the article had nothing to do with white or black American composers or the "race question"; on its face, the article addressed the frustrating prejudice against American composers expressed by orchestra leaders, opera producers, theater managers, and band directors in the United States. Since American musicians failed to give American compositions a fair hearing, Mathews argued, American music never got a chance to "catch on" in this country. But the argument did not end by lamenting the misfortunes of American composers. Rather, Mathews began to explore the problem of defining a distinctive school of American music, and here he got into the problem of race. Like most serious musicians and commentators of his day, Mathews engaged musical literature that drew on Indian and Negro motifs as sources for a national music, and like many of his contemporaries, Mathews deplored their use. "Indian and Negro motives," he concluded, "are almost completely foreign to the average American. They suggest nothing at all."[9]

According to Mathews, national music had to speak to and for the "average" citizen of the nation. And the problem for the United States was determining what constituted the "average American." As a nation of immigrants, the United States included millions of people who had come from Europe. But it was from European music that Americans wanted their musical arts to be distinguished. So, the argument went, America must look to its folk— Indians and African Americans—for unique styles and sounds. The problem with that solution, as Mathews pointed out, was that those "folk" were minorities—"almost completely foreign"— and they spoke in no meaningful way for average (white) Americans.

While Mathews's essay implied the connection between race and national music, others were much more explicit, though no more satisfying in their analysis. Months after Mathews's article appeared, for example, H. J. Wilson published an essay entitled "The Negro and Music" in *The Outlook* that openly addressed the "negro problem." Arguing that African Americans were particularly acute in their appreciation and expression of music, Wilson believed that musical education could be enlisted as a means of socializing African Americans into the mainstream of American life. He applauded efforts "to preserve the folk music" of African Americans and to cultivate the "musical instinct" of people of color. But "if music is so absorbing to the negro," he wondered, "why not devise some way of making it serve systematically to promote his rational activities and to turn to account his exuberance. . . . Surely the best results may be expected," he concluded, "when that genius shall arise who, while feeling the full value to the negro of the more conservative, finely tempered, and intellectual music of the white man, will yet give recognition to the unique musical aestheticism of the black man."[10] Although no more specific than Mathews in defining the national music to which African Americans should be introduced, Wilson was trying to imagine ways of incorporating African American people and art into a society and culture that he believed was essentially defined by whites.

E. R. Kroeger was even more open about his racial agenda. Writing in 1899, Kroeger responded to Antonin Dvorak's controversial assertion that American music would arise from the appropriation of African American rhythms and melodic motifs. "Is it true that we must accept the music of another race (the negro) as being that which is American?" Kroeger asked. "Have not the white Americans sufficient individuality to develop a characteristic style of composition?" For Kroeger it was troubling to imagine that African Americans could speak musically for their countrymen, though obviously the reverse would not have bothered him.[11]

Embedded in most discussions of American music were comments that established a racial hierarchy. Edward Baxter Perry, for example, openly called for "a hierarchy of taste" in a 1904 article for *The Etude*. At the bottom of the ladder of taste, one found ragtime, and at the top rung was stationed a symphony or an opera. "The boy who enjoys only 'rag-time' at ten, only lovelyrics at twenty, may, at thirty, revel in the Beethoven symphony or the Wagner opera," he argued. But this "growth" would occur only "if he has a chance to develop and is not too stupid or too hidebound to take it."[12] Likewise, Henry T. Finck, writing about Edward MacDowell in 1906, reported that the composer of *Indian Suite, From an Indian Lodge,* and *Woodland Sketches,* "never indorsed [*sic*] the view . . . that a great American Temple of Music might and will be built with Indian songs as the foundation-stones. Nor has he ever countenanced the widely prevalent opinion that negro melodies form the only other possible basis of a distinctively American school of music." African American music, he insisted, represented "a crazy quilt . . . of tune from the stores of European nations" for which "the negro has received credit" he did not deserve. MacDowell's "own creative imagination," Finck believed, "would have easily yielded melodies more beautiful" than any-thing derived from Indians or Negroes. Finck's assessment of MacDowell's music ranked the composer's strains higher than those of Indians or African Americans. Moreover, he tried to convince his readers that the latter were unable to have produced anything of merit on their own. Thus, he indicted African Amer-icans for their inferior imitation of European music.[13]

Even those who saw great potential in the appropriation of African American music sometimes ranked it beneath white com-positions. Arthur Farwell, one of the staunchest supporters of African American foundations for American music, nevertheless saw it as a lesser form of art. After urging the American composer of the future to draw on "folk-songs peculiar to American soil, chiefly the negro and Indian," he advised him to "stoop to con-quer," to "come down from the clouds of European refinement and understand the crude but inexhaustibly vital realities of his people . . . their music and their independence." While the musical elements of the folk were "crude," the American composer could "stoop" or "come down" to that level, supply "brains and ideals," and could then make something worthy out of these fragments of music.[14]

Others established a racial hierarchy by warning of the physical debilitation that befell auditors of African American music. In the early 1900s, a rash of attacks against ragtime appeared that used physiological analogies to make African American music seem unhealthful. Frank Damrosch, the director of the Institute of Mu-sical Arts, for instance, denounced ragtime on these grounds in 1913. "If Europe really adopts ragtime," he told a reporter for the New York *Evening Sun,* "it will deserve all the injury it will receive. Ragtime tunes are like pimples. They come and go. They are impurities in the musical system which must be got rid of before it can be considered clean." William George Bruce, secretary of the Merchants and Manufacturers Association of Milwaukee, made an impassioned plea for the "strains of the old masters" at a summer concert at the Schenuit Conservatory of Music in 1913. He held the "wild Apache dance" and "jiggery ragtime" responsible for such "physical and mental disturbances" as a "frenzied mind" and abnormal "heart action." R. J. O'Hanlon condemned the "ragtime craze" as "animalism." And *The Negro Music Journal,* while denying that ragtime represented their race alone, also damned it as a "low and degrading class of music" and described it variously as a "dangerous epidemic" and "not of a healthful nature."[15]

Ragtime, of course, invited particularly demeaning comments on its origin, which in turn reflected on the race that introduced it to Americans. When *The Etude* struggled to define ragtime for one of its readers in 1900, it immediately associated the music with "bands of colored musicians." "These bands are not usually organized, not uniformed, being volunteer affairs," the explanation continued. "The colored race is extremely imitative, and, all playing mostly 'by ear,' any mistake or peculiarity made by one band, which happens to take their fancy, is readily taken up by all the others. This music got its name from the rough appearance of the bands, which are called rag-bands, and the music rag-music, or 'rag-time' music." Similarly, the definition of ragtime offered in the 1908 edition of *Grove's Dictionary of Music* presented ragtime as a musical depiction of "negro life in modern America" and associated it with "coon songs," a term that is implicitly degrading of African Americans.[16]

Thus critical commentary on African American music, in general, and ragtime, in particular, contributed to the ranking of races in the United States. Whether defined as a lower form of art or as injurious to the physical well-being of its auditors, ragtime and other African American forms of music, ironically, were enlisted in the battle over the race question in the United States.

One of the consequences of this kind of use of commentary on African American music was a discussion of national character that managed to exclude African Americans from this group identity— even though African Americans had generated the music that prompted the discussion in the first place. The question of American character ostensibly was not bound to race. E. R. Kroeger, for instance, wrote of the typical American, "He is quick of perception, alert, prompt to act, resourceful, daring, imaginative, optimistic.

He is forever trying to improve upon existing conditions; he is courteous and considerate of the opposite sex, and he is sincere in his efforts to better himself spiritually." Kroeger hoped that a national music would eventually emanate from that character.[17] Those who commented on ragtime insisted that it had captured some important elements of that character. Daniel Gregory Mason, though hardly fond of ragtime, believed that it expressed some of these traits—"restlessness," "optimism," and "fondness of hustling." Similarly J. Lawrence Erb referred to American striving, hurrying, and a quest for "new fields to conquer" as parts of "American life" in 1899 that were reflected in popular ragtime. Hiram K. Moderwell identified the "jerk and rattle" of most American cities that gave them "a personality different from that of any European capital," and he believed that ragtime gave musical expression to that vigor.[18]

In each of these examples, the characteristics assigned to Americans include ambition, energy, youth, and vigor and implicitly suggest that progress is peculiarly American. These laudable traits provided the impetus of American development. But the discussions and stereotypes of African Americans in the popular press at the turn of the century denied their embrace of these traits. African Americans were often portrayed as lazy and lacking initiative, slovenly and complacent. Moreover, lynch mobs were the ultimate tools of critics who found African Americans insolent, sexually menacing, and barbaric. Even popular lyrics contributed to this image of African Americans as razor-toting, chicken-stealing, fun-loving members of an irresponsible race. So even though African American musicians had created a form of music that spoke so eloquently to the ambition and drive of white Americans, it was widely believed that they themselves were devoid of those positive qualities.

In an article for *The Etude,* Constantin von Sternberg addressed this seeming contradiction. African American music, he argued, was a sound basis for American music, not because it bore "Ethiopian traits," but because most African American songs "dwell chiefly upon the white 'massa.'" In a chilling analogy, Sternberg insisted that "speech is the father of song" but that the "mother may come from some other country or race." Thus, while the mother of American music—African American in this case—expressed "accommodativeness," "suffering," and lack of self-interest, the "father is white." He was also "heroic, bold, enter-prising, venturesome, chivalric, romantic, loving . . . devout, masterful, and humane." Given this genesis of African American music and this set of traits, it was no wonder that African American music in general, and ragtime in particular, could speak to whites and at the same time deny African Americans their birth-right.[19] One is forced to conclude that African American com-posers, like children born to slaves, followed the condition of their mother.

Even that unfortunate irony, however, does not diminish the great contributions made by Joplin and other African American musicians. Their creativity and music forced Americans of the early twentieth century to confront an enormous challenge to their society and culture. White Americans in the Gilded Age and early twentieth century failed to rise to this great challenge with a resolution to the race question. Jim Crow laws, lynchings, and periodic race riots attest to their failure. Even the invention of "melting pot" mythology worked more successfully for Euro-pean immigrants than for American-born blacks. But determining the nature of a multiracial society was a difficult problem that simply would not go away. The success of African American ragtime promised a way of binding all Americans together through hybrid cultural forms, and though that promise was not realized at the dawn of the twentieth century, it continues to offer possibilities in the twilight of the century. As Houston Baker has written of black intellectuals and artists at the turn of the century, their particular African American expressions "created a space and an audience for black public speaking" and in the process made African American concerns part of the public conversation.[20]

Although ragtime could not inspire agreement on and resolu-tion of the race question in the United States, it could and did address growing dissatisfaction with the strictures of Victorian cultural imperatives. Many white Americans seem to have been drawn to the liberating possibilities of African American music, even though they were unwilling to countenance the "liberation" of its creators. By denying the social implications of dancing to a black man's tune and by using ragtime's racial origins for their own purposes, white Americans enlisted ragtime in the cause of undermining an increasingly stifling Victorianism.

## RAGTIME RHYTHM AND VICTORIAN BLUES

One of the critical cultural bywords of nineteenth-century America was self-control. It embodied the belief that individuals could become the architects of their destinies even as it prescribed restrained behavior. The idea of self-control also dovetailed with an emerging democratic ethos in Jacksonian America that reflected a belief in self-government—collective, political self-control—and it reinforced liberal economic imperatives to pursue self-interest and to arrive at the common good through private enterprise. As a personal ideal, self-control—which was implicit in everything from dietary reform to sexual repression to religious conversion to self-culture—offered a guide to behavior in the liberal market society and democratic polity of antebellum America. It was understood as a guiding principle in a matrix of social, cultural, political, and economic relationships that shaped national life.[21]

As the century drew to a close, however, the world in which self-control offered both inspiration and comfort was much changed. Political divisions, civil war, and national reunion had complicated the political world by making African American men citizens. Moreover, women's activism in the cause of antislavery had engendered a suffrage movement. This political transformation demanded a rethinking of antebellum "democracy" and of the nature of collective self-rule. Similarly, the tremendous growth and expansion of American businesses that had incorporated the entrepreneurial spirit of prewar America dwarfed individual efforts to control either labor or destiny. The larger workplaces that began to replace the artisanal workshops of the early nineteenth century undercut the notion that an individual controlled any or all of the forces that affected the chance of success and social mobility. Likewise intellectual and philosophical currents of the period offered explanations of life and the universe that called into question providential notions of a design for the universe and that recognized social or natural forces—"rationalization," "class conflict," or "natural selection"—that had much greater force in determining human society than did the individual. Under the conditions prevailing at the end of the century, it was hard to embrace the ideal of self-control without some kind of modification.[22]

According to numerous cultural historians, Americans experienced a "reorientation" of their culture in the decade of the 1890s.

New sights and sounds, forms of work and leisure, art and literature began to appear in this critical period, and all of it contributed to the central national conversation. All in one way or another helped Americans loosen their hold on various dimensions of the Victorian ethos of striving, repression, progress, and morality. Whether a celebration of team spirit, collective politics, emotional expressiveness, or the possibility of consumer abundance, many of the cultural expressions of the late nineteenth century offered ways of constituting society and organizing interior life that recognized the limitations of self-control and repression.[23]

One of the important legacies of ragtime was its role in this transition from Victorianism to modern culture in America. Indeed, it may well be that one of the reasons ragtime gained such tremendous popularity in the 1890s and early 1900s was that its liberating rhythm offered an escape from the burden of self-control. As Hiram Moderwell wrote of ragtime in 1915, "You simply can't resist it"; it appeals to the "primitive love of the dance." He lauded the "rollicking fun," "playful delicacy," "sensual poignancy," and "tender pathos" of various popular rags, which, he concluded, "have no more than commenced their job of expressing a generation."[24] The adjectives Moderwell selected for his description of ragtime bear little resemblance to the language of restraint associated with Victorian self-control, and his reference to a generation is suggestive of the "reorientation" of American culture in these years.

The role played by Joplin and ragtime music in this cultural shift, however, is neither simple nor unambiguous. While ragtime rhythms may have resulted in a gay, physical response—judging from some of the commentary, a nearly involuntary response—it is much less clear that composers like Joplin intended to inspire such a response in their listeners. Nor is it clear that the sexual implications of this unrestrained music were advocated by African American ragtime composers. Moreover, it must be remembered that syncopation was not brand new in the 1890s. It had been a part of African American music for generations. But it was not until the last decade of the nineteenth century that popular music that featured sustained syncopation enjoyed wild favor in the United States. Joplin himself noted in 1913, "There has been ragtime music in America ever since the Negro race has been here, but the white people took no notice of it until about twenty years ago."[25] Finally, though the embrace of ragtime both signified and contributed to the demise of Victorianism, it does not imply that ragtime composers were self-conscious "moderns" or even necessarily hostile to Victorian ideals.

At the bottom of ragtime's appeal was a rhythm that invited movement and expression rather than order and restraint. Musicologists have noted the African American origins of the distinctive rhythm in ragtime music. Its presence in works by African American composers is evidence of their fashioning art from the raw materials of their experience and culture. But the way cultural commentators wrote about these rhythms suggests that other meanings were derived from them (or attached to them) that spoke for a different social experience.

From the early popularity of ragtime in the 1890s to its heyday in the 1910s, one finds a certain consistency in the commentary on the physical effect of ragtime on listeners. C. Crozat Converse, writing in 1899, noted that it "set the head to nodding and the foot to stamping," and fourteen years later, Natalie Curtis described "heads swaying and feet tapping" at a ragtime concert in New York City. These observations are not particularly remarkable; surely it is not unusual for people to respond to many kinds of music in this fashion. The meaning each writer attached to this observation, however, is revealing. Converse, a critic, attributed the popularity of this music and rhythm to the "Simian descent" of the "ordinary music listener," a comment that refers to primitive residues in modern humanity. Curtis, an advocate, thought the performance she witnessed significant because it represented "a novelty to the whites" that elicited "a very storm of tumultuous applause" followed by "a broad smile of enjoyment." Their response, she implied, was something both new and pleasurable.[26]

Others who echoed the observations of Converse and Curtis attached additional meaning to the "primitive" exuberance that suggests a climate of self-control that conditioned the hearing of ragtime. In 1900, for example, *The Etude* reprinted a screed against ragtime from the *Choir Music Journal* that argued that compositions catering to "the insane craze for 'rag-time' music" would "stifle the nostrils of decency." The writer deplored the "double-jointed, jumping-jack airs" and their references to "hot town," "warm babies," "blear-eyed coons," and "blood-letting razors"—indecent terms that well-bred young people "daily roll around their tongues in gluttonous delight." The contrast was clear: ragtime songs "fairly stagger in the drunkenness of their exaggerations," and what was needed was music of a more "sober" variety.[27] Here ragtime rhythm bore the moral burden of having lost control—"insanity," indecency, "drunkenness" and "gluttony." The author's critique had very little musicological content, but it was loaded with cultural freight.

Similarly, Constantin von Sternberg linked ragtime to vulgarity and cultural regression. "Vulgarity in 'rag-time' is, of course, undeniable," he insisted, and called "the vogue of 'ragtime' a case of musical atavism" that appealed to everyone from "the billionaire and billionairesse down to the slums." Preston Ware Orem linked all popular music together with language that suggested both its lack of restraint and its "dash and go, typical undoubtedly of the spirit of the age and country in which we live. . . . The 'Imperial Edward' of Sousa, with its blaring trombones standing up to face the audience; the sinuous 'Salome,' with its suggestion of the Orient; the swaying 'Floradora' sextette; the jerky 'Toreador' song of the nimble and spasmodic Francis Wilson; the 'rag-time' ditty of the black-face comedian, have all this family trait—rhythm," he concluded. In each of these examples, Orem identified and applauded characteristics or actions that violated Victorian axioms of self-control, public decorum, and sensual restraint.[28]

Some musical commentators, like Harold Hubbs, identified more precisely what they believed were the moral and cultural implications of ragtime. "Perhaps the most vigorous objection against ragtime," he argued, "comes from those who, by their loftier instincts detest its favorite haunts, namely, popular dance halls, places of ill repute, cabarets, etc. Another serious objection is its frequent adaptation in vulgar and suggestive songs." Ragtime, like the outcast, found "refuge among the rough and worldly;" it was music for the wise and experienced. Daniel Gregory Mason equated ragtime with "nickel thrillers," "low theater," and "cheap whisky," all of which led to the "relaxation of brains and wills in America." This critique arose in part from the restricted vision of the critics. For while ragtime music did accompany immoral activities in the places they described, it also found its way into parlors, cotillions, fashionable parties, popular recordings, and the respectable theaters. The positive spin on these manifestations denounced by Mason could be found in Lawrence Gilman's review of "The New American Music" being produced by Arthur Farwell, an advocate of incorporating African American and syncopated themes in serious music. The "vivid new impulse in our native musical art," Gilman insisted, was "liberation." Freed from "traditional restrictions," these American musicians sought "a broader range of content and an expansion of the expressional vehicle." In the modern spirit, they broke free from stifling restrictions, taboo subjects, and a narrow range of acceptable forms. Like their ragtime contemporaries, these new musicians sought a music that was not hemmed in by Victorian assumptions, experience, or limitations.[29]

Two matters should be noted at this point. The first involves a curious paradox. On the one hand, late-Victorians, frustrated with the imperative of self-control in a world over which individuals seemingly could exert so little control, took their cues for "liberation"—including sexual liberation—from African American music and rhythm. Such music did indeed introduce them to new forms, rhythms, and worlds clearly outside the experience of respectable, white, middle-class life. On the other hand, one of the greatest fears—expressed frequently in grisly newspaper accounts of rape and lynching—was the monstrous sexuality of African American men. Freudians might well be tempted to speculate on the "return of the repressed" or on the deep significance of the expurgation of a class of people who symbolized alluring, but forbidden, desires. But short of such analysis, it seems reasonable to suggest that in spite of racial fears, white Americans found themselves drawn to African American music and rhythm in part because of preconceived notions about black sensuality. But their *experience* of this music in their own parlors, society dances, concert and theater halls, or arenas of amusement remained decidedly respectable, safe, and managed. In other words, they used their beliefs about African Americans to serve their own ends. As James Weldon Johnson put it,

> On occasion, I have been amazed and amused watching white people dancing to a Negro band in a Harlem cabaret; attempting to throw off the crusts and layers of inhibitions laid on by sophisticated civilization; striving to yield to the feel and experience of abandon; seeking to recapture a taste of primitive joy in life and living; trying to work their way back into that jungle which

was the original Garden of Eden; in a word, doing their best to pass for colored.[30]

Johnson's comments lead to the second matter, which involves the objectives of African American composers themselves. While Johnson's comments demonstrate a willingness to accept certain of the designations for African American music assigned by white critics—its primitive, liberating dimensions—at bottom, that African American cultural leader took pride in the music of his people for its beauty as a "distinctive form of art."[31] Like so many cultural expressions—literature, art, sermons, advice, and architecture— music enjoys a life of its own unfettered by the hopes, intentions, and purposes of its creator. A good example, can be found in *The Outlook,* when in 1914 it reported on a concert at Carnegie Hall given by the Music School Settlement for Colored People in New York. J. Rosamond Johnson, Harry T. Burleigh, and Will Marion Cook starred in the program that featured only African American music and performers. Although the reporter recognized that the African American composers "were proud of their musical inheritance" and "proud of their race," the language used to describe the concert performance reflected suppositions that had nothing necessarily to do with racial pride. Johnson's "music-hall songs" for example, were "not of a very high order" but had "the merit of spontaneity and rhythm and melody." Burleigh offered a rendition of *Father Abraham* replete with "almost barbaric harmonization." And under Cook's direction, the "Afro-American Folk-Song Singers" took the audience "right into the midst of the black belt." The music, presented as an expression of and tribute to a racially particular heritage, served nonetheless to inspire commentary laden with racial and cultural assumptions to which the composers and performers may or may not have assented.[32]

Like these African American musicians, Scott Joplin hoped to introduce his countrymen to the music and rhythm of his people through his performances, his sheet music, and his opera. He liked Joseph Lamb's compositions because they bore characteristics of "regular Negro" music. Joplin may have desired liberation from social conditions that bound people of color to second-class status and that restricted their movements and opportunities, but he, like some of the critics cited above, deplored the vulgarity of ragtime songs. He was as offended by the unnecessary vulgarity as he was by the hostile critics who rejected the music along with the vile words. As early as 1908, Joplin had tried to distinguish his compositions from "what is scurrilously called ragtime" in *School of Ragtime.* In 1911, he characterized the music for *Treemonisha* as "strictly Negro," but two years later he told a reporter for the *New York Age,* "I am a composer of ragtime music, but I want it thoroughly understood that my opera . . . is not ragtime. In most of the strains I have used syncopation (rhythm) peculiar to my race, but the music is not ragtime and the score is grand opera."[33] The interview with Joplin was rather short, and Joplin's comments provided few details for this distancing from ragtime. But it is plausible that Joplin was trying to distinguish his work from the cultural commentary on and associations with ragtime made by contemporary critics.

Joplin and other African American composers of ragtime unquestionably wanted to broaden American culture from the narrow limits of Victorianism in order to make space for a fair hearing of their work, but that does not mean they were either thoroughgoing modernists or anti-Victorian. Joplin himself seems like a transitional figure who bridged the two cultural sensibilities. With the exception of the sexual indiscretion that resulted in his suffering from syphilis—an incident that most likely occurred between his marriages to Belle Jones Joplin and Lottie Stokes Joplin—Joplin respected the appearance of domestic fidelity and strove to maintain a reserved, decorous public persona. Unlike other Harlem entertainers of his day, Joplin projected a serious image. Photographs of the King of Ragtime present an unsmiling, stiff figure, impeccably dressed—no mugging for the camera, no burlesque, and no evocation of carefree gaiety. Moreover, Joplin embraced important dimensions of the Victorian ideal of self-control. The thrust of *Treemonisha* is that through hard work and education, African Americans can free themselves from ignorance and superstition that made them vulnerable to exploitation, fear, dependence, and submission. The language used to instruct students in the *School of Ragtime* also reflected a more old-fashioned sensibility. In Exercise No. 1, for example, Joplin reminded students of ragtime to give "each note its proper time" and to "scrupulously [observe] the ties" in order to play the composition accurately. He warned more than once against "carelessness."[34]

According to Daniel Singal, the unifying threads in various

manifestations of modernism were "a passion not only for opening
the self to new levels of experience, but also for fusing together
disparate elements of that experience into new and original
'wholes,'" and "to integrate once more the human and the animal,
the civilized and savage, and to heal the sharp divisions that the
nineteenth century had established in areas such as class, race,
and gender." Under modern conditions, culture would "free the
natural human instincts and emotions that the nineteenth century
had bottled up."[35] Viewed from the perspective of white American
culture critics, ragtime was seen as an appeal to the modern
temper. But African American musicians like Scott Joplin may not
have shared in that perception of their music, because that would
have entailed an acceptance of their culture as "animal," "savage,"
and "instinctive." Joplin and others did want to become part of a
new "whole" that included cultural elements with which they
could identify, but they wanted to do so on terms that reflected
the proper—equal—value of their cultural contribution.

## TREEMONISHA AND THE DIVERSITY OF THE AFRICAN AMERICAN COMMUNITY

The existence of multiple meanings for ragtime, as suggested by
the discussion just concluded, points to divisions in American
society that were reinforced by culture. To put the point another
way, racial divisions were not the result of apparent social differences alone; rather what people thought and articulated about
those differences provided the necessary underpinning for trans-
lating social difference into social inequality. Since the defining
difference in this study has been chiefly racial, it is tempting to
conclude that there are only two perspectives from which ragtime
and Joplin can be viewed—black and white. But such a conclusion
is not fair to the diversity within the African American community,
and it ignores obstacles for black artists that arose from within
their own community. And understanding the legacy of Scott
Joplin is incomplete without a consideration of the debate among
black leaders that some of his compositions attempted to engage.

One of the debates in the African American cultural community
of the early twentieth century involved the kind of language to
use for expressing black culture. One problem was whether or
not to attempt to represent Negro dialect; another problem re-

volved around the desirability of using terms and descriptions—
"coons,"razors, and watermelons, for example—that added to
white stereotyping of blacks. In his discussion of Joplin's use of
"objectionable terms" in some of his songs, Rudi Blesh notes that
it was part of a "shameful convention" at the turn of the century
in which people like Paul Laurence Dunbar and Bessie Smith,
among others, participated as well.[36] While correct in his observation of a trend, Blesh's comments suggest an anachronistic reading of turn-of-the-century black culture. Not all of Joplin's
contemporaries would have found his language "objectionable"
or "shameful," but most would have had plenty to say.

Like others of his generation, Joplin did not write solely in
dialect. Indeed, his first song, A *Picture of Her Face,* published in
1895, was indistinguishable from sentimental literature and ballads
of the period. The first verse, which follows, contains conventional
rhyming schemes and typical sentimentality:

> This life is very sad to me, a sorrow fills my heart,
> My story I will tell you, from me my love did part.
> The village church bell sadly tolled, the one I loved had died.
> She was a treasure more than gold, when she was by my side.
> But now she's gone beyond recall, in a silent tomb she sleeps.
> The one I loved yet best of all has left me here to weep.
> Tho' death so ruthless stole my love, my dear and only Grace,
> I've yet a treasure in this world, a picture of her face.

This composition, written in three-quarter time with no evidence
of syncopation, conformed to a style of writing prevalent in the
late nineteenth century. It is barely distinguishable from the following lyric of *After the Ball,* which became one of the big hits of
1893 and was written by a white songwriter, Charles K. Harris:

> A little maiden climbed an old man's knee
> Begged for a story: "Do Uncle please.
> Why are you single; why live alone?
> Have you no babies; have you no home?"
> I had a sweetheart, years, years ago.
> Where she is now, pet, you will soon know.
> List' to the story, I'll tell it all.
> I believed her faithless after the ball.[37]

It is also similar in style—though hardly the poetic equivalent—
of certain Paul Laurence Dunbar poems such as

Out of my heart, one treach'rous winter's day,
I locked young Love and threw the key away.
Grief, wandering widely, found the key,
And hastened with it, straightway, back to me,
With Love beside him. He unlocked the door
And bade Love enter with him there and stay.
And so the twain abide for evermore.[38]

Clearly, Joplin, Dunbar, and Harris—though aiming at different particular, critical audiences—chose to write these works in a language accessible to and reflective of the dominant culture. Nothing of the language or subject is an indicator of race.

At other times, however, African American artists and writers employed dialect to convey more accurately the speech of some of their people. These efforts differ very little from other "local color" writers of the Gilded Age who evoked particular regional dialects in their poems and stories.[39] Such writers—white and black—knew, of course, when it was appropriate to use such dialect and when it was not. Paul Laurence Dunbar, for instance, wrote some of his more famous poems with dialect. In "The Colored Band," for example, Dunbar captured one of the great institutions of African American life in small-town America at the turn of the century—the black band that often was a chief source of pride in towns dominated by whites. As the content of the following stanza indicates, blacks took pride in their music and used it as a point of comparison with whites:

Oh, de white ban' play hits music, an'
hit's mighty good to hyeah,
An' it sometimes leaves a ticklin' in yo' feet;
But de hea't goes into bus'ness fu' to he'p erlong de eah,
W'en de colo'ed ban' goes ma'chin' down de street.

Given the setting, the references, and racial overtones, Dunbar's use of dialect adds an air of authenticity to an experience known to many.[40]

James Corrothers had "always detested Negro dialect as smacking too much of '*niggerism*' which all intelligent coloured people detest." But after reading poetry by Dunbar, Corrothers found that "Negro dialect attained a new dignity and beauty," and he used it in the delightful poetry he himself began composing. He insisted, however, on rendering African American speech in ways that did not merely imitate Dunbar. At the same time, Corrothers recalled an infuriating experience he had as a journalist in which dialect was used inappropriately. He had interviewed prominent black Chicagoans for the *Chicago Tribune* in the 1890s and was horrified to see that an editor had completely rewritten his article. As he later recalled, "Nearly every sentence of my work had been recast into what was then the customary newspaper way of speaking of colored folk." In that instance, the dialect was being used to denigrate excellent and educated people, and Corrother's credibility in the black community suffered as a result.[41]

Unlike Corrothers, James Weldon Johnson wrote passionately in opposition to Dunbar. He believed that even a great artist like Dunbar was bound by "representations made of the Negro on the minstrel stage." The result, he argued, was a poetry filled with "geniality, childish optimism, forced conviviality, and mawkish sentiment" that elicited either humor or pathos. In addition to this limited range of expression, Johnson believed that dialect appealed most strongly to "the white American reading public." In another, unrelated passage in his autobiography, Johnson recalled conversations between black cultural leaders in which one would chide another for mispronunciations.[42] For Johnson, the ideal, for poetry at least, seemed to be proper usage of English and a content that reflected African American issues. But he, his brother, and their collaborator, Bob Cole, of course, employed Negro dialect liberally in their popular compositions.

Joplin's use of dialect is, perhaps, most revealing in *Treemonisha*. In this opera, Joplin identifies nondialect speech with educated characters and dialect with the ignorant or superstitious. In the opening scene, for instance, Ned and Monisha, the protagonist's parents, converse with a conjuror named Zodzetrick, who tries to sell them a "luck bag." While Monisha is tempted to buy, Ned angrily rejects the charm; all three characters speak in dialect. When Treemonisha speaks for the first time in this scene, her dialogue has no marks to indicate dialect. Likewise, Remus, one of her students—"to read and write she has taught me"—uses the same kind of speech. By the end of the opera, all of the people who have come under the influence of Treemonisha use standard English—only the conjurors continue to use dialect.

Dialect serves two functions for Joplin. The first is to lend an

The cover of Joplin's extant opera, *Treemonisha*

air of authenticity to his opera. It is, after all, set in a rural region of southwestern Arkansas in the 1880s. The dialect thus helps to evoke the time and place—reverberations from Joplin's childhood—for audiences less familiar with that particular region. The second is Joplin's use of language as a gauge of education. As it did to Johnson and some of his friends, standard English in serious discussions marked the speaker as worthy, whereas mispronunciations served as evidence of poor education or ignorance. While Johnson was willing to use dialect in some of the musical comedy he helped write, Joplin used dialect for two serious purposes, both of which served to educate more than entertain the audience.

References to such things as coons, razors, watermelons, and chicken-stealing are more difficult to analyze. To be sure, many popular songs written about or by African Americans contained such references. Indeed, an entire genre of popular songs—coon songs—bears a term of derision in its title. African American songwriters used this language as well—the black comedian and songwriter Ernest Hogan, for instance, wrote *All Coons Look Alike to Me,* which became emblematic of the vicious stereotypes embedded in song lyrics and pervasive in American life. According to Lester A. Walton, Hogan "often expressed regret that he wrote the composition," but he also acknowledged that "the song made him a big sum of money and was instrumental in putting him forward in the theatrical business."[43] In other words, Hogan's song, though distasteful, had launched his career at a time when it was difficult for any black performer to gain a national audience and when the only representations of blacks were made by white performers wearing blackface.

According to James Dormon, the coon song craze was more complex than mere stereotyping. It began in the 1890s at the height of black minstrelsy and early black vaudeville. In these fields, African American artists were forced to "black up," which meant that they were actually imitating whites imitating blacks. The object of the humor and stereotyping is far less clear. While these songs and the language fueled prejudice, they also provided material for black satire. Joplin's use of similar terms should be viewed in the context of the early 1900s—much as Hogan's problematic song has been seen. Like Hogan, Joplin hoped to create a popular hit that melded certain musical and lyrical conventions with musical and dance innovations. And if Dormon is correct, it may have added a peculiar twist to the white expectations of blacks. For in Joplin's *Ragtime Dance* (1902), where these lyrics appear, the stock language is juxtaposed with ballet, traditionally a province of white performers and an art appreciated by a cultivated elite.[44]

Perhaps the most important debate within the African American community—at least to Joplin—had to do with education and black advancement. His lengthiest and most serious work—*Treemonisha*—focused on the twin problems of ignorance and superstition in rural black communities. As Joplin no doubt remembered from his childhood in northeastern Texas, the lack of formal education combined with folk practices and belief in "haunts" not only hindered African Americans from being prepared to take advantage of employment opportunities but also made them susceptible to terrorism by white supremacist groups like the Ku Klux Klan. One of the great advantages of moving to Texarkana for the Joplin family had been the increased chances to learn. Thanks both to private schooling sponsored by activists in the black community and to the informal teaching provided by Joplin's German music teacher, Joplin had succeeded in leaving Texarkana, avoiding a life of menial work and deprivation, and earning a national reputation in the entertainment business.

As others have argued, the plot of *Treemonisha* parallels many events in Joplin's life. The opera is set "on a plantation somewhere in the State of Arkansas, Northeast of the Town of Texarkana." The cast—like Joplin's early childhood on the farm owned by the Caves family—consists largely of "several negro families living on the plantation." Treemonisha's parents, Ned and Monisha, like Joplin's parents, Jiles and Florence, had lived through the dark days of slavery and civil war and all four lacked any formal education. Although Treemonisha is said to have been born in 1866, two years before Joplin, both were born free, and their experiences are strikingly similar. Both children gained the advantages of education because of their parents' willingness to do manual labor. Both were educated by white people. And in the 1880s, each started a "career as a teacher and leader."[45]

Autobiographical elements, however, are far less important than the overall thrust of the opera. Its fundamental message is that education is essential for freedom. Although Treemonisha as a young girl is "the only educated person in the neighborhood," she eventually teaches others—like Remus—how to read and write. So education to Joplin referred pretty specifically to the rudiments of learning. Moreover, Joplin contrasts literacy with "conjury," which he develops in act 2 with "Superstition," a song by the conjurors about "black cats," "sneezes," "itching," and "graveyards," all omens to be heeded for personal guidance, and in "Treemonisha in Peril" where the conjurors have captured Treemonisha and declare: "Dis here gal don't believe in superstition. She don't believe in conjury. She's been tellin' de people dat dey should throw away their bags o' luck. Now, how are you goin' to get food to eat, if you can't sell yo' bags o' luck? . . . Dat gal mus' be punished."[46] Before they can actually carry out any punishment, however, the conjurors are outwitted by their own fears. Remus, who has donned scarecrow clothes, appears, and the conjurors, believing him to be "de Devil," all run away.

In act 3, Treemonisha completes the lesson by discouraging her neighbors from punishing her kidnappers. In such lecture songs as "Treemonisha's Return" and "Wrong Is Never Right," Joplin blends simple morality with logical thinking as a lesson for the African American community. Hard work is celebrated as are Christian forgiveness and educated leaders. While the final scene revolves around a dance to celebrate Treemonisha's safe return to the community, the lyric, "Marching onward, marching onward, marching onward to that lovely tune," implies that the combination of education, hard work, and morality will translate into progress for the race.

The message and the story were both quite simple and straightforward pleas for education, a subject of great importance to the African American community of the early twentieth century. In 1895, Booker T. Washington had addressed a predominantly white audience at the Atlanta Exposition with the conviction that blacks could advance by beginning "at the bottom of life" with manual labor and industrial education. He believed that schools like the Hampton Institute and Tuskegee served the interests of the African American community more realistically than higher education or demands for social equality. The underlying assumption in Washington's address was that success should come through struggle and that education should be practical. Within the following decade an opposing view took shape and was articulated by W. E. B. Du Bois in *The Souls of Black Folk* (1903). While acknowledging the great contributions Washington had made toward the advancement of the race, Du Bois accused him of asking African

Americans to give up political power, civil rights, and higher education—sacrifices Du Bois believed too enormous to make. In addition to "a broad system of Negro common schools supplemented by thorough industrial training," Du Bois advocated the establishment and support of "the well-equipped college and university . . . to train the best of the Negro youth as teachers, professional men, and leaders."[47]

Education of African Americans was a subject of great concern and consequence in the early twentieth century. It was tied inextricably to the race question and to the desire of blacks for social equality. Generally, participants in the debate attracted considerable attention. Joplin's opera, which was devoted to education, however, failed to excite any comment from cultural and intellectual leaders in Harlem. Their silence reveals a great deal about the nature of black leadership in early twentieth-century New York. First, the intellectual leader most closely associated with Harlem was, of course, W. E. B. Du Bois, whose ideas on education were furthest from Joplin's. Du Bois *assumed* that literacy was good, but he went on to advocate the establishment of institutions devoted to advanced learning and professional training. Thus, one reason for ignoring *Treemonisha* perhaps lies in the Harlem leaders' lack of sympathy with Joplin's view.

That lack of sympathy, however, points to a second reason for the critical silence—divergent social backgrounds of Joplin and the intellectual and cultural leaders of Harlem. Du Bois, for example, a northerner by birth, had learned of conditions in the South only as an outsider. Southern white oppression of blacks, reliance on potions and superstitions, and complete lack of literacy were not parts of his formative experience. Nor did these figure in the lives of other cultural arbiters. Lester Walton, the editor of the music and drama section of the *New York Age,* had come to New York from St. Louis a little more than a year before Joplin, but he was younger, better educated, and had worked as a reporter for a white newspaper by the time he arrived in the city. Likewise, James Weldon and J. Rosamond Johnson, Will Marion Cook, and James Reese Europe had all received fine educations in good institutions, and they simply could not identify with Joplin's advocacy of literacy. They were not "the typical Harlem audience . . . sophisticated enough to reject their folk past but not sufficiently so to relish a return to it in art," as Rudi Blesh has argued.[48] The cultural leaders who likely would have commented on *Treemonisha* had no such past at all. They simply could not appreciate the importance of Joplin's message, because it did not speak to their experience.

Joplin's disappointment over *Treemonisha*'s failure illuminates important divisions in the African American community. Regional differences served as barriers to a shared culture and affirm the existence of diverse experiences within the African American community in the United States.[49] When W. E. B. Du Bois outlined contributions by African Americans in *The Gift of Black Folk* in 1924, for example, he excluded Joplin from the list of important musicians and included such people as Rosamond Johnson, Harry Burleigh, R. Nathaniel Dett, Maud Cuney Hare, Edmund T. Jenkins, and R. Augustus Lawson, all of whom, like him, had grown up outside of the rural communities of the deep South and had received a traditional, formal education.[50] Similarly, Joplin's inability to penetrate the inner circle of popular entertainers in New York undoubtedly owed a great deal to his presence, speech, and beliefs, all of which reflected an alien experience. His music—viewed aesthetically, purely as music—won popular acclaim from blacks and whites alike, but Joplin, as a potential cultural leader in the dynamic center of New York, presented problems that ultimately could not be overcome. In the end it was almost as difficult for Joplin to participate in the making of African American culture as it was to be included in the mainstream of American life.

Regardless of the outcome for Joplin, this recognition of divisions in African American life helps to break down a dichotomous view of American culture and must be considered a significant legacy of Joplin's work. For the sooner Americans can weigh the merits of art and argument by some standard besides race or region, the sooner a multiracial *society* will reflect the popular embrace of a multiracial *culture* and the sooner we will be able to dance to one another's tunes without fear, oppression, or prejudice.

## SCOTT JOPLIN AND AMERICAN CULTURE

Scott Joplin's life story has provided a view of Gilded Age America that enriches our understanding of the making and meanings of culture in the United States. The music that represented his life's work became accepted as one of the first genuinely American musical expressions, and his rise from obscurity in Cass County, Texas, to national fame symbolizes the American dream of success. And the discrepancy between the popularity of his music and the continued unequal treatment of African Americans points to the most important and stubborn problem of twentieth-century America. Perhaps the most important conclusion one can draw about the life of Scott Joplin and the ragtime era is to acknowledge the mutual dependence of American and African American culture. Neither makes much sense without the other, and one can find more than one understanding of each within the national community and racial subcommunities. Scott Joplin was intimately involved in the making of American music; the distinctive American sound depended on the artistry of African Americans.

In the late twentieth century, Americans find themselves embroiled in debates over "multiculturalism," as if the existence of multiple voices, experiences, and expressions somehow represents a new problem to be debated in popular magazines, in public school curriculum meetings, or in the halls of the academy. But Joplin's life provides evidence that this issue has a long past. Even ragtime—the happy-go-lucky music from a supposedly simpler bygone era—shows how the quintessential American music owes its existence to the presence, creativity, and persistence of African American musicians. The challenge in the last years of the twentieth century, as it was in the century's beginning, is to conceive of an American identity in terms large enough to recognize the many sources of national, public culture.

# NOTES

## Introduction

1. Monroe Rosenfeld wrote an article on Joplin that appeared in the *St. Louis Globe-Democrat* in 1903. In it he lauded the African American's achievements as a composer of popular piano rags and noted that he aspired to more serious works. While this article was great promotion for Joplin, it contained a number of errors, which became the bases for inaccurate reports later in his career. Indeed, when the editor of the *Sedalia Times* reprinted Rosenfeld's article and commented on it, he replaced some of the errors with new errors of his own. Neither writer, for example, knew (or bothered to learn) Joplin's place of birth or his musical training. After his death, the *New York Age* printed a short obituary that contained vague references to his childhood in Missouri and otherwise focused mostly on his years in New York City. Many years later, when a retired newspaper reporter in Sedalia, Hazel Lang, published an informal history of Pettis County, she perpetuated some of the myths about how Joplin was discovered. See "The King of Rag-Time Composers Is Scott Joplin, a Colored St. Louisan," *St. Louis Globe-Democrat,* June 7, 1903, Sporting Section, 5, col. 1–3; "Scott Joplin a King," *Sedalia Times,* June 13, 1903, 1, col. 1–2; "Scott Joplin Dies of Mental Trouble," *New York Age,* April 5, 1917, 1, col. 7; and Hazel N. Lang, *Life in Pettis County: 1815–1973.*

2. The following are examples of the writings that kept Joplin's memory alive. The first three are based on reminiscences of people who knew Joplin, and the last is a scholarly essay based on primary research. Each writing is extremely valuable, but the paucity of work on Joplin and the relatively small audiences for these works emphasize how obscure Joplin had become in the post–world war period. I should note that the article in the *Sedalia Democrat* is not singular, but rather is exemplary of articles on Joplin that periodically appeared whenever groups within the city sponsored events that explored the

history of Sedalia. In the early 1960s, for example, Robert Darch frequently wrote short pieces on ragtime in Sedalia that mentioned or discussed Joplin's role. See S. Brunson Campbell, "Ragtime Begins: Early Days with Scott Joplin Recalled," 8, 18; Rudi Blesh and Harriet Janis, *They All Played Ragtime: The True Story of an American Music;* "Swipsey [*sic*] Cake Walk Result of a Famous Collaboration," *Sedalia Democrat,* November 24, 1954, 2, col. 5–6; and Trebor Jay Tichenor, "Missouri's Role in the Ragtime Revolution," 239–44.

3. Jesse Lemisch is the scholar most often associated with the concept of writing history "from the bottom up." In the late 1960s, he published a number of pieces about obscure and inarticulate people in American society who nonetheless left records of their beliefs and experiences. See for example, "Listening to the 'Inarticulate': William Widger's Dream and the Loyalties of American Revolutionary Seamen in British Prisons." Lemisch's work sparked interest in other groups heretofore left unexamined, among them, African Americans. African Americans, of course, had not been completely ignored, but most of the scholarship examined the "peculiar institution." While studies on slavery continued to be written, books like John Blassingame's *The Slave Community* and Eugene Genovese's *Roll, Jordan, Roll: The World the Slaves Made* focused on the problem of slavery from the perspective of the slaves themselves rather than from the slaveowners' point of view. And in the wake of such research, studies in African American life and culture soon followed, creating a context in which people like Joplin could be "rediscovered."

4. This information came from the jacket of *Piano Rags by Scott Joplin,* performed by Joshua Rifkin, Piano, vols. 1 and 2 (New York: Nonesuch Records, 1970).

5. T. J. Anderson is quoted in Dominique-Rene de Lerma, *Reflections on Afro-American Music,* 74, 85.

6. See Addison W. Reed, "The Life and Works of Scott Joplin." Reed, as a student of music rather than of history, provided important insights into the musical influences on Joplin's work. His work is less helpful in understanding the social and cultural context in which Joplin lived and wrote music. This work relies heavily on Joplin's compositions, interviews with family members and friends, who by that time were fairly old, and the collections of materials by local historians. Reed did not consult such sources as censuses—published or manuscript—or local newspapers from the turn of the century.

7. James Haskins and Kathleen Benson, *Scott Joplin,* xi.

8. Lawrence took on a tremendous challenge when she began to put together all of Joplin's published works. She had to sift through copyright files, publishers' records, and various versions and printings

of the same compositions to present, with as much confidence as possible, the definitive collected works of Joplin. In spite of her best efforts, Lawrence was unable to secure permission from Jerry Vogel to include *Fig Leaf Rag, Rose Leaf Rag,* and *Searchlight Rag* in the collection. Nevertheless, her work is an essential starting point for Joplin researchers. It consists of two volumes: *Works for Piano* and *Works for Voice.* See Vera Brodsky Lawrence, ed., *The Collected Works of Scott Joplin.*

9. Peter Gammond, *Scott Joplin and the Ragtime Era* and Edward A. Berlin, *Ragtime: A Musical and Cultural History.* Berlin's book includes hundreds of citations from popular musical periodicals from the early twentieth century. From this mass of material, he discovered that critics of ragtime cited songs rather than piano rags for their immoral and vulgar character. This study raises important questions for a study of Joplin: namely, did critics consider his compositions to be of the same class as those they denounced? Is the lack of mention evidence that Joplin essentially was ignored by his contemporaries? With the word *rag* in the title of so many of his compositions, were Joplin's compositions automatically lumped in with the others? Did the songs come under attack because of the words or the music, and if because of the music, would not Joplin's music also be considered bad?

10. William J. Schafer and Johannes Riedel, *The Art of Ragtime: Form and Meaning of an Original Black American Art;* David Jasen and Trebor Jay Tichenor, *Rags and Ragtime: A Musical History;* and John Edward Hasse, ed., *Ragtime: Its History, Composers, and Music.*

11. In a popular book on music appreciation, Sigmund Spaeth addressed these issues head-on: "Just as any message requires the co-operation of the sender, the bearer, and the receiver, so every musical performance has as its necessary factors the music itself, the composer, the interpreter, and the listener." I am indebted to Spaeth for these important insights. Spaeth acknowledges the slippery relationship between all of these "necessary factors." So even with these categories of analysis, deducing the meaning of music remains difficult. He wrote, "Every composer had his own definite ideas and intentions, and he probably took it for granted that the mechanical difficulties of his work would be adequately overcome, and that his tonal conceptions would receive their just due from the interpreting instruments or voices.

But beyond this he must have hoped for an intimate understanding and an inevitable revelation on the part of his interpreters. He must have dreamed of the perfect performance which would transfer directly to the listener the inner meaning of his entire composition, and in most cases he probably never heard such a performance actually given." See Sigmund Spaeth, *The Common Sense of Music,* 258–59, 264.

12. In a sense, many of the new studies in cultural history explore the gray areas in which intellectual, social, and cultural history overlap. Though some of the new cultural history has evolved from a Marxian analysis that relies on the relationship between "base" and "superstructure" and suggests that the two are intimately intertwined, recent work in the field has moved away from both the deterministic element of Marxist cultural analysis and the rigid division between materiality and the ideal. Rather than exploring base and superstructure or social and intellectual dimensions of a historical problem, many cultural historians, following the interpretive path of such anthropologists as Clifford Geertz, conceptualize the problem in terms of "experience" and "meaning." For more insight into these concepts see: Clifford Geertz, *The Interpretation of Cultures;* John E. Toews, "Intellectual History after the Linguistic Turn: The Autonomy of Meaning and the Irreducibility of Experience"; T. J. Jackson Lears, "The Concept of Cultural Hegemony: Problems and Possibilities"; and Lynn Hunt, ed., *The New Cultural History.*

13. "What Can Music Do for People?" *Chicago Daily Tribune,* June 12, 1893, 8, col. 1; Walter R. Spalding, *Music: An Art and a Language,* 1, 5; and Eric Clarke, *Music in Everyday Life,* 24.

14. Aaron Copland, *What to Listen For in Music,* 12.

15. For brief discussions of the musicological analysis of Joplin's music, see Haskins, *Scott Joplin,* 63–86; and Blesh, *They All Played Ragtime,* 51–53. For a longer, fuller treatment, see Reed, "The Life and Works of Scott Joplin."

16. Sandra S. Sizer, *Gospel Hymns and Social Religion: The Rhetoric of Nineteenth-Century Revivalism;* James Dormon, "Shaping the Popular Image of Post-Reconstruction American Blacks: The 'Coon Song' Phenomenon of the Gilded Age"; Berlin, *Ragtime: A Musical and Cultural History;* and Nicholas Tawa, *The Way to Tin Pan Alley: American Popular Song, 1866–1910.*

17. Though twenty-five years old now, David Brion Davis's discussion of cultural history is still one of the best places to begin thinking about ways to conceptualize the relationships between society and culture and between the individual and culture. More recent developments in cultural history incorporate the idea of "cultural hegemony" introduced by Antonio Gramsci. Jackson Lears and Raymond Williams are largely responsible for acquainting other historians with the term and its potential for clarifying important relationships in the past. Lynn Hunt has recently brought together a variety of

essays that apply some of these insights to particular cultural issues. Questions about language and intellectual history are effectively discussed by Dominick LaCapra, though one might want to consult work by Terry Eagleton for a clear introduction of the evolution of literary theory in the twentieth century. See David Brion Davis, "Some Recent Directions in American Cultural History"; Raymond Williams, "Base and Superstructure in Marxist Cultural Theory"; T. J. Jackson Lears, "The Concept of Cultural Hegemony: Problems and Possibilities"; Hunt, *The New Cultural History;* Dominick La Capra, *Rethinking Intellectual History: Texts, Contexts, Language;* and Terry Eagleton, *Literary Theory: An Introduction.*

18. Elie Siegmeister, *Music and Society.* Siegmeister himself was a fascinating figure. After studying at Columbia College and Juilliard, he worked with Nadia Boulanger to learn composition. In his own work, he seems to have been interested in the ways folk music could nourish serious composition, for his own compositions included *American Folk Suite, May Day,* and *North Pole Flight,* which incorporate folk or commonplace themes in serious music. In addition, he co-authored a compilation of Negro protest songs, conducted the music for a film called *People of Cumberland,* and lectured in the New School for Social Research in New York. For a general overview of intellectuals in the 1930s, see Richard Pells, *Radical Visions and American Dreams: Culture and Social Thought in the Depression Years* and Warren Susman, *Culture as History: The Transformation of American Society in the Twentieth Century,* especially chapters 9–11.

19. See for example, Theodor Adorno, "Popular Music," in *Introduction to the Sociology of Music.* The English version was translated from German by E. B. Ashton. For an introduction to the Frankfurt School's critical theory, see Stephen Eric Bronner and Douglas MacKay Kellner, eds., *Critical Theory and Society: A Reader,* Part 3: Cultural Criticism and the Critique of Mass Culture.

20. A good example of recent work in the sociology of music, which follows Adorno's interpretive lead, can be found in Fabio Dasilva, Anthony Blasi, and David Dees, *The Sociology of Music,* 5.

21. Christopher Ballantine, *Music and Its Social Meanings.*

22. W. E. B. Du Bois, *The Souls of Black Folk,* 16–17.

23. Hiram K. Moderwell, "Ragtime"; "Ragtime as a Source of National Music"; "Idealized Ragtime." For other similar discussions see the following articles: T. Carl Whitmer, "The Energy of American Crowd Music"; H. E. Krehbiel, "The Distinctive Note in American Music"; J. Lawrence Erb, "Where Is the American Song?"; David Bispham, "Music as a Factor in National Life"; Arthur Farwell, "The Struggle toward a National Music"; Constantin von Sternberg, "What

Is American Music?"; Untitled Editorial, *The Etude* 17 (December 1899): 379–80; and Olin Downes, "An American Composer."

24. "Our Musical Condition," 138.

25. Kelly Miller, "The Artistic Gifts of the Negro."

26. "Theatrical Comment," *New York Age,* April 3, 1913, 6, cols. 1–2.

27. Werner Sollors, ed., *The Invention of Ethnicity,* xiv.

28. In addition to Sollors's *The Invention of Ethnicity,* see the following works for a discussion of ethnicity and American culture: Werner Sollors, *Beyond Ethnicity: Consent and Descent in American Culture;* Philip Gleason, *Speaking of Diversity: Language and Ethnicity in Twentieth-Century America;* and Luther S. Luedtke, ed., *Making America: The Society and Culture of the United States.*

29. Eric Foner, *Reconstruction: America's Unfinished Revolution, 1863–1877.*

30. The following secondary works have illustrated Americans' perceptions of themselves as Protestant, Anglo-Saxon, and middle class: Joseph J. Ellis, *After the Revolution: Profiles of Early American Culture;* Steven Watts, *The Republic Reborn: War and the Making of Liberal America, 1790–1820;* Daniel Walker Howe, *The Political Culture of the American Whigs;* Ronald G. Walters, *American Reformers, 1815–1860;* Ann Douglas, *The Feminization of American Culture;* Karen Halttunen, *Confidence Men and Painted Women: A Study of Middle-Class Culture in America, 1830–1870;* T. J. Jackson Lears, *No Place of Grace: Antimodernism and the Transformation of American Culture, 1880–1920;* and David Brion Davis, *Antebellum American Culture.*

31. Perhaps the best example of Anglo-Saxon Protestant concern and defensiveness appeared in print in 1885, when Josiah Strong published *Our Country: Its Possible Future and Its Present Crisis* (New York: Baker & Taylor, 1885), which he wrote at the behest of the American Home Missionary Society.

32. The following citations are only a sampling of the articles published at the turn of the century on some aspect of American culture and society. William O. Partridge, "The American School of Sculpture"; P. A. Bruce, "The American Negro of To-day"; J. W. Dow, "American Renaissance"; Jessie Trimble, "The Founder of an American School of Art"; "Americans in the Rough"; William Archer, "America To-day: The Republic and the Empire"; Helen Campbell, "Is American Domesticity Decreasing, and if so, Why?"; Nicholas Paine Gilman, *Socialism and the American Spirit;* George A. Gordon, "The Real America"; Ian Maclaren, "The Restless Energy of the American People—An Impression"; John Clark Ridpath, "Shall the United States Be Europeanized"; J. E. Rankin, "Pride of American Citizenship"; and "What Is the American Spirit?"

33. "Music in America," 108–9.

34. Henry F. Gilbert, "The American Composer," 170, 178. The italics are Gilbert's.

35. "Dvorak on Negro Melodies."

36. Two typical responses were letters to the *Musical Record* that appeared in the same issue that reprinted Dvorak's comments on Negro Melodies. See an anonymous letter entitled "An African School of Music" and John Francis Gilder's letter entitled "Dvorak's American Theory."

37. The following articles represent a sampling of essays on the problem of American music at the turn of the century: Sternberg, "What Is American Music?"; Farwell, "The Struggle toward a National Music"; Constantin von Sternberg, "National Music"; Bispham, "Music as a Factor in National Life"; Lawrence Gilman, "The New American Music"; Erb, "Where Is the American Song?"; Richard Aldrich, "American Composers"; E. Irenaeus Stevenson, "Will American Composition Ever Possess a Distinctive Accent?"; E. R. Kroeger, "On 'American' Music"; Krehbiel, "The Distinctive Note in American Music"; W. S. B. Mathews, "The Great American Composer: The Where, the Why, and the When"; "Music in America"; Gilbert, "The American Composer."

## Chapter 1. Reconstructing a Childhood; Reconstructing the Nation

1. James Haskins's diligent work with census material provides convincing evidence that Joplin's father was a slave belonging to Charles Moores and brought to Texas from South Carolina. Joplin's mother reputedly was a freewoman from Kentucky, but as Haskins points out, no records confirm or dispute this family story. Nevertheless, both of Joplin's parents were acquainted with the "peculiar institution" firsthand. Jiles was freed sometime before the outbreak of the Civil War and married Florence sometime during the war. See James Haskins, *Scott Joplin*, 19–36.

2. Ibid., 24–27.

3. Ibid.

4. Randolph B. Campbell, *An Empire for Slavery: The Peculiar Institution in Texas, 1821–1865*, 57.

5. Ibid., 231; and Leon F. Litwack, *Been in the Storm So Long: The Aftermath of Slavery*, 184.

6. James W. Smallwood, *Time of Hope, Time of Despair: Black Texans during Reconstruction*, 25–37; Litwack, *Been in the Storm So Long*, 184; and Campbell, *An Empire for Slavery*, 231.

7. Much has been written about the aftermath of the Civil War and the efforts to rebuild the nation. One of the best synthetic treatments to appear in recent years is Foner, *Reconstruction*.

8. For more information on the ratification of the Fourteenth Amendment and the votes in each state, see Horace Edgar Flack, *The Adoption of the Fourteenth Amendment,* 190, 191. For excellent studies of Reconstruction in Texas see: Lawrence D. Rice, *The Negro in Texas, 1874–1900;* James Marten, *Texas Divided: Loyalty and Dissent in the Lone Star State, 1856–1874;* William L. Richter, *The Army in Texas during Reconstruction;* W. C. Nunn, *Texas under the Carpetbaggers;* and Smallwood, *Time of Hope.*

9. Powell Clayton, *The Aftermath of the Civil War in Arkansas,* 68, 69, 64.

10. Litwack, *Been in the Storm So Long,* 184–85.

11. Foner, *Reconstruction,* 119.

12. Litwack, *Been in the Storm So Long,* 184–85.

13. George P. Rawick, *The American Slave: A Composite Autobiography,* Supplement, Series 2, Vol. 2, Part 1, 403.

14. Litwack, *Been in the Storm So Long,* 308–9.

15. Richter, *The Army in Texas during Reconstruction,* 159–161; Smallwood, *Time of Hope,* 64.

16. See the narratives of Will Adams, Campbell Davis, and Bill Collins in Rawick, *The American Slave,* Vol. 4, Part 1, 3, 287; and Supplement, Series 2, Vol. 3, Part 2, 882.

17. Quoted in Smallwood, *Time of Hope,* 165.

18. W. D. Wood, *Reminiscences of Reconstruction in Texas,* 5, 14–15. Wood was a prominent resident of Centreville in Leon County, Texas, at the end of the Civil War.

19. Smallwood, *Time of Hope,* 65; and "The Need of Vigilance," *The Jefferson Radical,* December 11, 1869, 1, col. 2–3.

20. Foner, *Reconstruction,* 200.

21. Ibid., 205. See also Smallwood, *Time of Hope,* 54–56.

22. Smallwood, *Time of Hope,* 60–61.

23. Rawick, *The American Slave,* Supplement, Series 2, Part 4, Vol. 5, 1823. Barbara Susan Overton Chandler included some material on Cullen Baker in her 1937 Master's Thesis entitled "A History of Bowie County." Written from an apologist's perspective, Chandler's thesis argued that Baker was hired by whites interested in protecting "the weak and oppressed" against "unscrupulous carpetbaggers," "vicious negro[es]," and "undesirable men." Even after he escaped arrest by shooting his would-be captors and killing one man, "Baker was hailed as a hero by many people." See Chandler, "A History of Bowie County," 49–50.

24. Smallwood, *Time of Hope,* 61, 142.

25. See Gus Bradshaw's comments in Rawick, *The American Slave,* Supplement, Series 2, Vol. 2, Part 1, 393. This was true throughout

the South as Genovese noted in *Roll, Jordan, Roll*. Of course, it is important to recognize that Rawick's oral histories, on which Genovese based his work and which I cite here, were recorded in the 1930s well after the end of the Civil War. Perhaps one can account for some of the rosiness of the portrayal of slavery by remembering that African Americans in 1930 had survived decades of lynchings, discrimination, two severe economic depressions, and social ostracism as free citizens.

26. 1870 Manuscript Census, Davis County, Linden, Texas, 14–15.

27. *Tenth Census, 1880: Report on Cotton Production in the United States*, 5:161. The "Report on the Cotton Production in the State of Texas" was prepared by R. H. Loughridge, Ph.D. For the testimony of A. M. Moore of Harrison County, see Rawick, *The American Slave*, Vol. 5, Part 3, 119.

28. *Tenth Census, 1880: Report on Cotton Production in the United States*, 5:161–62.

29. Rawick, *The American Slave*, Supplement, Series 2, Vol. 2, Part 1, 395, 392.

30. Ibid., Vol. 3, Part 2, 597.

31. Chandler, "A History of Bowie County," 58.

32. *Ninth Census, 1870: A Compendium of the Ninth Census of the United States*, 840–41. Cass County itself reported to the census taker that no industrial or lumbering establishments existed in the county. This may be somewhat misleading, because the area now known as Cass County was in the midst of being renamed from Davis County—in a few instances in the 1870 census, one can find information from Cass County, but more often it is still listed as Davis County. Davis County reported the existence of 6 lumber mills employing 26 men. For a breakdown of productive establishments and the number of workers employed in each by counties, see statistics for Davis (now Cass), Harrison, Bowie, Marion, Red River, Upshur, and Titus Counties in *Ninth Census, 1870: The Statistics of the Wealth and Industry of the United States*, 735–36.

33. Smallwood, *Time of Hope*, 73–74, 80; for school attendance see *Ninth Census, 1870: The Statistics of the Population of the United States*, 1:429.

34. For Louis Cain's narrative, see Rawick, *The American Slave*, Supplement, Series 2, Vol. 3, Part 2, 597.

35. Litwack, *Been in the Storm So Long*, 305.

36. See A. M. Moore's narrative in Rawick, *The American Slave*, Vol. 5, Part 3, 123; and J. Mason Brewer, *Negro Legislators of Texas and Their Descendants: A History of the Negro in Texas Politics from Reconstruction to Disfranchisement*.

37. See Lee Pierce's narrative in Rawick, *The American Slave,* Vol. 5, Part 3, 186–87.

38. See Nancy King's narrative in Rawick, *The American Slave,* Vol. 4, Part 2, 289.

39. Chandler, "A History of Bowie County," 87.

40. See Betty Powers's narrative in Rawick, *The American Slave,* Vol. 5, Part 3, 192.

41. Rice, *The Negro in Texas,* 265–68; and Smallwood, *Time of Hope,* 119–23. See *Daily Texarkana Independent,* August 19, 1884, 4, col. 3; September 4, 1884, 4, col. 2; and October 24, 1884, 4, col. 4.

42. Rawick, *The American Slave,* Supplement, Series 2, Vol. 3, Part 2, 518.

43. Ibid., Vol. 2, Part 1, 129.

44. See narratives by Simp Campbell and Lucius Cooper in Rawick, *The American Slave,* Supplement, Series 2, Vol. 3, Part 2, 615, 930.

45. Workers of the Writers' Program of the Works Projects Administration, *Arkansas: A Guide to the State,* 121.

46. Rawick, *The American Slave,* Supplement, Series 2, Vol. 3, Part 2, 517.

47. Rawick, *The American Slave,* Supplement, Series 2, Vol. 3, Part 2, 693.

48. Haskins, *Scott Joplin,* 46–47; and Addison W. Reed, "The Life and Works of Scott Joplin," 7–8.

49. Chandler, "A History of Bowie County," 68–69.

50. Barbara Overton Chandler and J. E. Howe, *History of Texarkana and Bowie and Miller Counties Texas-Arkansas,* 75.

51. Rice, *The Negro in Texas,* 187–88.

52. *Tenth Census, 1880: Report on Cotton Production in the United States,* 5:104. According to the tenth census, black farmers in Miller County, Arkansas, just across the border from where Joplin had been working in Texas, earned about ten dollars a month, which was roughly the equivalent of working on shares. Differences undoubtedly existed in the two states, but the census taker on the Texas side did not accumulate the same anecdotal information about African Americans' livelihood in that state that he reported in Arkansas. Nevertheless, it is probably safe to assume that the Joplins' financial situation improved substantially when they moved to Texarkana.

53. *Tenth Census, 1880: The Newspaper and Periodical Press,* 8:338. Although none of these newspapers from the 1870s is extant, I assume their contents were similar to those in other parts of the country in the same period and to the *Daily Texarkana Independent,* of which numerous issues from the 1880s have survived.

54. Chandler, "A History of Bowie County," 54–55.

55. See advertisements for these schools in the *Daily Texarkana Independent,* August 19, 1884.

56. "Sensible Colored People," *Daily Texarkana Independent,* September 12, 1884, 4, col. 2.

57. *Daily Texarkana Independent,* September 1, 1884, 1, col. 1.

58. Haskins, *Scott Joplin,* 46, 205. For information on the Joplins and their neighbors, see the 1880 Manuscript Census, Bowie County, Texarkana, Texas, 29.

59. Albrecht has done the kind of primary source research that makes his case a strong one for Julius Weiss as Joplin's German piano teacher. Rudi Blesh reported what family members told him: namely, that Joplin began receiving piano lessons from a German teacher about the time he was eleven years old. Blesh did not attempt to identify the teacher. Addison Reed discounted the story altogether in his dissertation on Joplin and in the articles that were published from that research. James Haskins argues in favor of Alfred Ernst because of an interview that appeared in the *St. Louis Post-Dispatch* in 1901 in which Ernst praised the unpolished musical potential of Joplin. As Albrecht shows, however, too many facts conflict with the family recollections to make Ernst a likely candidate for Joplin's German music teacher. Moreover, as I suggest in Chapter 5 below, Ernst was named the official conductor of the Louisiana Purchase Exposition orchestra and chorus in 1904, just three years after his interview praising Joplin. In spite of that earlier enthusiasm, Ernst apparently did nothing to help his "protege" during the fair. In 1880, Ernst was a young man, which further contradicts reports from Joplin's family that his teacher was old. Though the identity of Joplin's teacher probably never will be known for sure, Albrecht's case for Weiss is quite compelling. See Theodore Albrecht, "Julius Weiss: Scott Joplin's First Piano Teacher."

60. Though Robert W. Rodgers played the prominent, public role of pushing for public schools in the community, much of the driving force came from his wife, Frances. Seventeen years her husband's junior, Frances came from a family dedicated to education, and she was remembered by Texarkanans as the energetic advocate for education who informed her husband's public stance. See Chandler and Howe, *History of Texarkana,* 276–77.

61. According to Albrecht, the Rodgers family replaced their old square piano with a new grand piano shipped from St. Louis while Weiss was the children's tutor. He speculates that Weiss may have arranged for the Joplins to purchase the old instrument on installments or in exchange for labor. Extrapolating backward from Joplin's opera *Treemonisha,* Albrecht conjectures that the parents in the opera, who

arrange for their daughter's education by working for white people in exchange for lessons, may have been modeled after Joplin's own parents. It is an interesting theory, but Albrecht acknowledges that no evidence has turned up to corroborate it. An equally plausible scenario that Albrecht does not entertain is that the Rodgers advertised their old piano when the new one arrived, and the Joplins, in the market for an instrument for Scott, may have approached them to see if they could work out some way of acquiring it. Albrecht does point out that in a community as recently founded as Texarkana, old used pianos would not have been readily available. It may have been that Weiss heard Scott play when the Joplins tried to purchase the Rodgers' piano, after which time, the German offered to teach the naturally talented African American lad.

62. Haskins, *Scott Joplin,* 58; Albrecht, "Julius Weiss," 103–4. A number of stories about the Joplins' family life have appeared in various biographical writings. In his dissertation, Addison Reed inexplicably wrote that the Joplins had been separated while Scott was a boy, but census information indicates that they were living together in 1870 and 1880. Family stories suggest that Jiles Joplin was not exactly a faithful husband, but whatever disagreements the two parents had, they did not result in Scott's being raised by a single parent.

63. Haskins, *Scott Joplin,* 59–60.

64. Ibid.

65. (Marshall, Texas) *Tri-Weekly Herald,* June 10, 1875, 2, col. 2; and December 18, 1875, 1, col. 6. It was common practice in local nineteenth-century newspapers to reprint news from neighboring towns and publications. The article about Mrs. Duncan explains that the event occurred in Texarkana, but does not attribute it to any particular source. The second shooting incident is a reprint from the *Texarkana Democrat.*

66. "The Texarkana Excitement," (Marshall, Texas) *Tri-Weekly Herald,* June 5, 1880, 2, col. 2. The article was reprinted from the *Texarkana Visitor.*

67. Haskins, *Scott Joplin,* 75; Reed, "Life and Works of Scott Joplin," 14; and Albrecht, "Julius Weiss," 104–5.

68. W. C. Handy, *The Father of the Blues: An Autobiography,* 17–18, 24–25; and Rice, *The Negro in Texas,* 265, 268. For an example of an excursion train running between Texarkana and Marshall, Texas, see "The Texarkana Train," (Marshall, Texas) *Tri-Weekly Herald,* March 2, 1876, 3, col. 1. For announcements of arriving entertainers, see (Marshall, Texas) *Tri-Weekly Herald,* November 4, 1875, 3, col. 3; and *Daily Texarkana Independent,* September 20, 1884, 1, col. 3–4.

69. Rawick, *The American Slave,* Supplement, Series 2, Vol. 2, Part 1, 351–54.

70. Rice, *The Negro in Texas,* 187–88.

71. Luther G. Williams, "Early Jazz Piano and the Black Migration: A Sociocultural Approach," 6–7. Paper presented at the American Culture Association Meeting, Louisville, Kentucky, March 19, 1992.

72. Maud Cuney Hare, *Negro Musicians and Their Music,* 45; Marshall W. Stearns, *The Story of Jazz,* 109–22.

73. Cuney Hare, *Negro Musicians,* 44–45.

**Chapter 2. 1893: The Columbia Exposition, Economic Depression, and the Embrace of Ragtime**

1. For descriptions—negative and positive, respectively—of Sedalia's room in the Missouri Building at the Fair, see "Sedalia Room," *Sedalia Bazoo,* June 30, 1893, 4, col. 3; and "The State Building," *Sunday Morning Bazoo,* July 16, 1893, 2, col. 1–4.

2. James Haskins, *Scott Joplin,* 80–82; Blesh, *They All Played Ragtime,* 41–42; "Did You Know Ragtime Music Was Born in Sedalia?" *Sedalia Democrat,* June 29, 1947, 6, col. 6; and Reed, "Life and Works of Scott Joplin," 19–21.

3. The observer was Florence Kelley, who included this comment in her autobiographical writings. See Kathryn Kish Sklar, ed., *The Autobiography of Florence Kelley: Notes of Sixty Years,* 87.

4. "Theatrical Comment," *New York Age,* April 3, 1913, 6, col. 1–2.

5. Isaac Goldberg, one of the first historians of ragtime, made essentially the same point in 1930. He argued that ragtime was not new, rather it "was inherent in the oldest spirituals" and "latent in the songs of the minstrel era." So "far from being an invention of the Mauve Decade," ragtime, he believed, was "a rediscovery." See Goldberg, *Tin Pan Alley: A Chronicle of the American Popular Music Racket,* 139.

6. One of the earliest studies to recognize the 1890s as a critical watershed was John Higham's essay on the reorientation of American culture in that decade. Jackson Lears made a more pointed analysis of that transformation in his book on antimodernism, in which he explores fully the quest for authenticity. More recently still, Miles Orvell has investigated the layered meaning of a search for authenticity. He argues, in part, that the "real thing" became crucial at a time when so much in cultural expression and social relations rested on artifice. See John Higham, "The Reorientation of American Culture in the 1890s"; Lears, *No Place of Grace*; and Miles Orvell, *The Real Thing: Imitation and Authenticity in American Culture, 1880–1940.*

7. The following articles provide a sampling of comments on Indians and African Americans as the sources for American music at the turn of the century: Henry Finck, "Edward MacDowell: Musician and Composer"; Olin Downes, "An American Composer"; Sternberg, "What Is American Music?"; Farwell, "The Struggle toward a National Music"; David Bispham, "Music as a Factor in National Life"; Krehbiel, "The Distinctive Note in American Music"; Kroeger, "On 'American' Music."

8. "World's Columbian Exposition: Bulletin of Exposition Concerts to July 28th." The program did not exclude American composers altogether. According to the Bulletin, the program included works by Americans John K. Paine, George W. Chadwick, Arthur Foote, and George F. Bristow. None of the Americans, however, were African Americans.

9. "Personal Remarks," *Sedalia Bazoo,* May 24, 1893, 2, col. 2.

10. "Musical Items," *The Etude* 11 (July 1893): 143.

11. "Popularize the Fair," *Chicago Tribune,* June 15, 1893, 12, col. 2.

12. "Musical Items," *The Etude* 11 (September 1893): 175. After the fair closed, a writer to the editor of the *Musical Record* asked for an assessment of the effect of the Columbian Exposition on "the progress of musical culture in America." The editor replied as follows: "It can hardly be claimed that classical music received an impetus. There was much good orchestral and organ music heard, but the audiences were neither large nor appreciative. Popular selections by military bands seemed to be the music most in demand." See "Music at the World's Fair," *Musical Record* (December 1893): 14. Theodore Thomas's tenure as the director of music at the fair was troubled from the outset by a controversy over piano manufacturers and advertising. The lack of patronage at the concerts, which charged one dollar for admission, undermined his plans for an uplifting program as well. By the time he resigned in August, Thomas had faced a fairly constant stream of criticism. For more details on Thomas's problems, see Ray Ginger, *Altgeld's America: The Lincoln Ideal versus Changing Realities,* 20–21; "Theodore Thomas's Defense," *Chicago Tribune,* May 11, 1893, 12, col. 3; "Adverse to Thomas—The Investigation Commissioners Report against Him," *Chicago Tribune,* May 12, 1893, 2, col. 6–7; Lloyd Lewis and Henry Justin Smith, *Chicago: The History of Its Reputation,* 209–10; and "What Theodore Thomas Thinks," 7.

13. "Gamblers in Disarray: All Crap Games in Saloons Are Closed by the Police," *Chicago Tribune,* May 19, 1893, 6, col. 1; "After the Saloons," *Chicago Tribune,* June 26, 1893, 6, col. 1; Lewis and Smith,

*Chicago: The History of Its Reputation,* 177–78; and Ginger, *Altgeld's America,* 23.

14. Carl Bowen Johnson, "World's Fair Letter," *The Independent* 45 (July 6, 1893): 9.

15. "The White City," *Sedalia Bazoo,* May 25, 1893, 4, col. 5.

16. Robert Rydell offers the best analysis of the racial implications of the World's Columbian Exposition. See *All the World's a Fair: Visions of Empire at American International Expositions, 1876–1916,* 38–71.

17. Frederick Douglass, "Inauguration of the World's Columbian Exposition," 602.

18. Frederick Douglass, "Introduction to the Reason Why the Colored American Is Not in the World's Columbian Exposition." According to Robert Rydell, "Colored People's Day," which was to be celebrated on August 25, 1893, attracted only about a thousand African American visitors. See Rydell, *All the World's a Fair,* 52–55. *The Independent* also reported in August that a "Negro Congress" had been held and had been considered by observers "the most interesting and attractive of all the congresses thus far held." See "The Negro Congress at Chicago."

19. Frederick Douglass, "Why Is the Negro Lynched," 508; Elliott M. Rudwick and August Meier, "Black Man in the 'White City': Negroes and the Columbian Exposition, 1893."

20. The cartoon of Mr. Johnson and the "heathen" appeared in *Harper's Weekly* 37 (August 19, 1893): 797. For additional cartoons in the series see the following issues of Volume 37 of *Harper's Weekly:* (July 15): 681; (August 12): 770; (September 2): 849; (September 9): 868; (September 23): 914; (September 30): 940; and (October 14): 976.

21. Rydell, *All the World's a Fair,* 53–54.

22. A good example of different expectations occurred in May 1893. Restaurateurs, hoping to augment the enormous profits to be made during the Fair, reduced the wages of black waiters. Without notice, the waiters went on strike. According to the *Chicago Tribune,* the waiters were almost immediately rehired at their old (higher) wages. Moreover, when some proprietors resisted paying back wages due, the Union of Colored Waiters hired a lawyer to sue for the money to which their members were entitled. Such agency, labor organization, and assertiveness was not that common among the sharecroppers and day laborers Joplin had grown up among in Texas. For an account of this incident, see "Waiters Go Out and Come Back," *Chicago Tribune,* May 11, 1893, 11, col. 5. For information on the Illinois antidiscrimination law and on the black community in late-

nineteenth-century Chicago, see Bessie L. Pierce, *A History of Chicago,* 3:48–50.

23. Lorenzo J. Greene, Gary R. Kremer, and Anthony F. Holland, *Missouri's Black Heritage,* 94–97; C. Vann Woodward, *Origins of the New South, 1877–1913,* 211–12, 351–54; C. Vann Woodward, *The Strange Career of Jim Crow.* According to Greene, Kremer, and Holland, African Americans in St. Louis called for a "national day of 'humiliation, fasting, and prayer' to accent their plea" for protection against racial violence. On May 31, 1892, around fifteen hundred blacks participated in what they called "Lamentation Day."

24. I have found no primary documentation that Joplin visited the World's Fair. This account relies on work by Reed, Rudi Blesh, and James Haskins, who, in turn, relied on the memories and oral testimonies of Joplin's family, friends, and acquaintances. For their accounts of Joplin in Chicago, see Addison Reed, "The Life and Works of Scott Joplin," 20–22; Haskins, *Scott Joplin,* 80–82; and Blesh, *They All Played Ragtime,* 149–52.

25. Haskins, *Scott Joplin,* 81.

26. "Did You Know Ragtime Music Was Born in Sedalia?" *Sedalia Democrat,* June 29, 1947, 6–7, col. 6 and col. 3, respectively.

27. Frederick Jackson Turner, "The Significance of the Frontier in American History," American Historical Association, *Annual Report for the Year 1893* (Washington, 1894), 199–227. See also comments on the setting of, content of, and reactions to Turner's address in Ginger, *Altgeld's America,* 22.

28. "Seen at the Fair," *Sedalia Democrat,* August 20, 1893, 7, col. 2.

29. Carl Bowen Johnson, "World's Fair Letter," *The Independent* 45 (July 1893): 9.

30. "Yesterday at the Fair," *Chicago Tribune,* June 18, 1893, 28, col. 2–3.

31. The quote is from "Bitter against the Act," *Chicago Tribune,* May 29, 1893, 5, col. 5. For additional commentary from ministers for and against Sunday opening, see "The Boycotters," *Chicago Tribune,* May 28, 1893, 29, col. 1; "Pleads for Open Gates," *Chicago Tribune,* June 5, 1893, 3, col. 4; "Lessons of an Open Sunday," *Chicago Tribune,* June 13, 1893, 4, col. 3; "Oppose Sunday Opening," *Chicago Tribune,* June 19, 1893, 2, col. 2; "Says It Will Yet Be Closed," *Chicago Tribune,* June 19, 1893, 3, col. 3; "Sunday Closing Comes Up Again," *Chicago Tribune,* June 1, 1893, 5, col. 1; "American Sunday Not in Danger," *Chicago Tribune,* June 18, 1893, 4, col. 6.

32. "All Fakirs Flourish: Sideshows which Fatten on the Crowd Outside the Gates," *Chicago Daily Tribune,* May 8, 1893, 1, col. 3–4.

33. Lewis and Smith, *Chicago: The History of Its Reputation*, 203, 177–78.

34. "They Say," *Sedalia Democrat*, October 15, 1893, 7, col. 3–4.

35. "Popularize the Fair," *Chicago Tribune*, June 15, 1893, 12, col. 1.

36. "Yesterday at the Fair," *Chicago Tribune*, June 18, 1893, 28, col. 3; "Art in the 'White City,'" *Sedalia Democrat*, August 24, 1893, 2, col. 4; and "The White City," *Sedalia Bazoo*, May 25, 1893, 4, col. 5.

37. "Viewed from Above: The Crowd and Its Motions," *Chicago Tribune*, May 2, 1893, 5, col. 4.

38. "Another Gala Day at the Fair," *Chicago Tribune*, June 17, 1893, 12, col. 4.

39. Ibid.

40. Bicycling, dancing, amusement parks, the Trilby fad, all represent ways that Americans in the 1890s participated in activities that called into question traditional Victorian assumptions about amusement. I do not mean to imply here that ragtime alone, or even most importantly, offered Americans an escape from respectable amusement; it clearly represents one form of diversion among many that provided Americans such release. For excellent discussions of other crazes in this period and their relation to American social and cultural life, see Lewis Erenberg, *Steppin' Out: New York Nightlife and the Transformation of American Culture, 1890–1930*; John F. Kasson, *Amusing the Million*; Gregory W. Bush, *Lord of Attention: Gerald Stanley Lee and the Crowd Metaphor in Industrializing America*, 8–30; and Higham, "The Reorientation of American Culture."

41. These references come from a *Chicago Tribune* article that appeared after it was decided to keep the fair open on Sundays. The article described the kind of people who attended on the first Sunday and concluded that the opening did not appall churchgoers as critics of the plan had feared. Later in the article, the writer noted that "Of course Midway Plaisance was a jam. It always is." See "White City Filled," *Chicago Tribune*, June 12, 1893, 2, col. 5.

42. Rupert Hughes, "A Eulogy of Rag-Time."

43. W. H. A. "'Rag Time,' The Music of the Hour," *The Metronome* 15 (May 1899): 4.

44. For a discussion of the connection between the World's Fair and the unraveling of Victorian culture, see Justus D. Doenecke, "Myths, Machines and Markets: The Columbian Exposition of 1893." Alan Trachtenberg devotes a chapter to the relationship between the White City and the process of incorporation in the American economy in the 1890s in *The Incorporation of America: Culture and Society in the Gilded Age*, 208–34.

45. There is, to my knowledge, no book-length treatment of the depression of 1893. Some of the best evidence of its severity and significance still remains in the primary sources. It often is discussed in the context of more complicated analyses of such developments as government regulation of big business, the consolidation of big business, the "long depression" of the late nineteenth century, or the business cycle. For discussions of the depression of 1893 see, David Thelen, *The New Citizenship: Origins of Progressivism in Wisconsin, 1885–1900*, 55–85; Nell Irvin Painter, *Standing at Armageddon: The United States, 1877—1919*, 110–40; Robert L. Heilbroner, *The Economic Transformation of America*, 105–25; Gilbert C. Fite and Jim E. Reese, *An Economic History of the United States*, 296–527; Carlos A. Schwantes, *Coxey's Army: An American Odyssey*, 23–33.

46. Gompers's comments were part of the president's report, published in *Report of Proceedings of the Thirteenth Annual Convention of the American Federation of Labor, held at Chicago, Ill. December 11th to 19th Inclusive 1893*, 11. Gompers was also mindful of meeting in the World's Fair City: "Here in the fading shadow of the colossal, magnificent 'White City,' where the genius and noble handicraft of man reared the World's Columbian Exposition of 1893, surpassing in reality the flights of fancy and the poet's dream, here, may we, representatives of those who made this wondrous project and achievement possible, not take counsel with each other and determine upon such action that shall forever obliterate the dark shades, the injustice and the cruel wrongs perpetrated on the toiling masses, the wealth producers of America?"

47. For discussions of agriculture and populism in the late nineteenth century see John D. Hicks, *The Populist Revolt: A History of the Farmers' Alliance and the People's Party*; Richard Hofstadter, *The Age of Reform from Bryan to F. D. R.*; Lawrence Goodwyn, *Democratic Promise: The Populist Movement in America*; Bruce Palmer, *"Man Over Money": The Southern Populist Critique of American Capitalism*; Norman Pollack, *The Populist Response to Industrial America: Midwestern Populist Thought*; and "The Omaha Platform," the official program of the People's Party in 1892, which articulated the frustrations with prevailing economic conditions and visions of the future of American populists.

48. Sean Wilentz, *Chants Democratic: New York City and the Rise of the American Working Class, 1788–1850*.

49. Much work has been published in recent years defining the texture and contours of American Victorianism in the nineteenth century. The following list is not anywhere near exhaustive, but it does include important works that have explored key issues. Walter E. Houghton, *The Victorian Frame of Mind, 1830–1870*; Daniel Walker

Howe, ed., *Victorian America;* Kathryn Kish Sklar, *Catharine Beecher: A Study in Domesticity;* Steven Mintz, *A Prison of Expectations: The Family in Victorian Culture;* Halttunen, *Confidence Men and Painted Women;* Howe, *The Political Culture of the American Whigs;* Neil Harris, *Humbug: The Art of P. T. Barnum;* and Douglas, *The Feminization of American Culture.* For discussions of republicanism in America, see Gordon Wood, *The Creation of the American Republic;* Drew McCoy, *The Elusive Republic;* Watts, *The Republic Reborn;* and Wilentz, *Chants Democratic.*

50. The following three books deal with the tension between the conditions of work in the late nineteenth century and the work ethic itself. They explore in differing degrees the pervasive dissatisfaction with work and its meaning in an incorporating economy. See Daniel Rodgers, *The Work Ethic in Industrial America, 1850–1920;* Harry Braverman, *Labor and Monopoly Capitalism: The Degradation of Work in the Twentieth Century;* and Susan Curtis, *A Consuming Faith: The Social Gospel and Modern American Culture,* Chapter 2.

51. Thelen, *The New Citizenship,* 55–85; Stephan Thernstrom, *Poverty and Progress: Social Mobility in a Nineteenth-Century City;* Curtis, *A Consuming Faith;* Erenberg, *Steppin' Out;* Rodgers, *The Work Ethic in Industrial America;* Higham, "The Reorientation of American Culture in the 1890s"; Kasson, *Amusing the Million;* Lawrence Levine, *Highbrow/ Lowbrow: The Emergence of Cultural Hierarchy in America;* Elaine Tyler May, *Great Expectations: Marriage and Divorce in Post-Victorian America;* Jean Strouse, *Alice James: A Biography.*

52. For good discussions of literature in the late nineteenth century, see Fred Lewis Pattee, *A History of American Literature Since 1870;* Larzer Ziff, *The American 1890s: Life and Times of a Lost Generation;* Eric J. Sundquist, *American Realism: New Essays;* and H. Wayne Morgan, *American Writers in Rebellion: From Mark Twain to Dreiser.*

53. Goldberg, *Tin Pan Alley,* 32–33, 139. Goldberg's comments on ragtime are quite insightful. One must overlook the racial divisions implied in his text as a reflection of the 1920s. At another point in the book, Goldberg insists that American music is the product, not of white incorporation of black, but an interaction between the two races in a process of culture, a comment that captures the spirit of respect, admiration, and affection toward African Americans in Goldberg's book that is more characteristic than the implied racism.

54. This argument appeared in an untitled editorial in *The Etude* 17 (December 1899): 379–80. Another connection between ragtime and the depression has been posited by some music scholars. After a decade of hard times, they argue, Americans were ready for "happy" music. I think the appeal of ragtime went much deeper than its cheeriness and cannot be accounted for in this way. For evidence of

this interpretation see Stearns, *The Story of Jazz,* 140; and Blesh, *They All Played Ragtime,* 4.

### Chapter 3. Joplin and Sedalia: The King of Ragtime in the Queen City of Missouri

1. For a discussion of the number of copies of *Maple Leaf Rag* sold and of the meaning of "classic" ragtime, see Jasen and Tichenor, *Rags and Ragtime,* 77–78.

2. The story of the discovery of *Maple Leaf Rag* has been related in the following works: Addison W. Reed, "Scott Joplin, Pioneer" in *Ragtime: Its History, Composers, and Music.* Hasse, ed., 126; Gammond, *Scott Joplin and the Ragtime Era,* 63; Blesh and Janis, *They All Played Ragtime,* 44–52; and Lang, *Life in Pettis County,* 736.

3. For the Stark version of the discovery of *Maple Leaf Rag,* see "Missouri Was the Birthplace of Ragtime," *St. Louis Post-Dispatch,* January 18, 1961, 3F, col. 2.

4. Joplin had written a couple of ballads earlier in the 1890s, both of which were published in 1895 in Syracuse, New York. M. L. Mantell published *Please Say You Will,* which was billed as a "Song and Chorus" by Scott Joplin, "of the Texas Medley Quartette." Leiter Brothers published *A Picture of Her Face.* The two pieces were published in Syracuse as a result of Joplin and the Texas Medley Quartette going on tour "to see how the general public would receive Joplin's new music," according to S. Brunson Campbell. Unless the performances were considerably different than the printed music, Joplin's early compositions lacked the distinctive syncopation that marked his later work. The absence of syncopation in the compositions may have been a consequence of Joplin's not having learned how to notate that rhythm, for it was not until his return to Sedalia that he enrolled in music courses at the George R. Smith College for Negroes. See Lawrence, ed., *Collected Works of Scott Joplin,* 2:273–83; and "Did You Know Ragtime Music Was Born in Sedalia?" *Sedalia Democrat,* June 29, 1947, 7, col. 3.

5. Ben Harney and Brun Campbell, both white pioneers in ragtime music, acknowledged their indebtedness to black musicians. Harney is often credited with the first published ragtime composition, but that accomplishment takes nothing away from the essentially African American origin and character of ragtime music.

6. This brief sketch of Sedalia's development relies mostly on Michael Cassity, *Defending a Way of Life: An American Community in the Nineteenth Century,* 36–50, quote is from 55; and to a much lesser degree on Mark A. McGruder, *History of Pettis County Missouri.*

7. Cassity, *Defending a Way of Life,* 56, 64–67.

8. For material on Sedalia's growth, see "Something of Sedalia," *Sedalia Bazoo,* January 29, 1893, 12, col. 3. Marshall's impressions were recorded in "Ragtime Era Revival Set Here Monday," *Sedalia Democrat,* October 16, 1960, 1, col. 1.

9. Information on the city's population comes from published census reports for 1890 and 1900. *Twelfth Census, 1900: Report on the Population of the United States,* Vol. 1, Part 1, xlviii, 546, 626; For information on the age breakdown and indications of living conditions, see *Eleventh Census, 1890: Report on the Population of the United States,* Vol. 1, Part 1, 882, 923. According to the eleventh census, families in Pettis County averaged 4.95 people, while 5.12 people lived in each dwelling. This would suggest either that people occasionally took in a boarder or servant, or it may indicate an averaging of boarding houses into the total. In either case, the numbers differ dramatically from statistics in urban areas like New York, Boston, or Philadelphia, where the number of people per dwelling outnumbered by 4 or 5 the number of people per family.

10. Burton W. Peretti, "Emerging from America's Underside: The Black Musician from Ragtime to Jazz," in *America's Musical Pulse: Popular Music in Twentieth-Century Society,* Kenneth J. Bindas, ed., 66.

11. Lang, *Life in Pettis County,* 477.

12. "Swipsey [*sic*] Cake Walk Result of a Famous Collaboration," *Sedalia Democrat,* November 24, 1959, 2, col. 5; Reed, "Life and Works of Scott Joplin," 24–25.

13. *Sedalia Bazoo,* June 16, 1893, 2, col. 1.

14. *Sedalia Times,* September 29, 1901, 1, col. 4.

15. "Police Court," *Sedalia Bazoo,* December 12, 1892, 1, col. 4.

16. "The Cake Walk," *Sedalia Democrat,* August 6, 1897, 1, col. 4.

17. "Among the Justices," *Sedalia Sentinel,* November 16, 1899, 5, col. 5.

18. The entry for Joplin can be found in the 1900 Manuscript Census for Pettis County, Missouri, Sedalia City, 214A. The practice in the late nineteenth century was for census takers to go from door to door, recording the address of each dwelling, indicating the head of each household and any boarders. Even boarders were divided by families. This arrangement permits researchers to see who lived on the same street as the subject of their inquiry. In this particular case, the census taker assigned to Joplin's neighborhood must have been either inexperienced or inattentive to details or both. At some point, the recorder noticed that the addresses, number of dwellings, and number of households were incorrect, so emendations were made by crossing through original entries and entering new information in the space remaining. If the changes are correct, the census shows

that Scott Joplin, a single, black man, aged 27, occupation Musician, was the head of a household that also included Belle Jones, a single, black woman, aged 25, occupation laundress. They lived with the Michael Seethaler family at 801 Washington Street. In addition to Joplin and Jones, Susan Hawkins and her daughter, Lena Smith, boarded with the Seethalers. Since Joplin's birthdate is incorrectly recorded as October 1872, I think Belle Jones answered the census taker's questions. It is significant to note that she made no effort to hide the fact that she and Joplin, two single people, cohabited in the boardinghouse. Most biographies note that Joplin was married twice, first to a woman named Belle who was related to the family of Scott Hayden, one of Joplin's protégés, and later to Lottie Stokes Joplin in New York. No biographer, to my knowledge, has any documentary evidence of a marriage between Belle Jones and Scott Joplin. Jones also declared herself to be the mother of three children, only one of whom was living. Her only living child did not reside with her and Joplin.

19. Juhl was lampooned by the reporter who regularly spiced up the police reports for the *Sedalia Bazoo* in 1892. Two months after his arrival in Sedalia, Juhl was arrested for carrying a concealed weapon, to which he pleaded guilty and paid a fine of $50. After recounting the bare bones of Juhl's recent history, the journalist offered a poem:

> With music I can make you laugh,
> And cause to dance the big Giraffe,
> And e'en the coons I teach to play
> The festive 'Ta-ra-Boom-ty-eh.
>
> Oh! Once I played upon a horn,
> And almost made a fiddle talk,
> But now foresaken and forlorn,
> I'm forced to play upon a rock.

See "Police Court," *Sedalia Bazoo,* December 12, 1892, 1, col. 4. For G. T. Ireland's account of Juhl, see Lang, *Life in Pettis County,* 477–78.

20. "A Dandy Coon," *Sedalia Sentinel,* July 20, 1899, 2, col. 4.

21. *Sedalia Bazoo,* November 28, 1893, 2, col. 1.

22. "A New Order," *Sedalia Capital,* June 27, 1895, 3, col. 3.

23. "Colored People Protest," *Sedalia Capital,* August 24, 1895, 4, col. 6.

24. "A Rousing Meeting," *Sedalia Capital,* August 23, 1895, 2, col. 2.

25. Ibid. For information about occupation and property owner-ship, see the 1900 Manuscript Census for Pettis County, Missouri, Sedalia City, 184A, 172B, 160B for Steele, Ireland, and Gravitt, re-spectively. W. H. Carter founded and edited the *Sedalia Times* in the 1890s. The *Times* was one of the most influential African American newspapers in the city in that period. For more information on Ireland, see "Tom Ireland Dies Friday; Known for Varied Talents," *Sedalia Capital*, August 31, 1963, 5, col. 3–4.

26. "Did You Know Ragtime Music Was Born in Sedalia?" *Sedalia Democrat*, June 29, 1947, 7, col. 5–6.

27. The following newspaper articles represent a small sampling of reports on the Queen City Band in Sedalia newspapers: "Snap Shots," *Sedalia Capital*, July 29, 1897, 8, col. 2 and July 31, 1897, 5, col. 1–2; "Band Went to Fayette," *Sedalia Democrat*, September 22, 1897, 1, col. 3; "Return of the Band," *Sedalia Democrat*, September 23, 1897, 5, col. 4; "Is To Be No Guying," *Sedalia Democrat*, October 10, 1897, 1, col. 3; "Decided to Play," *Sedalia Democrat*, October 11, 1897, 1, col. 3; "In Colored Society," *Sedalia Sentinel*, August 14, 1899, 2, col. 4; "Band Entertainment," *Sedalia Times*, October 26, 1901, 1, col. 2; "Band Entertainment," *Sedalia Times*, November 16, 1901, 1, col. 1; and "Band Concert," *Sedalia Times*, May 10, 1902, 1, col. 1.

28. Campbell, "Ragtime Begins," 8.

29. "The Date Is Fixed," *Sedalia Capital*, March 28, 1899, 8, col. 3.

30. The following citations from Sedalia newspapers include re-ports of Tony Williams's various entertainment activities at the end of the 1890s: "The Date Is Fixed," *Sedalia Capital*, March 28, 1899, 8, col. 3; "The Unlucky Coons," *Sedalia Capital*, March 31, 1899, 1, col. 3; "A Hot Time Tonight," *Sedalia Evening Democrat*, April 11, 1899, 7, col. 3–4; "A Creditable Entertainment," *Sedalia Evening Democrat*, April 12, 1899, 6, col. 3; "The Closing Ball," *Sedalia Capital*, May 30, 1899, 1, col. 3; *Sedalia Evening Sentinel*, July 13, 1899, 4, col. 3; January 30, 1900, 4, col. 5; and January 31, 1900, 6, col. 3; "Personal Para-graphs," *Sedalia Evening Sentinel*, October 10, 1899, 4, col. 5.

31. Lang, *Life in Pettis County*, 478; "The Street Fair," *Sedalia Dem-ocrat*, September 3, 1899, 1, col. 4.

32. "The Band at Home Again," *Sedalia Times*, October 26, 1901, 1, col. 1.

33. "Perfect Jam Today," *Sedalia Democrat*, September 7, 1899, 4, col. 3.

34. In the 1900 manuscript census for Pettis County, Missouri, Sedalia City, Joplin gives his occupation as "musician" and reports 0 months of unemployment. As mentioned earlier in one of the notes,

it is likely that Belle Jones, who cohabited with him, gave this answer. But her answer that he was fully employed in 1899 reflects a perception of regular engagement. The St. Louis city directories for 1902 and 1903 also list him as a musician. See *Gould's St. Louis Directory for 1902* and *Gould's St. Louis Directory for 1903*.

35. According to Addison Reed, Tony Williams ran the Maple Leaf Club, where Joplin began playing when he arrived with his friend Otis Saunders. Williams and Saunders urged him to learn how to compose and publish so he could leave a permanent mark on the world of music. See Reed, "Life and Works of Scott Joplin," 22–23. Brun Campbell corroborates Reed's argument. See "Did You Know Ragtime Music Was Born in Sedalia?" *Sedalia Democrat,* June 29, 1947, 1, col. 3–6 (cont'd. on pages 6 and 7).

36. Marshall was about thirteen years younger than Joplin. His family moved to Sedalia, where he was born, because they had heard of George R. Smith's easy terms for African American settlers in his town and because they were able to send their children to school for nine months instead of only three months each year. In 1900, nineteen-year-old Marshall was employed as a porter, and two years later, he was a driver for a local company. He attended the George R. Smith College for Negroes for two years after high school. For information on Marshall see *W. H. McCoy's Twentieth Century Sedalia, Missouri, City Directory for 1900–1901; Hoye's Sedalia, Missouri, City Directory*; and "Ragtime Era Revival Set Here Monday," *Sedalia Democrat,* October 16, 1960, 1, col. 2.

Scott Hayden was a schoolmate of Marshall's, born about a year later in 1882. In June 1900, the census taker who surveyed Sedalia listed eighteen-year-old "Scottie Hayden" as one of the school-age children living at 133 N. Osage Street. Further down on the list (which suggests that it was taken at a later time and possibly by another person) eighteen-year-old "Scott Hayden" appears as the head of a household, a tenant in an apartment. Hayden probably was just beginning to look for a place of his own after graduating from high school; his mother may well have listed her son without knowing that he was about to live on his own. See 1900 Manuscript Census, Pettis County, Missouri, Sedalia City, 161A and 164B; "Hayden a Protege: Joplin's Impact on Ragtime Increased by His Influence," *Sedalia Democrat,* November 25, 1959, 10, col. 1–2.

37. Alonzo Hayden's memories were recorded in the following article published when he was 85 years old. Kathy Cochran, "Great Scott," *Vibrations: Sunday Magazine of the Columbia Missourian,* December 14, 1980, 3–5.

38. Lang, *Life in Pettis County,* 741, 738; "Ragtime Era Revival Set Here Monday," *Sedalia Democrat,* October 16, 1960, 1–2.

39. Lang, *Life in Pettis County,* 738; "Ragtime Era Revival Set Here Monday," *Sedalia Democrat,* October 16, 1960, 1–2; "Swipsey [*sic*] Cake Walk Result of a Famous Collaboration," *Sedalia Democrat,* November 24, 1959, 2, col. 5–6.

40. Editorial comment in the *Sedalia Times,* March 11, 1902, 2, col. 2–3.

41. S. Brunson Campbell, "A Silver Half-Dollar and the 'Ragtime Kid,'" 1, in the S. Brunson Campbell Papers, Collection #995, Vol. 12, #355, Western Manuscripts Collection, Columbia, Missouri.

42. "Sedalia's Opportunity," *Sedalia Democrat,* January 1, 1893, 2, col. 3.

43. "Minter Bros. Assign," *Sedalia Bazoo,* January 9, 1893, 4, col. 3. Less than a week earlier, the Minters had advertised a "January Clearance Sale" in the *Sedalia Democrat.* "WE NEED MONEY!" their ad had proclaimed, but apparently, cash and solvency were not forthcoming. See their advertisement in the *Sedalia Democrat,* January 4, 1893, 1, col. 2–3.

44. "Will Leave the City," *Sedalia Democrat,* February 8, 1893, 2, col. 4.

45. The August 10, 1893 edition of the *Sedalia Bazoo* was drastically reduced, and the reduction was explained on the editorial page as a cost-saving measure. The next day's edition was its last until November 20, 1893. The comment about railroad conditions appears on page 4, column 1 of the August 11, 1893 edition. See also "Sold at Auction," *Sedalia Bazoo,* February 2, 1893, 4, col. 5; and "A Surprising Failure," *Sedalia Bazoo,* May 23, 1893, 3, col. 2 for details of other bankruptcies.

46. Frank B. Meyer advertised his newly acquired stock in the *Sedalia Democrat,* June 13, 1893, 4, col. 2–3, and announced his summer sale in the *Sedalia Democrat,* July 20, 1893, 4, col. 2–4. In the same July issue of the *Sedalia Democrat,* the following companies also announced summer sales: Holcomb's "Great Discount Sale," 2, col. 5–7; Kraesel's "Grand Clearing Sale," 3, col. 4–6; St. Louis Clothing Company "Mid-Summer Clearing Out Sale," 3, col. 2–7; and a notice appeared on page 3, col. 7 that all insurance policies whose premiums had not been paid by 20 July would be considered "null and void."

47. "Pulling 'Vags,'" *Sedalia Bazoo,* November 23, 1892, 1, col. 3 offers a typical pre-depression treatment of vagrants in the Queen City. "Police Court," and "A Tough Citizen," *Sedalia Democrat,* January 15, 1893, 7, col. 5 both articulate concerns over changing conditions

and the dilemma faced by a city devoted to order but overrun by unemployed men.

48. *Rosa Pearle's Paper,* May 19, 1894, 4, col. 1.

49. "The Woman of To-Day," *Rosa Pearle's Paper,* June 16, 1894, 4, col. 3.

50. "Questions: Out-of-Date and Up-to-Date," *Rosa Pearle's Paper,* June 16, 1894, 6, col. 1.

51. The quoted material comes from the *Sedalia Democrat,* June 16, 1893, 2, col. 2. For examples of Sedalians cavorting about in Chicago, see "They Say," *Sedalia Democrat,* October 15, 1893, 7, col. 3–4.

52. "They Say," *Sedalia Democrat,* August 6, 1893, 3, col. 3–4; and "Two Cases of Adultery," *Sedalia Bazoo,* February 16, 1893, 4, col. 1.

53. "Two Disreputable Negroes," *Sedalia Democrat,* February 8, 1893, 2, col. 4.

54. Compare the notices of "The Spider and the Fly" in these two newspapers: *Sedalia Bazoo,* December 26, 1892, 2, col. 2; and *Sedalia Sentinel,* November 29, 1899, 4, col. 4.

55. For an editorial defense of theaters, see *Rosa Pearle's Paper,* February 2, 1895, 4, col. 1–2. For the article on summer amusements, see *Sedalia Bazoo,* June 23, 1893, 2, col. 1.

56. *Sedalia Bazoo,* July 5, 1893, 2, col. 3.

57. "Society," *Sedalia Evening Sentinel,* June 9, 1899, 5, col. 2–4.

58. "The Palace Hotel," *Sedalia Bazoo,* November 11, 1892, 3, col. 2. See the 1900 manuscript census for Pettis County, Missouri, Sedalia, for listings of various brothels and resident prostitutes.

59. "A Watermelon Social Last Night," *Sedalia Democrat,* September 1, 1897, 2, col. 2; "Society," *Sedalia Sentinel,* August 19, 1899, 5, col. 1–2.

60. Ibid.; "Will Dance Tonight," *Sedalia Democrat,* April 7, 1899, 4, col. 2; and "Sweet Charity," *The Review and Plain Talker,* September 18, 1898, 1, col. 4.

61. "A Society Minstrel Entertainment," *Sedalia Democrat,* January 7, 1900, 10, col. 3; "Minister Objects to a Cake-Walk," *Sedalia Evening Democrat,* April 17,1899, 4, col. 6.

62. "Band Concert Tonight," *Sedalia Capital,* June 29, 1897, 1, col. 2.

63. "Will Honor a Local Club," *Sedalia Evening Democrat,* January 2, 1900, 1, col. 2; "Will Give a Masque Ball," *Sedalia Sunday Democrat,* February 4, 1900, 5, col. 1.

64. *W. H. McCoy's Sedalia, Mo., City Directory 1898–1899*; *W. H. McCoy's Twentieth Century Sedalia, Mo., City Directory for 1900–1901*; and *Hoye's Sedalia, Mo., City Directory.*

65. This brief sketch of John Stark and his family is based on information provided by Rudi Blesh and Hazel Lang. See Blesh, *They All Played Ragtime,* 45–48; and Lang, *Life in Pettis County,* 738–39.

66. Notice in *Rosa Pearle's Paper,* August 4, 1894, 1, col. 3; and "Starke (sic) Musicale," *Sedalia Gazette,* April 5, 1895, 5, col. 3.

67. "Will Open a Studio," *Sedalia Capital,* November 11, 1899, 1, col. 2.

68. "Appointed Musical Director," *Sedalia Democrat,* June 16, 1893, 2, col. 3.

69. "Nellie Stark," *Sedalia Democrat,* September 12, 1897, 8, col. 2. Two years later, *Rosa Pearle's Paper* reprinted an article from the *Kansas City Star,* which reviewed Stark's performance in a concert in that city. Local readers must have been thrilled to read the last sentence: "Miss Stark pleased beyond ordinary measure and Kansas City would welcome a return." See *Rosa Pearle's Paper,* January 14, 1899, 4, col. 2.

70. According to a 1903 city directory for St. Louis, Eleanor Stark resided with her parents and brother at 4509 Shenandoah Avenue, but her music studio was located at 1042 North Grand Avenue. See *Gould's St. Louis Directory for 1903.*

71. "Missouri Was the Birthplace of Ragtime," *St. Louis Post-Dispatch,* January 18, 1961, 3F, col. 4. See also Rudi Blesh, "Scott Joplin: Black-American Classicist," in Lawrence, ed., *Collected Works of Scott Joplin,* 2:xxiii.

72. "Will Honor a Local Club," *Sedalia Democrat,* January 2, 1900, 1, col. 2.

73. I suspect the interest in Joplin's budding career was keener in Sedalia than is suggested in extant records. Two African American newspapers in Sedalia, the *Times* and the *Weekly Conservator,* contain gaps that eerily coincide with dates one expects to find some comment on Scott Joplin. For example, the *St. Louis Post-Dispatch* carried a long article on Joplin on February 28, 1901 in which a German conductor, Alfred Ernst, calls him "an extraordinary genius as a composer of ragtime music." The editions of the two black papers in Sedalia that would have followed the *Post-Dispatch* article are missing. Likewise, after promising a performance of his opera, *A Guest of Honor,* in Sedalia in August 1903, the issues of the paper that likely would have contained a report of this event have disappeared. As I conducted this research, I had the strange feeling that someone had gotten to the record before me and had removed important commentary and memories. I have no evidence for my theory, but I think it is reasonable to suspect that Joplin's many friends in the newspaper

business hoped to preserve his memory by removing issues or articles that pertained to Joplin. Their faith in his talent and their interest in his career may have prompted their desire to have full documentation of his Sedalia beginnings by the time he hit it big or to have treasured souvenirs of the career that they had nurtured and that blossomed after he moved to St. Louis. A closely related possibility is that newspapers that ran on a shoestring budget routinely had leftover copies of run-of-the-mill issues, which were saved by the editor. But when demand for the paper was especially great, the editor may have sold all existing copies. If true, then issues with special reports on Joplin may have sold out, which accounts for the gap in the record.

It is not certain that Joplin had a five-year exclusive contract with John Stark. Stark implied as much after Joplin's death, and S. Brunson Campbell reported that such a contract existed. If Joplin did sign a five-year contract with Stark, he violated it more than once. Unquestionably, a special relationship existed between Joplin and Stark, but it may not have rested on a contractual basis. See Haskins, *Scott Joplin*, 100–101, 216–17.

74. "The King of Rag-Time Composers Is Scott Joplin, a Colored St. Louisan," *St. Louis Globe-Democrat*, June 7, 1903, Sporting Section, 5, col. 1–3; "Scott Joplin a King," *Sedalia Times*, June 13, 1903, 1, col. 1–2.

75. "Sedalians in St. Louis and What They Are Doing," *Sedalia Weekly Conservator*, June 20, 1903, 2, col. 2.

76. *Sedalia Times*, April 11, 1903, 2, col. 2; "Scott Joplin's Opera," *Sedalia Weekly Conservator*, August 22, 1903, 2, col. 3. Rosenfeld also alluded to the opera in his review of Joplin's work. Though some insisted that they remembered his performance, no record of it has survived, and unfortunately, the book and score for *A Guest of Honor* have subsequently disappeared.

77. "Our Trip to the World's Fair City," *Sedalia Times*, April 26, 1902, 1, col. 1.

78. Ibid.

79. *Sedalia Times*, September 29, 1901, 2, col. 2.

80. *Sedalia Sentinel*, January 2, 1900, 8, col. 1.

81. "He Used His Gun," *Sedalia Evening Democrat*, January 15, 1900, 5, col. 1; "Tough Colored Clubs," *Sedalia Sentinel*, January 15, 1900, 5, col. 3; and "Rough House on Main Street," *Sedalia Sentinel*, March 8, 1900, 4, col. 4.

82. "Clubs Must Close," *Sedalia Democrat*, January 25, 1900, 1, col. 1; *Sedalia Times*, September 22, 1901, 1, col. 4.

## Chapter 4. The Incorporation of Ragtime

1. The advertisement appeared in the *Sedalia Evening Sentinel,* February 3, 1900, 6, col. 1. The association between pianos, Victorian culture, and morality has been made in the following work: Craig H. Roell, *The Piano in America, 1890–1940*; and Leon Plantinga, "The Piano and the Nineteenth Century," in *Nineteenth-Century Piano Music,* ed. R. Larry Todd.

2. Theodor Adorno, "Popular Music," in *Introduction to the Sociology of Music.* This book was originally published under the title *Einleitung in die Musiksoziologie* (Frankfurt-am-Main: Suhrkamp Verlag, 1962). Theodor Adorno and Max Horkheimer, *Dialectic of Enlightenment,* 120–67. For additional essays on this subject by Adorno and other members of the Critical School, see Bronner and Kellner, eds., *Critical Theory and Society,* 77–212.

3. The juxtaposition of these two discourses on popular music was first suggested to me by Eric Lott in a paper entitled "Marlon Brando, Pocahontas, and Me: Pop Music between Folk and Commerce," which he delivered at the 1992 annual meeting of the Sonneck Society of American Music, held in Baton Rouge, Louisiana, February 15, 1992. For examples of the celebration of popular music as authentic expression, see Peter Guralnick, *Lost Highway: Journeys and Arrivals of American Musicians*; and LeRoi Jones, *Blues People: Negro Music in White America.*

4. The best book on this dual phenomenon of incorporation is Trachtenberg, *The Incorporation of America.* An excellent essay that defines Modernism as the incorporation of unlikes into single cultural entities at the turn of the century is Daniel Joseph Singal, "Towards a Definition of American Modernism." For more specific discussions of economic incorporation, see Alfred Chandler, *The Visible Hand: The Managerial Revolution in American Business*; Braverman, *Labor and Monopoly Capital*; Hofstadter, *The Age of Reform*; Rodgers, *The Work Ethic in Industrial America, 1850–1920*; and Robert Wiebe, *The Search for Order, 1877–1920.*

5. Luther G. Williams, "Early Jazz Piano and the Black Migration: A Sociocultural Approach," a paper presented at the American Culture Association Meeting, Louisville, Kentucky, March 19, 1992; Eileen Southern, *The Music of Black Americans: A History,* 310–26; Jervis Anderson, *This Was Harlem, 1900–1950,* 152–57; and Wallace Thurman, "Negro Life in New York's Harlem," in *Speech and Power: The African-American Essay and Its Cultural Content from Polemics to Pulpit,* ed. Gerald Early, 1:82–87.

6. Rawick, *The American Slave,* Supplement, Series 2, Vol. 3, Part 2, 693.

7. H. E. Krehbiel, *The Pianoforte and Its Music,* 34.

8. Arthur Loesser, *Men, Women, and Pianos: A Social History,* 441–45.

9. Krehbiel, *The Pianoforte,* 36; Loesser, *Men, Women, and Pianos,* 460–64, 469; and Leon Plantinga, "The Piano and the Nineteenth Century," 6. According to an early twentieth-century encyclopedia of music, between 1796 and 1896, nearly 500 patents were issued for improvements on pianos, and all of them helped make the American-made instruments among the best pianos in the world and increasingly affordable to ordinary working or middle-class families. See W. L. Hubbard, Emil Liebling, et al., eds., *The American History and Encyclopedia of Music,* 315.

10. Loesser, *Men, Women, and Pianos,* 466.

11. Most of the myriad studies on Victorianism as a culture note prominently its moral/religious character. For an introduction to Victorian Culture, see Houghton, *The Victorian Frame of Mind*; and Howe, ed., *Victorian America.* For discussions of the importance of this Victorian morality on home life, see Halttunen, *Confidence Men and Painted Women*; Sklar, *Catharine Beecher*; Christopher Lasch, *Havens in a Heartless World*; Mintz, *A Prison of Expectations*; Gwendolyn Wright, *Moralism and the Model Home: Domestic Architecture and Cultural Conflict in Chicago, 1873–1913*; and Harvey Green, *The Light of the Home: An Intimate View of the Lives of Women in Victorian America.*

12. Loesser, *Men, Women, and Pianos,* 468.

13. The 1890 census reported that most piano manufacturers were located in Massachusetts, New York, Maryland, and Connecticut. Altogether, 169 establishments, capitalized at over 16 million dollars, operated in those four states. In all the other states combined, 71 establishments existed and were capitalized at something under 2 million dollars. See *Eleventh Census, 1890: Report on Manufacturing Industries in the United States,* Vol. 6, Part 1, 256–57.

14. Leonard Liebling, "The Music Trades of America," 143–44.

15. Hubbard, et al., *American History and Encyclopedia of Music,* 325.

16. *Rosa Pearle's Paper,* June 16, 1894, 6, col. 2; "Was a Banner Day," *Sedalia Democrat,* September 30, 1897, 2, col. 3.

17. *Rosa Pearle's Paper,* February 2, 1895, 7, col. 2.

18. Ibid., May 19, 1894, 8, col. 3. The same ad ran two times a month through the summer of 1894 and twice in February 1895.

19. *Sedalia Sentinel,* December 20, 1899, 4, col. 5–6. This ad ran December 20–23, 1899, undoubtedly in an effort to make a few last-minute Christmas sales.

20. In the article, the writer provides seemingly commonsense advice on the best way to care for a piano so as to avoid damage to

the exterior and the inner workings of the instrument. The article thus seemed to be aimed at first-time piano owners. See "Care of the Piano," *Sedalia Bazoo,* December 30, 1892, 4, col. 3.

21. Robert Braine, "A Piano for Everybody," 7.

22. J. Hillary Taylor, "History of the Pianoforte," 73.

23. Charles M. Skinner, "The Home Piano," 49. This piece originally appeared in the *Saturday Evening Post,* but was reprinted in *The Etude,* where it spoke directly to the piano-playing public.

24. Arthur Weld, "The Invasion of Vulgarity in Music," 52.

25. Charles Kassell Harris, *After the Ball: Forty Years of Melody, an Autobiography*; Tawa, *The Way to Tin Pan Alley*; and Goldberg, *Tin Pan Alley.*

26. Goldberg, *Tin Pan Alley,* 1; and Liebling, "The Music Trades of America," 143–44.

27. I first noticed this technique when I began looking at the Starr Music Collection in the Lilly Library in Bloomington, Indiana, which has a handful of Joplin compositions. Subsequently, I have noticed that it must have been a common practice in the early 1900s that has continued on into the century.

28. Starr Music Collection, Lilly Library, Joplin File, item 1, *Maple Leaf Rag,* 1.

29. These words were used to publicize *Kismet Rag,* which was published in 1913. The ad appeared on a later printing of *Maple Leaf Rag.* See Starr Music Collection, Lilly Library, Joplin File, Item 1, *Maple Leaf Rag,* 6.

30. "The King of Rag-Time Composers Is Scott Joplin, a Colored St. Louisan," *St. Louis Globe-Democrat,* June 7, 1903, Sporting Section, 5, col. 1–3.

31. "Ragtime," *The Outlook* 104 (May 24, 1913): 137; Axel Christensen, "Can Ragtime Be Suppressed?" 3–4.

32. "Questions and Answers," *The Etude* 16 (October 1898): 285.

33. *The Etude* 17 (November 1899): 340; "Our Musical Condition," 138; Theodore Stearns, "Don't Rush into Print," 126; "Dr. Damrosch Hits Ragtime," 7; and "Ragtime Causing Mental Ailments," 28.

34. "The Rag Time Is Doomed," *Sedalia Sentinel,* October 17, 1899, 3, col. 4–5.

35. "Scott Joplin Is Dead," 13.

36. Advertisement in *Christensen's Ragtime Review* 1 (May 1915): 25.

37. Starr Music Collection, Lilly Library, Joplin File, Item 4, *Maple Leaf Rag,* 6.

38. This interpretation is based on work by Warren Susman and Jackson Lears on the personal repercussions of a modernizing society at the turn of the century. See Susman, "'Personality' and the Making

of Twentieth-Century Culture"; and Lears, "From Salvation to Self-Realization: Advertising and the Therapeutic Roots of the Consumer Culture, 1880–1930."

39. Starr Music Collection, Lilly Library, Joplin File, Item 4, *Maple Leaf Rag,* 6.

40. Ibid., 2.

41. Ibid., 6.

42. Lawrence Levine recently has argued that at the turn of the century, American culture began to bifurcate along class lines between high culture of the fine arts and low culture of popular entertainmer.t. He shows how various institutions such as symphonies, opera houses, theaters that presented Shakespeare as serious and edifying entertainment, and art museums, all of which expected a certain kind of dress, decorum, and exclusivity, emerged. They represented important cultural markers that divided classes from one another and that redefined the place and meaning of such art in American culture. See Levine, *Highbrow/Lowbrow: The Emergence of Cultural Hierarchy in America.*

43. In the following article, Arthur Larkin argued that "Some think [ragtime] easily handled by the average classical player. But it is a horrible defeat to some of the classical students who, after taking music lessons for two or three years, don't really know how to play a good ragtime piece as well as a ragtime player who has studied ragtime only a short while. . . . Classical students should bear in mind that ragtime played properly will not hurt their classical playing. Ragtime has to be played in good time and just as perfectly as classical music." See Arthur D. Larkin, "Does Real Ragtime Spoil the Classical Student," 12.

44. "Can You Imagine This?" 2.

45. Ad in *Christensen's Ragtime Review* 1 (January 1915): 23.

46. Rayner Dalheim & Co. advertised in *Christensen's Ragtime Review* 1 (March 1915): 30, and on the next page of the same issue, Mellinger Music Co. offered similar services. J. Forrest Thompson, who was one of the teachers in Axel Christensen's Louisville, Kentucky, school, advertised in *Christensen's Ragtime Review* 1 (May 1915): 19.

47. Adorno, "Popular Music" in *Introduction to the Sociology of Music;* some of Joplin's contemporaries would have agreed: Wilson G. Smith, "The Vagrant Philosopher," 181–83; Theodore Stearns, "Don't Rush Into Print," 126–27; and "The Rag Time is Doomed," *Sedalia Evening Sentinel,* October 17, 1899, 3, col. 4–5.

48. Hubbard, et al., *American History and Encyclopedia of Music,* 69. See also Natalie Curtis, "The Negro's Contribution to the Music of

America: The Larger Opportunity of the Colored Man of Today,"
660–69.

### Chapter 5. Lost in Urban America

1. To see the original covers of Joplin's compositions, see
Lawrence, ed., *Collected Works of Scott Joplin,* 1:29, 35, 41, 245.

2. "To Play Ragtime in Europe," *St. Louis Post-Dispatch,* February
28, 1901, 3, col. 2–3.

3. The *Post-Dispatch* article concluded by saying that "A trip to
Europe in company with Prof. Ernst is the dream of [Joplin's] life. It
may be realized." None of Joplin's biographers, however, has been
able to discover any evidence that the King of Ragtime accompanied
Ernst across the Atlantic in 1901. A few years later, when Joplin had
moved to New York City, he became friends with performers who
dubbed themselves the "Five Musical Spillers." In honor of their
friendship, Joplin "Respectfully Dedicated" *Pineapple Rag* (1908) to
them. In late 1912 and early 1913, the Spillers made a short trip to
London, where they performed at the Alhambra Theater. I thought
it might be possible that Joplin accompanied the Spillers, because in
a letter to the *New York Age,* one of the Spillers reported: "London
is a great city. They are singing everything here that is popular in
New York. Ragtime is the craze here. *Everybody* is working and seem
to be getting along. *Everybody* reads the Age." In the context of the
letter, these references to "Everybody" seemed to suggest that performers other than the ones in their group were also in London. The
London *Times,* which did advertise the Spillers' act at the Alhambra,
did not include any indication that Scott Joplin was featured there
or in any other theater at the time. For the Spillers' letter, see "The
Spillers Abroad," *New York Age,* January 2, 1913, 6, col. 3. A few
months later, Joplin commented that "Ragtime rhythm is a syncopation original with the colored people, . . . But the other races
throughout the world are learning to write and make use of ragtime
melodies. It is the rage in England." See "Theatrical Comment," *New
York Age,* April 3, 1913, 6, col. 1.

4. "Ragtime Era Revival Set Here Monday," *Sedalia Democrat,* October 16, 1960, 2, col. 3; and *Sedalia Times,* April 11, 1903, 2, col. 2.

5. "A Silver Half-Dollar and the 'Ragtime Kid,'" in the S. Brunson
Campbell Papers, Collection #995, Vol. 12, #355, 1, Western Manuscript Collection, Columbia, Missouri.

6. A glance at early issues of the *St. Louis Palladium,* an African
American publication, indicates the wide range of opportunities for
African American entertainers in the city. Many of the advertisements
for bars and saloons indicate both the proprietor and the entertainer.

The *Palladium* also printed copies of new ragtime sheet music, which it included among more typical news stories and local reports. For an example of saloon advertising, see "The Jefferson Bar," *St. Louis Palladium,* August 1, 1903, 5, col. 4; and for sheet music, see "The Deserted Coon," *St. Louis Palladium,* July 4, 1903, 8, entire page.

7. W. S. B. Mathews, "Art Music in the Middle West: The Large Cities," 96–97. According to census takers, there were considerably more music teachers than the number of whom Mathews was made aware. In 1900, 1,255 women and men reported being employed as musicians or teachers of music, and in 1910, 1,986 reported being so employed. According to the 1900 census, Joplin was one of about one hundred African American men who were either musicians or music teachers. See *Twelfth Census, 1900: Occupations,* 706, 708; and *Thirteenth Census, 1910: Occupation Statistics,* 598–99.

8. Joplin's friends insist that Joplin and Jones married in Sedalia. Unfortunately no corroborating documentary evidence has yet come to light. Perhaps they had become common-law spouses by the time they arrived in St. Louis. Joplin and Jones eventually parted—a break-up that was painful to both. I have found no formal evidence of either a marriage or a divorce.

9. See *Gould's St. Louis Directory for 1902;* and *Gould's Directory for 1903* for entries for Scott Joplin. The first places him at 2658-A Morgan, and the second places him at 2117 Lucas Avenue. Both identify him as a musician. Though he was in Sedalia in the 1890s when several city directories were published, his name appears in none of them. He probably was on the road when the surveys were made or had no permanent residence of his own.

10. "To Play Ragtime in Europe," *St. Louis Post-Dispatch,* February 28, 1901, 3, col. 2–3.

11. "The King of Rag-Time Composers Is Scott Joplin, A Colored St. Louisan," *St. Louis Globe-Democrat,* June 7, 1903, Sporting Section, 5, col. 1–3.

12. *The Ragtime Dance* in Lawrence, ed., *Collected Works of Scott Joplin,* 2:293–301.

13. For a full discussion of *The Ragtime Dance,* see Lawrence, ed., *Collected Works of Scott Joplin,* 1:xxii–xxiv. For the Sedalia "boosting" of Joplin's ballet, see "Our Trip to the World's Fair City," *Sedalia Times,* April 26, 1902, 1, col. 1.

14. Marshall was interviewed in 1949 for Blesh, *They All Played Ragtime,* 71, and his comment there is repeated in Lawrence, ed., *Collected Works of Scott Joplin,* 1:xxvi–xxvii, which also includes a full discussion of *A Guest of Honor* and its sad fate. For references to

Joplin's preparations, see "Scott Joplin's Opera," *Sedalia Weekly Conservator,* August 22, 1903, 2, col. 3.

15. Joplin biographers speculate that Joplin essentially "cannibalized" the opera for various of the pieces that he published in the next few years. Given the amount of work that went into the composition of music for an opera, Joplin may well have done this, so as to get some kind of return on his investment of time and energy. If he did so, however, Joplin never indicated as much or which pieces came from the opera.

16. "Music at the World's Fair," *World's Fair Bulletin* 3 (July 1902): 21. Ernest Kroeger returned to the comparisons two years later to justify the musical decisions made at the Louisiana Purchase Exposition. Indeed, he indicated in the following article that he and others on the Bureau of Music consulted their counterparts from the World's Columbian Exposition to get advice to help avoid the disaster in Chicago in 1893. "The Chicago officials informed the St. Louis Bureau in the most emphatic manner," Kroeger wrote, "that a scheme of high-class music at any Exposition would be a serious mistake; that the crowd in attendance would not have it at all; that the energy, enthusiasm, and money spent in this direction would be largely thrown away." See E. R. Kroeger, "Music and Musicians at the World's Fair, St. Louis, U.S.A.," *World's Fair Bulletin* 5 (September 1904): 15–18.

17. *World's Fair Bulletin* 3 (September 1902): 1; "World's Fair Music: Professor Ernest R. Kroeger Appointed Director of Programmes and Awards," 18.

18. "Alfred Ernst: Official Conductor of Orchestra and Chorus," 44. It is possible that Ernst knew of Joplin's difficulty finding backing for his serious works. Perhaps he attended the performance of *A Guest of Honor* and decided that Joplin was not turning out to be worthy of his praise and endorsement from three years earlier. It is not known whether he had actually broken with Joplin. James Haskins insisted in his biography of Joplin that the King of Ragtime continued to work under Ernst's tutelage, but he provides no concrete evidence of this. It would seem to me that Ernst's failure to promote Joplin when he could have from his official position in the music program makes his sponsorship of Joplin doubtful. As I indicated above, Theodore Albrecht's identification of Julius Weiss as Joplin's German music teacher makes all the more sense in light of this information about Ernst in St. Louis in 1904.

19. Jane Anne Liebenguth, "Music at the Louisiana Purchase Exposition," 27–34; "Announcement," *St. Louis Globe-Democrat,* May 1,

1904, Editorial Section, 8, col. 6–7. According to a notice in *The Etude,* Van der Stucken's *Louisiana March* contained themes from *Marseillaise, Hail Columbia, Dixie,* and *Old Hundredth,* so it was at once "new" and familiar. It also at least made an effort to acknowledge the diverse people who had settled in and developed the territory in the Louisiana Purchase. See "Musical Items," *The Etude* 22 (June 1904): 256.

20. "The Negro and the World's Fair," 32.

21. *World's Fair Bulletin* 2 (August 1901): 22.

22. "The World's Fair," *St. Louis Palladium,* January 16, 1904, 5, col. 1; "Plan to Care for Negro Visitors to World's Fair," *St. Louis Palladium,* March 19, 1904, 1, col. 3; and "To Exhibit This Newspaper at World's Fair," *St. Louis Palladium,* July 11, 1903, 1, col. 4. According to Greene, Kremer, and Holland, the *St. Louis Palladium* was one of the most successful of the black newspapers in Missouri at the turn of the century. John W. Wheeler edited it from 1897 to 1911. "Wheeler advocated black advancement through industry and self-help, a philosophy eminently consistent with that of his contemporary, Booker T. Washington, a national black leader," they wrote. "Wheeler shied away from the politics of confrontation and refused to abandon the Republican party when others of his race were doing so in the nineties and the early years of the twentieth century." See Greene, Kremer, and Holland, *Missouri's Black Heritage,* 102.

23. "The World's Fair," *St. Louis Palladium,* January 16, 1904, 5, col. 1.

24. "The World's Fair at Night," *St. Louis Palladium,* June 4, 1904, 1, col. 4.

25. Lilian Brandt, "The Negroes of St. Louis," 223–25; Emmett J. Scott, "The Louisiana Purchase Exposition," 310–11; W. S. Scarborough, "The Negro and the Louisiana Purchase Exposition," 312; and William H. Kenney, "James Scott and the Culture of Classic Ragtime," 156.

26. "Beauty, Size, and Sentiment of the World's Fair," *St. Louis Palladium,* May 7, 1904, 3, col. 3.

27. "Editorial," *World's Fair Bulletin* 5 (March 1904): 1.

28. "The Million Dollar Pike," 68. For additional commentary on the Pike, see Thomas R. MacMechen, "The True and Complete Story of the Pike and Its Attractions," 4–36; and Mark Bennitt and Frank Parker Stockbridge, *History of the Louisiana Purchase Exposition.*

29. The quote by the director of Admissions and Concessions and the examples both come from Robert Rydell, *All the World's a Fair,* 179–80. Rydell's analysis of the Louisiana Purchase Exposition is subtitled "The Coronation of Civilization," and in it he argues that the Fair was the perfect cultural accompaniment to American im-

perialism at the turn of the century, with its insatiable demand for new markets and its implied and overt racism. For the entire analysis, see Chapter 6.

30. "The Million Dollar Pike," 68.

31. "A Three Days' Tour," 25.

32. "Pike Celebration a Hummer," *St. Louis Post-Dispatch,* July 3, 1904, 2, col. 6.

33. Tichenor, "Missouri's Role in the Ragtime Revolution," 240, 242.

34. "The Rose Bud Ball," *St. Louis Palladium,* February 27, 1904, 1, col. 2.

35. This comment appeared on the back page of a later edition of Joplin's *The Cascades,* a copy of which is in the Starr Music Collection, Scott Joplin File, Lilly Library, Bloomington, Indiana.

36. Gammond, *Scott Joplin and the Ragtime Era*; and Blesh, *They All Played Ragtime,* 78. Some of the best recent work on James Scott has been produced by William H. Kenney. Offering an analysis of Scott's work that emphasizes the African American perspective, Kenney moves well beyond the time-worn arguments about ragtime and the underside of American cultural life. Kenney also problematizes the relationship between Joplin and Scott. While acknowledging that some kind of relationship existed between the two musicians, he has found no evidence to substantiate the claim made by other biographers that the two men actually met in St. Louis or elsewhere. See Kenney, "James Scott and the Culture of Classic Ragtime."

37. Rudi Blesh offers a very sensitive account of the problems between Joplin and his first wife, an account that is based on testimony from Arthur Marshall. See Blesh, *They All Played Ragtime,* 78–79.

38. Lawrence, ed., *Collected Works of Scott Joplin,* 1:xxx.

39. Ibid.

40. Blesh, *They All Played Ragtime,* 231.

41. Ibid., 79.

42. Ibid., 233. For additional information on Percy G. Williams, see Robert W. Snyder, *The Voice of the City: Vaudeville and Popular Culture in New York,* 37, 93, 194–95.

43. Lester A. Walton, "The Future of the Negro on the Stage," 439–42.

44. Lester A. Walton, "Music and the Stage," *The Colored American Magazine* 14 (September 1908): 459; and 14 (February/March 1908): 95. These were parts of a multi-part discussion of African Americans in the world of music and the theater that Walton published in the magazine in 1908.

45. Roell, *The Piano in America,* 44–45; Loesser, *Men, Women, and Pianos,* 584–85. Both Roell and Loesser offer excellent summaries of the invention and improvements of devices that played pianos mechanically at the turn of the century, and both refer to the many famous pianists who cut piano rolls for various of the companies that produced these player pianos. Their interpretations of these player pianos and rolls makes Joplin's cutting of piano rolls fairly significant at that stage in his career. Loesser hints at and Roell explicitly argues the consumer-orientation of player pianos.

Information about rolls cut by Joplin comes from two sources. Rudi Blesh listed many of the compositions for which piano rolls were cut, and he indicated with an asterisk the ones performed by the composer. In the case of Joplin, multiple rolls were cut of *Maple Leaf Rag,* and it is unclear which ones were actually made by Joplin. Vera Brodsky Lawrence addresses this ambiguity by including a rollography of Joplin works in her two-volume collection of his music. She has sorted through the rolls to identify the ones made by Joplin. According to Lawrence, Joplin is known to have cut at least one composition by another composer—*Ole Miss Rag* by W. C. Handy. See Blesh, *They All Played Ragtime,* 335–38; and Lawrence, ed., *Collected Works of Scott Joplin,* 1:297–98.

According to S. Brunson Campbell, Joplin "became very successful and cut quite a number of piano rolls of his own rags, which brought him in quite a revenue. He never made any phonograph records." Joplin may well have made some money cutting piano rolls, but it would be difficult to substantiate Campbell's claim. See "Did You Know Ragtime Music Was Born in Sedalia?" *Sedalia Democrat,* June 29, 1947, 7, col. 5.

46. The sources are not clear on when Scott Joplin married Lottie Stokes. Lottie Stokes Joplin told an interviewer in the 1950s that she married Joplin in 1907. Rudi Blesh wrote that the Joplins married in 1909, and S. Brunson Campbell reported that they married on June 18, 1910. See Kay C. Thompson, "Lottie Joplin," 8; Blesh, "Scott Joplin: Black-American Classicist," in Lawrence, ed., *Collected Works of Scott Joplin,* 1:xxxii; "Did You Know Ragtime Music Was Born in Sedalia?" *Sedalia Democrat,* June 29, 1947, 7, col. 5.

47. Quoted in Anderson, *This Was Harlem,* 10.

48. Ibid., 8. Anderson's work on Harlem documents its rise and evolution from 1900 to 1950. Blending an appealing narrative style with rich examples from contemporary observers, Anderson's early chapters provide an excellent context for viewing Joplin's experience in the city. As Anderson shows, Scott Joplin was one of many ambitious African Americans who sought fame and fortune in "Negro

Bohemia." For a discussion of the nature and extent of prostitution in this district, Timothy Gilfoyle's work is unsurpassed. He provides an interesting narrative on the evolution of prostitution in New York from the late eighteenth century into the early twentieth century and provides extremely useful maps that indicate the location of theaters and houses of prostitution. See Gilfoyle, *City of Eros: New York City, Prostitution, and the Commercialization of Sex, 1790–1920,* 203–10.

49. Noble Sissle is quoted in Anderson, *This Was Harlem,* 16.

50. James Weldon Johnson, *The Autobiography of an Ex-Colored Man,* 72.

51. "C.V.B.A. Entertainment," *New York Age,* February 3, 1910, 6, col. 1.

52. "Latest Ragtime Number," *New York Age,* May 19, 1910, 6, col. 4. A few weeks later, the same newspaper urged readers to "Get Scott Joplin's 'Euphonic Sounds,' the latest ragtime piece by Scott Joplin." See "Theatrical Jottings," *New York Age,* June 2, 1910, 6, col. 3.

53. The quoted material appears in Blesh, *They All Played Ragtime,* 236, but for more information on Lamb, see the entire passage, 235–40.

54. "Composer of Ragtime Now Writing Grand Opera," *New York Age,* March 5, 1908, 6, col. 4–5. It probably did not hurt Scott Joplin's cause that Lester Walton, the drama and music editor of the *New York Age,* had arrived in New York from St. Louis a little more than one year before Joplin. He may have known him or some of his St. Louis friends and may have given him a plug when he could. Later on, however, Walton did little to advance Joplin's career. As manager of the Lafayette Theater between 1914 and 1916, Walton did not extend an invitation to Joplin to perform *Treemonisha* in that establishment, even though he knew that Joplin had tried to stage it there in the autumn of 1913. Moreover, after it was performed in 1915, Walton offered no comment on it.

55. In "Negro Theatre at Columbus Opens to Standing Room," *New York Age,* March 19, 1908, 6, col. 2, details of opening night are provided to endorse the introduction of more such theaters. The article ends with a note that the stage manager of Clark's Theatre was Robert B. Joplin (possibly Joplin's brother). A few years later the newspaper noted the opening of the Walker-Hogan-Cole Theatre named for "three Negroes who, besides having been talented performers, possessed much executive ability and made it possible for hundreds of colored performers to get work at good salaries." For the entire account, see "Walker-Hogan-Cole Theatre," *New York Age,* March 7, 1912, 6, col. 1–2. For a notice on the founding of the Clef Club and a

list of charter members see "Musicians Organize Clef Club," *New York Age,* April 28, 1910, 6, col. 2–3. The material on the pervasiveness of ragtime appears in "Popularity of Ragtime," *New York Age,* January 13, 1910, 6, col. 1–2. The following two articles are examples of meetings on education in black New York that may have interested Joplin. "Educational Meeting Held at Bethel Church in the Interest of Wilberforce College—Good Speeches," *New York Age,* March 19, 1908, 3, col. 4, which reported the following concluding remarks from Charles W. Anderson: "If ever there was a time and people that needed colleges and universities, and the cultured leaders which they train, this is that time, and we are that people." "Educational Mass Meeting—For Morris Brown College," *New York Age,* May 12, 1910, 7, col. 2–3.

56. Lester A. Walton, "Colored Vaudevillians Organize," *New York Age,* June 10, 1909, 6, col. 1–3; "Motto of the C.V.B.A.," *New York Age,* January 6, 1910, 6, col. 4. In the article about the founding of the C.V.B.A., Walton makes it seem that the group was organized sometime in early June, but in a later article that reviewed the history of the association, Walton noted that it had been founded on May 24, 1909. Perhaps plans were made for or a constitution written and dated in late May 1909 for what eventually became the Colored Vaudeville Benevolent Association, but the group itself may not have met and ratified it until early June. For the history of the group, see Lester A. Walton, "In the Amusement World," *New York Age,* August 15, 1912, 6, col. 1.

57. "C.V.B.A. Entertainment," *New York Age,* February 3, 1910, 6, col. 1–2; "C.V.B.A. Benefit a Success," *New York Age,* February 16, 1911, 6, col. 4–5; and "C.V.B.A. Creole Dinner," *New York Age,* April 30, 1911, 6, col. 3.

58. "New C.V.B.A. Committees," *New York Age,* June 6, 1912, 6, col. 3; and Lester A. Walton, "In the Amusement World," *New York Age,* August 15, 1912, 6, col. 1–2.

59. Scott Joplin did take part in the association's annual entertainment in August 1912. He is mentioned in an article along with Leon Williams, W. N. Spiller, and D. Whiting as "leading a strenuous existence counting the [people in the audience?]." The report does not explicitly say that the entertainment took place in Harlem, but it probably did. See Lester A. Walton, "C.V.B.A. Entertainment," *New York Age,* August 22, 1912, 6, col. 1–2.

60. Lester A. Walton, "Negro Music," *New York Age,* January 1, 1914, 6, col. 1–2.

61. "Latest Negro Opera," *New York Age,* May 25, 1911, 6, col. 3; "Scott Joplin Honored," *New York Age,* June 22, 1911, 6, col. 3.

62. In a narrative of Joplin's life, it is difficult to know where to discuss this sensitive, yet critical, problem. It is known that Joplin died from the effects of syphilis in 1917 after a brief period of hospitalization for dementia. Since none of the people who knew Joplin reported seeing chancres associated with the first two stages of the disease, it is impossible to know with any certainty when Joplin became infected with the disease. Recent studies disagree on the timing of the various stages of the disease. According to C. B. S. Schofield, author of a general study entitled *Sexually Transmitted Diseases,* the tertiary stage appears usually three to ten years after the initial infection, but for as many as five to seven years, the effects are not apparent without medical tests. See Schofield, *Sexually Transmitted Diseases* (Edinburgh, London, New York: Churchill Livingstone, 1979), 85–86; and James H. Jones, *Bad Blood: The Tuskegee Syphilis Experiment* (New York: The Free Press, 1981), 2–4.

Biographers of Joplin are left to speculate. If Schofield is correct, then possibly Joplin became infected sometime after the break-up with Belle Jones Joplin and before his marriage to Lottie Stokes. Others have suggested that Joplin's disease caused the death of the child born to Belle Jones Joplin, but that theory has not been substantiated. Indeed, other explanations may be offered. According to the 1900 census for Sedalia, Missouri, Belle Jones had given birth to three children, of whom only one was living. She may have had some kind of medical ailment that contributed to the death of her children. Indeed, she may have contracted syphilis from the father of her first three children and may have transmitted the disease to Joplin.

Knowing after the fact that Joplin had syphilis for some part of his adult life prompts one to speculate on its effect on his creativity, production, performance, and social relations. But without sources, such speculation presents more problems than it solves. More than likely, Joplin lost dexterity in the later years of his life because of the effects of the disease, but it is hard to say when, to what degree, and how frequently such difficulties manifested themselves. I prefer to remain largely silent on an issue that is so nebulous. Joplin created some exquisite music in the early twentieth century, and at a time when he more than likely had syphilis. I prefer not to blame "failures" or "disappointments" on the disease, and I think it ill-advised to speculate on the relationship between ragtime and immorality on the grounds that Joplin died of syphilis.

63. Thompson, "Lottie Joplin," 18.

64. This review appeared in the June 24, 1911, issue of *The American Musician,* major excerpts of which appear in Haskins's *Scott Joplin,* 177–79.

65. "Press on Coleridge-Taylor," *New York Age,* October 10, 1912, 6, col. 3–5. For a revealing discussion of African American entertainment in Harlem in these years, see Carl Van Vechten, *In the Garret,* 312–24.

66. "Theatrical Jottings," *New York Age,* August 7, 1913, 6, col. 2.

67. Lester A. Walton, "Theatres in Harlem," *New York Age,* January 9, 1913, 6, col. 1.

68. Lester A. Walton, "An Evening at the Lafayette," *New York Age,* February 20, 1913, 6, col. 1–2; Lester A. Walton, "'The Traitor' Presented," *New York Age,* March 20, 1913, 6, col. 1–2; "Lafayette Theatre," *New York Age,* May 1, 1913, 6, col. 3 and May 8, 1913, 6, col. 3.

69. "Negro Players to Appear at Lafayette," *New York Age,* June 12, 1913, 6, col. 3; Lester A. Walton, "The Negro Players," *New York Age,* May 15, 1913, 6, col. 1–2. Walton's particular interest in the Lafayette is even more important considering he became its manager in 1914–1916 and 1919–1921. See Southern, *Biographical Dictionary of Afro-American and African Musicians,* 389.

70. Van Vechten, *In the Garret,* 315. For information on the Lafayette Theatre, see M. A. Harris, *A Negro History Tour of Manhattan,* 103. For an extended discussion of the importance of such black theaters as the Lafayette to African American culture in Harlem, see James Weldon Johnson, *Black Manhattan,* 170–81; and Anderson, *This Was Harlem,* 110–16.

71. Haskins, *Scott Joplin,* 188.

72. Lester A. Walton, "Outlook Much Brighter," *New York Age,* February 27, 1913, 6, col. 1–2.

73. "Theatrical Comment," *New York Age,* April 3, 1913, 6, col. 1.

74. "The Negro Musician," *New York Age,* September 30, 1915, 6, col. 2–3.

75. For Joplin's instructions on playing ragtime, see *School of Ragtime* and *Pine Apple Rag* in Lawrence, ed., *Collected Works of Scott Joplin,* 1:284, 176. Some critics have argued that Joplin was simply a poor performer because he played his works so precisely. For a typical comment along these lines, see Rex Harris, *Jazz,* 64. At the time, however, that accuracy was seen by some as a mark of his greatness. According to Harold E. Kimpton, for example, "Great stress should be laid on accuracy. A rag should be played exactly as its [sic] written, although we will admit that some might be able to improve a rag somewhat by a few additions. But don't knock down. The Scott Joplin and rags of like caliber demand perfect accuracy first, and then

comes the expression." See Harold E. Kimpton, "Ragtime, a Lasting Success," 7.

76. "Vaudeville," *Christensen's Ragtime Review* 1 (April 1915): 2.

77. Haskins, *Scott Joplin,* 194.

78. Advertisement in *New York Age,* October 22, 1914, 6, col. 5.

79. Van Vechten, *In the Garret,* 316–19. Though Van Vechten was a white man who had grown up in Cedar Rapids, Iowa, he eventually moved to New York and immersed himself in the black cultural community there. According to Jervis Anderson, "no one was more friendly or helpful to the Harlem Renaissance movement than Carl Van Vechten—some of whose work may even be said to belong to the canon of New Negro writing." For this reason, I have included his commentary on African American entertainment in Harlem in the 1910s as evidence of a sensibility contrary to that displayed by Joplin. See Anderson, *This Was Harlem,* 213.

80. Southern, ed., *Biographical Dictionary of Afro-American and African Musicians,* 81–82, 76–77, 210, 128–29; James Weldon Johnson, *Along This Way: The Autobiography of James Weldon Johnson* recounts his and his brother John Rosamond's education and careers, and in *Black Manhattan,* he describes a blossoming musical and entertainment community in Harlem that bore few of the marks of Reconstruction South. See Chapters 15–17.

81. J. Rosamond Johnson, ed., *Rolling Along in Song: A Chronological Survey of American Negro Music,* 18.

82. "Did You Know Ragtime Was Born in Sedalia?" *Sedalia Democrat,* June 29, 1947, 7, col. 5. Writing in 1928, Wallace Thurman described both the Lafayette and Lincoln Theatres, which, in the fifteen years since Joplin's efforts to stage *Treemonisha,* had declined considerably. "The Lafayette used to house a local stock company composed of all Negro players," he wrote of the better of the two theaters, "but it has now fallen into less dignified hands. . . . Cheap imitations of Broadway successes, nudity, vulgar dances and vulgar jokes are the box office attractions." By contrast, Thurman described the Lincoln as "smaller and more smelly than the Lafayette," whose "shows are even worse than those staged at the Lafayette. They are so bad that they are ludicrously funny." While conditions in the entertainment business can change quite rapidly, as is evident in the changes that occurred in the Lafayette Theatre in the year 1913, it is probably fair to conclude that even in 1915, performing at the Lincoln Theatre was a great comedown for an artist of Joplin's stature. For the complete discussion of the Lafayette and the Lincoln, see Thurman, "Negro Life in New York's Harlem," in *Speech and Power*

*The African-American Essay and Its Cultural Content from Polemics to Pulpit,*
ed. Gerald Early, 1:70–91.

83. "Theatrical Jottings," *New York Age,* December 17, 1914, 6,
col. 2.

84. It would seem likely to me that as a single man without roots
or ties, Joplin may have visited a prostitute in Chicago while he was
working with Louis Chauvin on *Heliotrope Bouquet* and in that way
became infected. Ten years later, the disease took its final toll. See
Haskins, *Scott Joplin,* 193–95. For other brief announcements of his
death see "Scott Joplin Dies of Mental Trouble," *New York Age,* April
5, 1917, 1, col. 7; "Things Theatrical," *New York Age,* April 5, 1917,
6, col. 1; and "Scott Joplin Is Dead," 13. See also the discussion in
footnote 62 above.

85. S. Brunson Campbell, one of the people responsible for keeping
alive the memory of Joplin's life, is partly responsible for either
starting or perpetuating the story of Joplin's funeral. See "Did You
Know Ragtime Was Born in Sedalia?" *Sedalia Democrat,* June 29, 1947,
6, col. 5.

## Chapter 6. The Legacy of Scott Joplin

1. Curtis, "The Negro's Contribution to the Music of America,"
660–69. In "Ragtime," *The Outlook* 104 (May 24, 1913): 137, one finds
a reprint of excerpts from Curtis's article with an implicit endorsement
of her ideas.

2. Moderwell, "Ragtime," 284–86; A. Walter Kramer, "Extols Ragtime Article," 122; James Cloyd Bowman, "Anti-Ragtime," 19.

3. Bessie Hanson, "Ragtime the American National Music," 8; Peter
Frank Meyer, "The Potency of Ragtime," 3–4; "Another Defender of
Ragtime," 3.

4. Krehbiel, "The Distinctive Note in American Music," 108.

5. Downes, "An American Composer," 28.

6. J. A. Fuller Maitland, ed., *Grove's Dictionary of Music and Musicians,* 4:16; Hubbard, et al., *The American History and Encyclopedia of
Music,* Vol. 10.

7. Haskins, *Scott Joplin,* 179.

8. Daniel Gregory Mason, "Folk-Song and American Music," 324.
J. Lawrence Erb noted a similar quality in the American character in
1899. Ragtime, for Erb, was a "direct result of the conditions that
obtain in our American life today. . . . We strive. We hurry. We seek
new fields to conquer." See Erb, "Where Is the American Song?" 154.

9. Mathews, "The Great American Composer," 422–23.

10. H. J. Wilson, "The Negro and Music," 823–26.

11. Kroeger, "On 'American' Music," 290.

12. Edward Baxter Perry, "Taste versus Prejudice," 148.

13. Finck, "Edward MacDowell," 983–89. Finck played fast and loose with history in this essay on MacDowell. He noted, as did many of his contemporaries, that the idea of an American school of music resting on African American folk influences arose with Antonin Dvorak in the early 1890s. "Dr. Dvorak adopted this view when he first came to New York as Director of the National Conservatory; but subsequently he abandoned it," wrote Finck. This is the only article I have seen that makes such a claim, but Finck obviously added it to strengthen his case against African American music incorporated into the mainstream of American art music. He was later criticized for this assertion by Sternberg in a letter to the editor entitled "National Music."

14. Farwell, "The Struggle toward a National Music," 565–70.

15. "Dr. Damrosch Hits Ragtime," 7; "Musical Materia Medica," 16; "Ragtime Causing Mental Ailments," 28; and "Our Musical Condition," 137–39.

16. "Questions and Answers," *The Etude* 18 (February 1900): 52; and Maitland, ed., *Grove's Dictionary of Music and Musicians,* Vol. 4, 16.

17. Kroeger, "On 'American' Music," 290.

18. Mason, "Folk-Song and American Music," 324–25; Erb, "Where Is the American Song?" 154; and Moderwell, "Ragtime," 285–86. Another article, "Ragtime Has Vitality," 8, argued, "It is becoming recognized more and more that the once-despised ragtime . . . possesses an energy and a vitality which expresses as no other music does the nervous, vigorous sweep of American life."

19. Sternberg, "What Is American Music?" 190. Any student of history cannot help but notice the uncomfortable similarity between Sternberg's coupling of a submissive "mother" with an assertive "father" and the situation on southern plantations before the Civil War. Slave laws, first codified in the seventeenth century, insisted that children of slave women were to follow in the condition of the *mother*. Such laws resulted in some cases in the enslavement by white men of their own children.

20. Houston Baker, "Modernism and the Harlem Renaissance," 94.

21. The following works explain most fully these concepts: Watts, *The Republic Reborn;* Marvin Meyers, *The Jacksonian Persuasion: Politics and Belief;* Harris, *Humbug: The Art of P. T. Barnum;* Walters, *American Reformers;* David J. Rothman, *The Discovery of the Asylum: Social Order and Disorder in the New Republic;* Halttunen, *Confidence Men and Painted Women;* Joseph Kett, *Rites of Passage: Adolescence in America, 1790 to the Present,* Parts I and II; and Michael Paul Rogin, *Fathers and Children: Andrew Jackson and the Subjugation of the American Indian.*

22. Thelen, *The New Citizenship;* Michael McGerr, *The Decline of Popular Politics: The American North, 1865–1928;* James T. Kloppenberg,

*Uncertain Victory: Social Democracy and Progressivism in European and American Thought, 1870–1920;* David Thelen, *Paths of Resistance: Tradition and Dignity in Industrializing Missouri;* Richard Sennett, *The Fall of Public Man;* Chandler, *The Visible Hand;* Rodgers, *The Work Ethic in Industrial America;* George Fredrickson, *The Inner Civil War: Northern Intellectuals and the Crisis of the Union;* Dorothy Ross, "Socialism and American Liberalism: Academic Social Thought in the 1890s"; and Daniel Rodgers, "In Search of Progressivism."

23. Higham, "The Reorientation of American Culture in the 1890s"; D. H. Meyer, "American Intellectuals and the Victorian Crisis of Faith"; Robert Crunden, *Ministers of Reform;* Curtis, *A Consuming Faith;* and Lears, *No Place of Grace.*

24. Moderwell, "Ragtime," 285.

25. "Theatrical Comment," *New York Age,* April 3, 1913, 6, col. 1–2.

26. C. Crozat Converse, "Rag-Time Music," 185; Curtis, "The Negro's Contribution to the Music of America," 664.

27. "Musical Impurity," 16.

28. Sternberg, "What Is American Music?", 190; Preston Ware Orem, "Popular Instrumental Music," 449.

29. Harold Hubbs, "What Is Ragtime?" 345; Daniel Gregory Mason, "Prefers Demonstration to Cheers," 122; Lawrence Gilman, "The New American Music," 871.

30. James Weldon Johnson, *Along This Way,* 328.

31. Ibid.

32. "Negro Music in the Land of Freedom," 611–12.

33. "Latest Negro Opera," *New York Age,* May 25, 1911, 6, col. 3; "Theatrical Jottings," *New York Age,* August 14, 1913, 6, col. 3–4.

34. *School of Ragtime* in Lawrence, ed., *Collected Works of Scott Joplin,* 1:284–86.

35. Singal, "Towards a Definition of American Modernism," 12–13.

36. Rudi Blesh, "Scott Joplin: Black American Classicist," in Lawrence, ed., *Collected Works of Scott Joplin,* 1:xxvi.

37. Harris, *After the Ball,* 58–60. Throughout Harris's autobiography, one can find lyrics to songs that made Harris one of the important actors in the field of popular music at the turn of the century.

38. "Love and Grief," in Lida Keck Wiggins, ed., *The Life and Works of Paul Laurence Dunbar,* 207.

39. Van Wyck Brooks, *New England: Indian Summer, 1865–1915* (New York: E. P. Dutton & Co., 1940). Brooks's book reviews the writers of New England in the Gilded Age who set about the task of evoking the character of a region that seemed to be fading in importance.

40. "The Colored Band," in Wiggins, ed., *The Life and Works of Paul Laurence Dunbar,* 262.

41. James Corrothers, *In Spite of the Handicap: An Autobiography,* 137, 82–85.

42. James Weldon Johnson, *Along This Way,* 159, 173.

43. "Theatrical Comment," *New York Age,* March 30, 1911, 6, col. 1. Walton's comments followed Hogan's untimely death.

44. Dormon, "Shaping the Popular Image of Post-Reconstruction American Blacks," 450–71.

45. Lawrence, ed., *Collected Works of Scott Joplin,* 2:5–7.

46. Ibid., 107–21.

47. Booker T. Washington, "The Atlanta Exposition Address," in *Up From Slavery,* 217–26; Du Bois, "Of Mr. Booker T. Washington and Others," in *The Souls of Black Folk,* 42–54.

48. Blesh, *They All Played Ragtime,* 249; and repeated in his essay on Joplin in Lawrence, ed., *Collected Works of Scott Joplin,* 1:xxxix. For biographical information on the Johnsons, Cook, Europe, and Walton, see Southern, *Biographical Dictionary of Afro-American and African Musicians.*

49. Excellent work in African American history in the last couple of decades has done a great deal to enrich our perceptions of the black experience in the past. Starting with studies on slavery, the historiography of African American history has expanded to include studies of black people and communities in other contexts. From studies of slavery such as Genovese's *Roll, Jordan, Roll* and Blassingame's *The Slave Community* to Levine's *Black Culture and Black Consciousness,* histories of African Americans have demonstrated a rich variety of ideas, cultural expressions, and lived experience within that community. At times, American historians have treated the black experience as something monolithic and distinct from other groups within American society by referring to a "black response" to events, for example. Because racism operates on the arbitrary standard of skin color, that designation makes some sense. Nevertheless, it is imperative to be as sensitive to variety within the African American culture and experience as ethnic studies have asked us to be in the case of white ethnics. For a discussion of the problem of ethnicity and race in American culture, see Sollors, *Beyond Ethnicity,* 20–39.

50. For information on the individuals singled out by Du Bois, see Southern, *Biographical Dictionary of Afro-American and African Musicians.* For the comment by Du Bois, see W. E. B. Du Bois, *The Gift of Black Folk: The Negroes in the Making of America,* 290–91.

# BIBLIOGRAPHY

## CENSUS REPORTS

Ninth Census, 1870, Manuscript Census for Davis (now Cass) County, Texas.

Tenth Census, 1880, Manuscript Census for Bowie County, Texas.

Twelfth Census, 1900, Manuscript Census for Pettis County, Missouri.

*Ninth Census, 1870: Statistics of the Population of the United States.* Vol. 1. Washington, D.C.: Government Printing Office, 1872.

*Ninth Census, 1870: A Compendium of the Ninth Census of the United States.* Washington, D.C.: Government Printing Office, 1872.

*Tenth Census, 1880: Statistics of the Population of the United States.* Vol. 1. Washington, D.C.: Government Printing Office, 1883.

*Tenth Census, 1880: Report on the Manufactures of the United States.* Vol. 2. Washington, D.C.: Government Printing Office, 1883.

*Tenth Census, 1880: Report on the Productions of Agriculture in the United States.* Vol. 3. Washington, D.C.: Government Printing Office, 1883.

*Tenth Census, 1880: Report on the Agencies of Transportation in the United States.* Vol. 4. Washington, D.C.: Government Printing Office, 1883.

*Tenth Census, 1880: Report on Cotton Production in the United States.* Vol. 5. Washington, D.C.: Government Printing Office, 1884.

*Tenth Census, 1880: The Newspaper and Periodical Press in the United States.* Vol. 8. Washington, D.C.: Government Printing Office, 1884.

*Eleventh Census, 1890: Report on Manufacturing Industries in the United States.* Vol. 6. Parts 1 and 2. Washington, D.C.: Government Printing Office, 1895.

*Eleventh Census, 1890: Report on the Population of the United States.*

Vol. 1. Part 1. Washington, D.C.: Government Printing Office, 1895.

*Eleventh Census, 1890: Report on the Population of the United States.* Vol. 1. Part 2. Washington, D.C.: Government Printing Office, 1897.

*Twelfth Census, 1900: Report on the Population of the United States.* Vol. 1. Part 1. Washington, D.C.: United States Census Office, 1901.

*Twelfth Census, 1900: Report on the Population of the United States.* Vol. 2. Part 2. Washington, D.C.: United States Census Office, 1902.

## NEWSPAPERS
### Texas

*Daily Texarkana Independent*
*Jefferson Radical*
(Marshall) *Tri-Weekly Herald*

### Missouri

*Sedalia Bazoo*
*Sedalia Capital*
*Sedalia Democrat*
*Sedalia Evening Sentinel*
*Sedalia Gazette*
*Sedalia Times*
*Sedalia Weekly Conservator*
(Sedalia) *Review and Plain Talker*
(Sedalia) *Rosa Pearle's Paper*
*St. Louis Globe-Democrat*
*St. Louis Palladium*
*St. Louis Post-Dispatch*

### Illinois

*Chicago Tribune*

### New York

*New York Age*
*New York Times*

## PRIMARY SOURCES
### Articles

"Advertising Again." *The Etude* 17 (November 1899): 362–63.

"An African School of Music." *Musical Record* (July 1893): 5.

Aldrich, Richard. "American Composers." *The Etude* 17 (May 1899): 135–37.

"Alfred Ernst: Official Conductor of Orchestra and Chorus." *World's Fair Bulletin* 5 (February 1904): 44.

"Americans in the Rough." *The Outlook* 81 (December 23, 1905): 956–57.

"And This Man Is Right." *Christensen's Ragtime Review* 1 (April 1915): 3.

"Another Defender of Ragtime." *Christensen's Ragtime Review* 1 (April 1915): 3.

Archer, William. "America To-day: The Republic and the Empire." *Pall Mall Magazine* 19 (September 1899): 95–105.

"A Battle of Pianos." *Everybody's Magazine* 9 (December 1903): 845.

Bispham, David. "Music as a Factor in National Life." *North American Review* 175 (December 1902): 786–99.

Bowman, James Cloyd. "Anti-Ragtime." *The New Republic* 5 (November 6, 1915): 19.

Braine, Robert. "A Piano for Everybody." *The Etude* 17 (January 1899): 7.

Brandt, Lilian. "The Negroes of St. Louis." *Southern Workman* 33 (April 1904): 223–28.

Bruce, P. A. "The American Negro of To-day." *Contemporary Review* 77 (February 1900): 284–97.

Campbell, Helen. "Is American Domesticity Decreasing, and if so, Why?" *Arena* 19 (January 1898): 86–96.

Campbell, S. Brunson. "Ragtime Begins: Early Days with Scott Joplin." *The Record Changer* 8 (March 1948): 8, 18.

"Can You Imagine This?" *Christensen's Ragtime Review* 1 (December 1914): 2.

Christensen, Axel. "Can Ragtime Be Suppressed?" *Christensen's Ragtime Review* 1 (June 1915): 3–4.

Converse, C. Crozat. "Rag-time Music." *The Etude* 17 (June 1899): 185.

———. "Rag-Time." *The Etude* 17 (August 1899): 256.

Curtis, Natalie. "The Negro's Contribution to the Music of America: The Larger Opportunity of the Colored Man of Today." *The Craftsman* 23 (March 1913): 660–69.

Davidson, Harry. "What Has 'Ragtime' To Do with 'American Music'?" *Ragtime Review* 2 (August 1916): 3.

Douglass, Frederick. "Inauguration of the World's Columbian Exposition." *World's Columbian Exposition Illustrated* 3 (March 1893): 602.

———. "Introduction to the Reason Why the Colored American Is Not in the World's Columbian Exposition." In *The Life and Writings of Frederick Douglass,* Vol. 4. Edited by Philip S. Foner. New York: International Publisher, 1955.

———. "Why Is the Negro Lynched?" In *The Life and Writings of Frederick Douglass,* Vol. 4. Edited by Philip S. Foner. New York: International Publisher, 1955.

Dow, J. W. "American Renaissance." *Nation* 79 (September 29, 1904): 266.

Downes, Olin. "An American Composer." *Musical Quarterly* 4 (January 1918): 23–36.

"Dr. Damrosch Hits Ragtime." *Musical America* 18 (July 26, 1913): 7.

"Ducasse Uses Ragtime in New Tone Poem." *Musical America* 37 (March 10, 1923): 15.

"Dvorak on Negro Melodies." *Musical Record* (July 1893): 13.

"Editorial." *The Negro Music Journal* 1 (October 1902): 30.

Erb, J. Lawrence. "Where Is the American Song?" *The Etude* 19 (January 1901): 6.

"Ethnological Value of Folk-Songs." *Musical Record* (July 1894): 9.

Farwell, Arthur. "The Struggle toward a National Music." *North American Review* 186 (December 1907): 565–70.

Finck, Henry T. "Edward MacDowell: Musician and Composer." *The Outlook* 84 (December 22, 1906): 983–89.

"Flays Rag-Time as Not Reflecting Americanism." *Musical America* 28 (July 20, 1918): 22.

Gates, W. F. "Ethiopian Syncopations—The Decline of Ragtime." *The Musician* 7 (October 1902): 341.

Gilbert, Henry F. "The American Composer." *Musical Quarterly* 1 (April 1915): 169–80.

Gilder, John Francis. "Dvorak's American Theory." *Musical Record* (July 1893): 5.

Gilman, Lawrence. "The New American Music." *North American Review* 179 (December 1904): 868–72.

Goodrich, A. J. "Syncopated Rhythm vs. 'Rag-Time.'" *The Musician* 6 (November 1901): 336.

Gordon, George A. "The Real America." *Arena* 20 (November–December 1898): 558–68.

Hanson, Bessie. "Ragtime the American National Music." *Christensen's Ragtime Review* 1 (March 1915): 8.

Harris, Henry J. "The Occupation of Musician in the United States." *Musical Quarterly* 1 (April 1915): 299–311.

Hubbs, Harold. "What Is Ragtime?" *The Outlook* 118 (February 27, 1918): 345.

Hughes, Rupert. "A Eulogy of Rag-Time." *Musical Record* (April 1899): 157–59.

"Idealized Ragtime." *Musical America* 18 (August 9, 1913): 20.

Johnson, Carl Bowen. "World's Fair Letter." *The Independent* 45 (May 18, 1893): 9; (July 6, 1893): 9; (August 24, 1893): 13.

Johnson, James Weldon. "The Negro of To-day in Music." *Charities* 15 (October 7, 1905): 58–59.

Kay, George W. "Reminiscing in Ragtime." *Jazz Journal* 17 (November 1964): 9.

Kimpton, Harold E. "Ragtime, A Lasting Success." *Ragtime Review* 1 (November 1915): 7.

Kramer, A. Walter. "Extols Ragtime Article." *The New Republic* 5 (December 4, 1915): 122.

Krehbiel, H. E. "The Distinctive Note in American Music." *The Etude* 24 (March 1906): 108.

Kroeger, E. R. "Music and Musicians at the World's Fair, St. Louis, U.S.A." *World's Fair Bulletin* 5 (September 1904): 15–18.

———. "On 'American' Music." *The Etude* 17 (September 1899): 290.

Larkin, Arthur D. "Does Real Ragtime Spoil the Classical Student?" *Ragtime Review* (July 1915): 12.

Liebling, Leonard. "The Music Trades of America." *The Etude* 17 (May 1899): 143–44.

"The Louisiana Purchase Exposition." *The Voice of the Negro* 1 (August 1904): 342.

Maclaren, Ian. "The Restless Energy of the American People—An Impression." *North American Review* 169 (October 1899): 564–76.

MacMechen, Thomas R. "The True and Complete Story of the

Pike and Its Attractions." *World's Fair Bulletin* 5 (April 1904): 4–36.

Mason, Daniel Gregory. "Folk-Song and American Music." *The Musical Quarterly* 4 (July 1918): 323–32.

———. "Prefers Demonstration to Cheers." *The New Republic* 5 (December 4, 1915): 122.

Mathews, W. S. B. "Art Music in the Middle West: The Large Cities." *The Etude* 23 (March 1905): 96–97.

———. "The Great American Composer: The Where, the Why, and the When." *The Etude* 24 (July 1906): 422–23.

———. "Opening Music of the Fair." *Musical Record* (June 1893): 12.

Meyer, Peter Frank. "The Potency of Ragtime." *Christensen's Ragtime Review* 2 (April 1916): 3–4.

Miller, Kelly. "The Artistic Gifts of the Negro." *The Voice of the Negro* 3 (April 1906): 252–57.

"The Million Dollar Pike." *World's Fair Bulletin* 5 (June 1904): 68.

Moderwell, Hiram, K. "Ragtime." *The New Republic* 4 (October 16, 1915): 284–86.

"Music at the World's Fair." *Musical Record* (December 1893): 14.

"Music at the World's Fair." *World's Fair Bulletin* 3 (July 1902): 21.

"Music in America." *The Outlook* 81 (September 16, 1905): 108–10.

"Musical Impurity." *The Etude* 18 (January 1900): 16.

"Musical Materia Medica." *Musical America* 18 (August 2, 1913): 16.

"The Negro and the World's Fair." *World's Fair Bulletin* 2 (October 1901): 32.

"The Negro Congress at Chicago." *The Independent* 45 (August 24, 1893): 10–11.

"Negro Melodies vs. Coon Songs." *The Etude* 23 (March 1905): 103.

"Negro Music in the Land of Freedom." *The Outlook* 106 (March 21, 1914): 611–12.

"Negroes and Music." *The Outlook* 75 (December 19, 1903): 967–68.

Oehmler, Leo. "Ragtime: A Pernicious Evil and Enemy of True Art." *Musical Observer* 11 (September 1914): 14–15.

Orem, Preston Ware. "Popular Instrumental Music." *The Etude* 20 (December 1902): 449.

"Our Musical Condition." *The Negro Music Journal* 1 (March 1903): 137–39.

Partridge, William O. "The American School of Sculpture." *Forum* 29 (June 1900): 493–500.

Perry, Edward Baxter. "Taste versus Prejudice." *The Etude* 22 (April 1904): 148.

"A Plea for Ragtime." *Ragtime Review* 1 (November 1915): 4.

"Popular Music—A Curse or a Blessing?" *Current Literature* 53 (September 1912): 335.

"Questions and Answers." *The Etude* 16 (October 1898): 285.

"Questions and Answers." *The Etude* 18 (February 1900): 52.

"Ragging and Jazzing." *The Metronome* 35 (October–November, 1919): 34.

"Ragtime." *The Outlook* 104 (May 24, 1913): 137.

"Ragtime." *Ragtime Review* 2 (May 1916): 4.

"Ragtime as Source of National Music." *Musical America* 17 (February 15, 1913): 37.

"Ragtime Begins." *Record Changer* 8 (March 1948): 8.

"Ragtime Causing Mental Ailments." *Musical America* 18 (July 15, 1913): 28.

"Ragtime Has Vitality." *Ragtime Review* 2 (February 1916): 8.

"A Ragtime Pioneer." *Ragtime Review* 1 (September 1915): 8.

Rankin, J. E. "Pride of American Citizenship." *The Independent* 52 (July 4, 1900): 1610–12.

Ridpath, John Clark. "Shall the United States Be Europeanized." *Arena* 18 (December 1897): 827–33.

"The St. Louis Fair." *The Outlook* 73 (April 25, 1903): 952–53.

Scarborough, W. S. "The Negro and the Louisiana Purchase Exposition." *The Voice of the Negro* 1 (August 1904): 312–15.

"Scott Joplin Is Dead." *Ragtime Review* 3 (July 1917): 13.

Scott, Emmett J. "The Louisiana Purchase Exposition." *The Voice of the Negro* 1 (August 1904): 305–12.

Sherlock, Charles Reginald. "From Breakdown to Rag-time." *Cosmopolitan* 31 (October 1901): 631–39.

Skinner, Charles M. "The Home Piano." *The Etude* 18 (February 1900): 49.

Smith, Wilson G. "The Vagrant Philosopher." *The Negro Music Journal* 1 (May 1903): 181–83.

Stark, John. "Respectability of Ragtime." *Ragtime Review* 2 (March 1916): 5–6.

Stearns, Theodore. "Don't Rush into Print." *The Etude* 18 (April 1900): 126–27.

Sternberg, Constantin von. "National Music." *The Outlook* 85 (March 16, 1907): 626.

————. "What Is American Music." *The Etude* 22 (May 1904): 190.

Stevenson, E. Irenaeus. "Will American Composition Ever Possess a Distinctive Accent?" *The Etude* 17 (May 1899): 146.

Taylor, J. Hillary. "History of the Pianoforte." *The Negro Music Journal* 1 (January 1903): 73–75.

"A Three Days' Tour." *World's Fair Bulletin* 5 (September 1904): 25.

Trimble, Jessie. "The Founder of An American School of Art." *The Outlook* 85 (February 23, 1907): 453–60.

Walton, Lester A. "The Future of the Negro on the Stage." *The Colored American Magazine* 6 (May/June 1903): 439–42.

————. "Music and the Stage." *The Colored American Magazine* 14 (February/March 1908): 95.

————. "Music and the Stage." *The Colored American Magazine* 14 (September 1908): 459.

Weld, Arthur. "The Invasion of Vulgarity in Music." *The Etude* 17 (February 1899): 52.

"What Is the American Spirit?" *The Independent* 53 (August 8, 1901): 1873–74.

"What the 'Concert-Goer' Says of 'The Negro Music Journal.'" *The Negro Music Journal* 1 (October 1902): 27–28.

"What Rags Will Live Forever?" *Ragtime Review* 1 (October 1915): 6.

"What Theodore Thomas Thinks." *Musical Record* (October 1893): 7.

Whitmer, T. Carl. "The Energy of American Crowd Music." *Musical Quarterly* 4 (January 1918): 98–116.

"Will Ragtime Turn to Symphonic Poems?" *The Etude* 38 (May 1920): 305.

Wilson, H. J. "The Negro and Music." *The Outlook* 84 (December 1, 1906): 823–26.

Winn, Edward. "'Ragging' the Popular Song-Hits." *Melody* 2 (May 1918): 8.

————. "Ragtime Piano Playing: A Practical Course of Instruction." *The Tuneful Yankee* 1 (January 1917): 42–44.

"World's Columbian Exposition: Bulletin of Exposition Concerts to July 28th." *The Etude* 11 (April 1893): 80.

"World's Fair Music: Professor Ernest R. Kroeger Appointed Director of Programmes and Awards." *World's Fair Bulletin* 4 (December 1902): 18.

## Books

Bennitt, Mark and Frank Parker Stockbridge. *History of the Louisiana Purchase Exposition*. St. Louis: Universal Exposition Publ. Co., 1905.

Clayton, Powell. *The Aftermath of the Civil War in Arkansas.* New York: The Neale Publishing Company, 1915.

Corrothers, James. *In Spite of the Handicap: An Autobiography.* New York: George H. Doran Co., 1916.

Dowd, Jerome. *The Negro in American Life.* New York: Negro Universities Press, 1926.

*The Dream City: A Portfolio of Photographic Views of the World's Columbian Exposition.* St. Louis: N. D. Thompson Publ. Co., 1893.

Du Bois, W. E. B. *The Gift of Black Folk: The Negroes in the Making of America.* 1924. Reprint. New York: AMS Press, 1971.

————. *The Souls of Black Folk.* 1903. Reprint. Greenwich, Conn.: Fawcett Publishing, Inc., 1961.

*Gazette's Sedalia City Directory for 1892–3.* Sedalia: Gazette Printing Company, 1893.

Gilman, Nicholas Paine. *Socialism and the American Spirit.* Boston: Houghton Mifflin, 1893.

*Gould's St. Louis Directory for 1901.* St. Louis: Gould Directory Co., 1902.

*Gould's St. Louis Directory for 1902.* St. Louis: Gould Directory Co., 1903.

*Gould's St. Louis Directory for 1903.* St. Louis: Gould Directory Co., 1904.

Handy, W. C. *The Father of the Blues: An Autobiography.* London: Sidgwick and Jackson, 1957.

Hare, Maud Cuney. *Negro Musicians and Their Music.* 1936. Reprint. New York: Da Capo Press, 1974.

Harris, Charles Kassell. *After the Ball: Forty Years of Melody, an Autobiography.* New York: Frank-Maurice, Inc., 1926.

Hitchcock, Benjamin W. *Musical, Pictorial and Descriptive Souvenir of the World's Columbian Exposition.* Chicago: National Music Co., 1892.

*Hoye's Sedalia, Mo., City Directory.* Sedalia: Sedalia Printing Co., 1903.

Hubbard, W. L., Emil Liebling, George W. Andrews, Arthur Foote, and Edward Dickinson, eds. *The American History and Encyclopedia of Music.* New York: Irving Squire, 1910.

Hughes, Rupert, ed. *Music Lovers' Encyclopedia.* Garden City, N.Y.: Garden City Publishing Co., 1947.

Johnson, J. Rosamond, ed. *Rolling Along in Song: A Chronological Survey of American Negro Music.* New York: Viking Press, 1937.

Johnson, James Weldon. *Along This Way: The Autobiography of James Weldon Johnson.* New York: Viking Press, 1933.

———. *The Autobiography of an Ex-Colored Man*. New York: Penguin Books, 1990.

———. *Black Manhattan*. New York: Arno Press and the New York Times, 1968.

Krehbiel, Henry Edward. *The Pianoforte and Its Music*. 1911. Reprint. New York: Cooper Square Publishers, Inc., 1971.

Lewis, Lloyd and Henry Justin Smith. *Chicago: The History of Its Reputation*. New York: Harcourt, Brace & Co., 1929.

McGruder, Mark A. *History of Pettis County Missouri*. Topeka, Indianapolis, Cleveland: Historical Publishing Co., 1919.

Maitland, J. A. Fuller, ed. *Grove's Dictionary of Music and Musicians*. New York: Macmillan, 1908.

*Report of Proceedings of the Thirteenth Annual Convention of the American Federation of Labor, Held at Chicago, Ill. December 11th to 19th Inclusive 1893*. Published by Direction of A. F. of L.

*Sedalia City Directory and Pettis County Directory for 1897*. Sedalia: Capen & Bowman, 1897.

*Sedalia City Directory for 1895*. Sedalia: Waller & Reynolds, 1895.

Sklar, Kathryn Kish, ed. *The Autobiography of Florence Kelley: Notes of Sixty Years*. Chicago: Charles H. Kerr Publishing Co., 1986.

Van Vechten, Carl. *In the Garret*. New York: Knopf, 1920.

*W. H. McCoy's Sedalia, Mo., City Directory 1898–1899*. Sedalia: Sedalia Printing Co., 1899.

*W. H. McCoy's Twentieth Century Sedalia, Mo., City Directory for 1900–1*. Sedalia: Sedalia Printing Co., 1901.

Washington, Booker T. *Up from Slavery*. New York: Magnum Books, 1968.

Wiggins, Lida Keck, ed. *The Life and Works of Paul Laurence Dunbar*. New York: Kraus Reprint Company, 1971.

Wood, W. D. *Reminiscences of Reconstruction in Texas*. n.p., 1902.

## SECONDARY WORKS
### Dissertations and Theses

Chandler, Barbara Susan Overton. "A History of Bowie County." Master's Thesis, University of Texas, 1937.

Reed, Addison W. "The Life and Works of Scott Joplin." Ph.D. diss., University of North Carolina, 1973.

### Articles

Albrecht, Theodore. "Julius Weiss: Scott Joplin's First Piano Teacher." *College Music Symposium* 19 (Fall 1979): 89–105.

Baker, Houston. "Modernism and the Harlem Renaissance." *American Quarterly* 39 (Spring 1987): 84–97.

Davis, David Brion. "Some Recent Directions in American Cultural History." *American Historical Review* 73 (February 1968): 696–707.

Doenecke, Justus D. "Myths, Machines and Markets: The Columbian Exposition of 1893." *Journal of Popular Culture* 6 (Spring 1973): 535–49.

Dormon, James H. "Shaping the Popular Image of Post-Reconstruction American Blacks: The 'Coon Song' Phenomenon of the Gilded Age." *American Quarterly* 40 (December 1988): 450–71.

Graham, Howard Jay. "The 'Conspiracy Theory' of the Fourteenth Amendment." In *Reconstruction: An Anthology of Revisionist Writings.* Edited by Kenneth M. Stampp and Leon F. Litwack. Baton Rouge: Louisiana State University Press, 1969.

Higham, John. "The Reorientation of American Culture in the 1890s." In *Writing American History.* Bloomington: Indiana University Press, 1972.

Kenney, William H. "James Scott and the Culture of Classic Ragtime." *American Music* 9 (Summer 1991): 149–82.

Lears, T. J. Jackson. "The Concept of Cultural Hegemony: Problems and Possibilities." *American Historical Review* 90 (June 1985): 567–93.

———."From Salvation to Self-Realization: Advertising and the Therapeutic Roots of the Consumer Culture, 1880–1930." In *The Culture of Consumption.* Edited by Richard Wightman Fox and T. J. Jackson Lears. New York: Pantheon Books, 1983.

Lemisch, Jesse. "Listening to the 'Inarticulate': William Widger's Dream and the Loyalties of American Revolutionary Seamen in British Prisons." *Journal of Social History* 3 (Fall 1969): 1–29.

Liebenguth, Jane Anne. "Music at the Louisiana Purchase Exposition." *Missouri Historical Society Bulletin* 36 (October 1979): 27–34.

Meyer, D. H. "American Intellectuals and the Victorian Crisis of Faith." *American Quarterly* 27 (1975): 585–603.

Rodgers, Daniel. "In Search of Progressivism." *Reviews in American History* 10 (December 1982): 113–32.

Ross, Dorothy. "Socialism and American Liberalism: Academic Social Thought in the 1890s." *Perspectives in American History* 11 (1977–1978): 5–79.

Rudwick, Elliott and August Meier. "Black Man in the 'White City': Negroes and the Columbian Exposition, 1893." *Phylon* 26

(1965): 319–37.

Singal, Daniel Joseph. "Towards a Definition of American Modernism." *American Quarterly* 39 (Spring 1987): 7–26.

Susman, Warren. "'Personality' and the Making of Twentieth-Century Culture." In *New Directions in American Intellectual History*. Edited by John Higham and Paul Conkin. Baltimore: Johns Hopkins University Press, 1979.

Thompson, Kay C. "Lottie Joplin." *The Record Changer* (October 1950): 18.

Tichenor, Trebor Jay. "Missouri's Role in the Ragtime Revolution." *Missouri Historical Society Bulletin* 17 (April 1961): 240–45.

Toews, John E. "Intellectual History after the Linguistic Turn: The Autonomy of Meaning and the Irreducibility of Experience." *American Historical Review* 92 (October 1987): 879–907.

Williams, Raymond. "Base and Superstructure in Marxist Cultural Theory." *New Left Review* 82 (November–December 1973): 3–16.


Books

Adorno, Theodor W. *Die Musikalischen Monographien*. Frankfurt am Main: Suhrkamp Verlag, 1971.

———. *Introduction to the Sociology of Music*. New York: Seabury Press, 1976.

——— and Max Horkheimer. *Dialectic of Enlightenment*. 1944. Reprint. New York: The Seabury Press, 1972.

Anderson, Jervis. *This Was Harlem, 1900–1950*. New York: Farrar Straus Giroux, 1981.

Ballantine, Christopher. *Music and Its Social Meanings*. New York: Gordon & Breach Science Publ., 1984.

Berlin, Edward A. *Ragtime: A Musical and Cultural History*. Berkeley: University of California Press, 1980.

Bindas, Kenneth J., ed. *America's Musical Pulse: Popular Music in Twentieth-Century Society*. Westport, Conn.: Praeger, 1992.

Blassingame, John. *The Slave Community*. New York: Oxford University Press, 1972.

Blesh, Rudi and Harriet Janis. *They All Played Ragtime: The True Story of an American Music*. New York: Knopf, 1950.

Bronner, Stephen Eric and Douglas MacKay Kellner, eds. *Critical Theory and Society: A Reader*. New York: Routledge, 1989.

Braverman, Harry. *Labor and Monopoly Capitalism: The Degradation of Work in the Twentieth Century.* New York: Monthly Review Press, 1974.

Brewer, J. Mason. *Negro Legislators of Texas and Their Descendants: A History of the Negro in Texas Politics from Reconstruction to Disfranchisement.* Dallas: Mathis Publishing Co., 1935.

Bush, Gregory W. *Lord of Attention: Gerald Stanley Lee and the Crowd Metaphor in Industrializing America.* Amherst: University of Massachusetts Press, 1991.

Campbell, Randolph B. *An Empire for Slavery: The Peculiar Institution in Texas, 1821–1865.* Baton Rouge: Louisiana State University Press, 1989.

Cassity, Michael. *Defending a Way of Life: An American Community in the Nineteenth Century.* Albany: State University of New York Press, 1989.

Chandler, Alfred. *The Visible Hand: The Managerial Revolution in American Business.* Cambridge: Harvard University Press, 1977.

Chandler, Barbara Overton and J. E. Howe. *History of Texarkana and Bowie and Miller Counties Texas-Arkansas.* Texarkana: J. E. Howe, Publisher, 1939.

Cheslock, Louis. *H. L. Mencken on Music.* New York: Knopf, 1961.

Clarke, Eric. *Music in Everyday Life.* New York: W. W. Norton & Co., Inc., 1935.

Copland, Aaron. *What to Listen For in Music.* New York: McGraw-Hill Book Co., 1957.

Crunden, Robert. *Ministers of Reform.* New York: Basic Books, 1982.

Curtis, Susan. *A Consuming Faith: The Social Gospel and Modern American Culture.* Baltimore: Johns Hopkins University Press, 1991.

Dasilva, Fabio, Anthony Blasi, and David Dees. *The Sociology of Music.* Notre Dame: University of Notre Dame Press, 1984.

Davis, David Brion. *Antebellum American Culture.* Lexington, Mass.: Heath, 1979.

de Lerma, Dominique-Rene, ed. *Reflections on Afro-American Music.* Kent, Ohio: The Kent State University Press, 1973.

Dickinson, Edward. *The Spirit of Music: How to Find It and How to Share It.* New York: Scribner's, 1925.

Douglas, Ann. *The Feminization of American Culture.* New York: Avon Books, 1977.

Eagleton, Terry. *Literary Theory: An Introduction.* Minneapolis: University of Minnesota Press, 1983.

Early, Gerald, ed. *Speech and Power: The African-American Essay and Its Cultural Content from Polemics to Pulpit.* Hopewell, New Jersey: Ecco Press, 1992.

Ellis, Joseph. *After the Revolution: Profiles of Early American Culture.* New York: Harper and Row, 1988.

Erenberg, Lewis. *Steppin' Out: New York Nightlife and the Transformation of American Culture, 1890–1930.* Chicago: University of Chicago Press, 1981.

Etzkorn, K. Peter, ed. *Music and Society: The Later Writings of Paul Honigsheim.* New York: John Wiley & Sons, 1973.

Ewen, David, ed. *Popular American Composers from Revolutionary Times to the Present.* New York: H. W. Wilson Co., 1962.

Fite, Gilbert C. and Jim E. Reese. *An Economic History of the United States.* Boston: Houghton Mifflin Co., 1965.

Flack, Horace Edgar. *The Adoption of the Fourteenth Amendment.* 1908. Reprint. Gloucester, Mass.: Peter Smith, 1965.

Foner, Eric. *Reconstruction: America's Unfinished Revolution, 1863–1877.* New York: Harper & Row, 1988.

Fredrickson, George. *The Inner Civil War: Northern Intellectuals and the Crisis of the Union.* New York: Harper and Row, 1965.

Gammond, Peter. *Scott Joplin and the Ragtime Era.* New York: St. Martin's Press, 1975.

Geertz, Clifford. *The Interpretation of Cultures.* London: Hutchinson & Co., 1975.

Genovese, Eugene. *Roll, Jordan, Roll: The World the Slaves Made.* New York: Random House, 1972.

Gilfoyle, Timothy. *City of Eros: New York City, Prostitution, and the Commercialization of Sex, 1790–1920.* New York: Norton, 1992.

Ginger, Ray. *Altgeld's America: The Lincoln Ideal Versus Changing Realities.* New York: Funk & Wagnalls, 1958.

Gleason, Philip. *Speaking of Diversity: Language and Ethnicity in Twentieth-Century America.* Baltimore: Johns Hopkins University Press, 1992.

Goldberg, Isaac. *Tin Pan Alley: A Chronicle of the American Popular Music Racket.* New York: The John Day Co., 1930.

Goodwyn, Lawrence. *Democratic Promise: The Populist Movement in America.* New York: Oxford University Press, 1976.

Green, Harvey. *The Light of the Home: An Intimate View of the Lives of Women in Victorian America.* New York: Pantheon Books, 1983.

Greene, Lorenzo J., Gary R. Kremer, and Anthony F. Holland. *Missouri's Black Heritage*. St. Louis: Forum Press, 1980.

Guralnick, Peter. *Lost Highway: Journeys and Arrivals of American Musicians*. New York: Vintage, 1979.

Halttunen, Karen. *Confidence Men and Painted Women: A Study in Middle-Class Culture in America, 1830–1870*. New Haven: Yale University Press, 1982.

Harris, M. A. *A Negro History Tour of Manhattan*. New York: Greenwood Pub., 1968.

Harris, Neil. *Humbug: The Art of P. T. Barnum*. Chicago: University of Chicago Press, 1973.

Harris, Rex. *Jazz*. New York: Penguin Books, 1956.

Haskins, James and Kathleen Benson. *Scott Joplin*. Garden City, N.Y.: Doubleday & Co., Inc., 1978.

Hasse, John Edward, ed. *Ragtime: Its History, Composers, and Music*. New York: Schirmer Books, 1985.

Heilbroner, Robert L. *The Economic Transformation of America*. New York: Harcourt Brace Jovanovich, Inc., 1977.

Hicks, John D. *The Populist Revolt: A History of the Farmers' Alliance and the People's Party*. Minneapolis: University of Minnesota Press, 1931.

Hofstadter, Richard. *The Age of Reform from Bryan to F. D. R.* New York: Vintage Books, 1960.

Houghton, Walter E. *The Victorian Frame of Mind, 1830–1870*. New Haven: Yale University Press, 1975.

Howe, Daniel Walker, ed. *Victorian America*. Philadelphia: University of Pennsylvania Press, 1976.

———. *The Political Culture of the American Whigs*. Chicago: University of Chicago Press, 1979.

Hunt, Lynn, ed. *The New Cultural History*. Berkeley: University of California Press, 1989.

Jasen, David A. and Trebor Jay Tichenor. *Rags and Ragtime, a Musical History*. New York: The Seabury Press, 1978.

Jones, LeRoi. *Blues People: Negro Music in White America*. New York: William Morrow & Co., 1963.

Kasson, John F. *Amusing the Million: Coney Island at the Turn of the Century*. New York: Hill & Wang, 1978.

Kett, Joseph. *Rites of Passage: Adolescence in America, 1790 to the Present*. New York: Basic Books, 1977.

Kloppenberg, James T. *Uncertain Victory: Social Democracy and Progressivism in European and American Thought, 1870–1920.* New York: Oxford University Press, 1986.

LaCapra, Dominick. *Rethinking Intellectual History: Texts, Contexts, Language.* Ithaca: Cornell University Press, 1983.

Lang, Hazel N. *Life in Pettis County: 1815–1973.* Privately published by Hazel Lang, 1975.

Lasch, Christopher. *Havens in a Heartless World.* New York: Basic Books, 1977.

Lawrence, Vera Brodsky, ed. *The Collected Works of Scott Joplin.* New York: New York Public Library, 1971.

Lears, T. J. Jackson. *No Place of Grace: Antimodernism and the Transformation of American Culture, 1880–1920.* New York: Pantheon Books, 1981.

Levine, Lawrence. *Black Culture and Black Consciousness: Afro-American Folk Thought from Slavery to Freedom.* New York: Oxford University Press, 1977.

———. *Highbrow/Lowbrow: The Emergence of Cultural Hierarchy in America.* Cambridge: Harvard University Press, 1988.

Litwack, Leon F. *Been in the Storm So Long: The Aftermath of Slavery.* New York: Vintage Books, 1979.

Locke, Alain. *The Negro and His Music.* Port Washington, N.Y.: Kennikat Press, 1936.

Loesser, Arthur. *Men, Women, and Pianos: A Social History.* New York: Simon and Schuster, 1954.

Luedtke, Luther S., ed. *Making America: The Society and Culture of the United States.* Chapel Hill: University of North Carolina Press, 1992.

McCoy, Drew. *The Elusive Republic.* New York: Norton, 1980.

McGerr, Michael. *The Decline of Popular Politics: The American North, 1865–1928.* New York: Oxford University Press, 1986.

Marten, James. *Texas Divided: Loyalty and Dissent in the Lone Star State, 1856–1874.* Lexington: University of Kentucky Press, 1990.

May, Elaine Tyler. *Great Expectations: Marriage and Divorce in Post-Victorian America.* Chicago: University of Chicago Press, 1980.

Meyers, Marvin. *The Jacksonian Persuasion: Politics and Belief.* Stanford: Stanford University Press, 1957.

Mintz, Steven. *A Prison of Expectations: The Family in Victorian Culture.* New York: New York University Press, 1983.

Morgan, H. Wayne. *American Writers in Rebellion: From Mark Twain to Dreiser.* New York: Hill & Wang, 1965.

Nunn, W. C. *Texas under the Carpetbaggers*. Austin: University of Texas Press, 1962.

Orvell, Miles. *The Real Thing: Imitation and Authenticity in American Culture, 1880–1940*. Chapel Hill: University of North Carolina Press, 1989.

Painter, Nell Irvin. *Standing at Armageddon: The United States, 1877–1919*. New York: Norton, 1987.

Palmer, Bruce. *"Man over Money": The Southern Populist Critique of American Capitalism*. Chapel Hill: University of North Carolina Press, 1980.

Pattee, Fred Lewis. *A History of American Literature since 1870*. New York: Century Co., 1915.

Pells, Richard. *Radical Visions and American Dreams: Culture and Social Thought in the Depression Years*. New York: Harper and Row, 1973.

Pierce, Bessie Louise. *A History of Chicago*. Vol. 3. New York: Knopf, 1957.

Pollack, Norman. *The Populist Response to Industrial America: Midwestern Populist Thought*. Cambridge: Harvard University Press, 1962.

Rawick, George P. *The American Slave: A Composite Autobiography*. 19 Vols. West Port, Conn.: Greenwood Press, 1972.

Rice, Lawrence D. *The Negro in Texas, 1874–1900*. Baton Rouge: Louisiana State University Press, 1971.

Richter, William L. *The Army in Texas during Reconstruction*. College Station: Texas A & M University Press, 1987.

Rodgers, Daniel. *The Work Ethic in Industrial America, 1850–1920*. Chicago: University of Chicago Press, 1974.

Roell, Craig, H. *The Piano in America, 1890–1940*. Chapel Hill: University of North Carolina Press, 1989.

Rogin, Michael Paul. *Fathers and Children: Andrew Jackson and the Subjugation of the American Indian*. New York: Vintage Books, 1975.

Rothman, David J. *The Discovery of the Asylum: Social Order and Disorder in the New Republic*. Boston: Little, Brown & Co., 1971.

Rydell, Robert W. *All the World's a Fair: Visions of Empire at American International Expositions, 1876–1916*. Chicago: University of Chicago Press, 1984.

Schafer, William J. and Johannes Riedel. *The Art of Ragtime: Form and Meaning of an Original Black American Art*. Baton Rouge: Louisiana State University Press, 1973.

Schwantes, Carlos A. *Coxey's Army: An American Odyssey*. Lincoln: University of Nebraska Press, 1985.

Sennett, Richard. *The Fall of Public Man*. New York: Vintage Books, 1974.

Siegmeister, Elie. *Music and Society*. New York: Critics Group Press, 1938.

Silbermann, Alphonse. *The Sociology of Music*. London: Routledge & Kegan Paul, 1963.

Sizer, Sandra S. *Gospel Hymns and Social Religion: The Rhetoric of Nineteenth-Century Revivalism*. Philadelphia: Temple University Press, 1978.

Sklar, Kathryn Kish. *Catharine Beecher: A Study in Domesticity*. New Haven: Yale University Press, 1983.

Smallwood, James M. *Time of Hope, Time of Despair: Black Texans During Reconstruction*. Port Washington, N.Y.: Kennikat Press, 1981.

Snyder, Robert W. *The Voice of the City: Vaudeville and Popular Culture in New York*. New York: Oxford University Press, 1989.

Sollors, Werner. *Beyond Ethnicity: Consent and Descent in American Culture*. New York: Oxford University Press, 1986.

―――. ed. *The Invention of Ethnicity*. New York: Oxford University Press, 1989.

Southern, Eileen. *Biographical Dictionary of Afro-American and African Musicians*. Westport, Conn.: Greenwood Press, 1982.

―――. *The Music of Black Americans: A History*. New York: Norton, 1971.

―――, ed. *Readings in Black American Music*. New York: Norton, 1971.

Spaeth, Sigmund. *The Common Sense of Music*. 1924. Reprint. Westport, Conn.: Greenwood Press, 1972.

Spalding, Walter R. *Music: An Art and a Language*. Boston and New York: The Arthur P. Schmidt Co., 1920.

Stearns, Marshall W. *The Story of Jazz*. New York: Oxford University Press, 1956.

Strouse, Jean. *Alice James: A Biography*. Boston: Houghton Mifflin Co., 1980.

Sundquist, Eric J., ed., *American Realism: New Essays*. Baltimore: Johns Hopkins University Press, 1982.

Susman, Warren. *Culture as History: The Transformation of American Society in the Twentieth Century*. New York: Pantheon Books, 1973.

Tawa, Nicholas. *The Way to Tin Pan Alley: American Popular Song, 1866–1910.* New York: Schirmer, 1990.

Thelen, David. *The New Citizenship: Origins of Progressivism in Wisconsin, 1885–1900.* Columbia: University of Missouri Press, 1972.

————. *Paths of Resistance: Tradition and Dignity in Industrializing Missouri.* New York: Oxford University Press, 1986.

Thernstrom, Stephan. *Poverty and Progress: Social Mobility in a Nineteenth-Century City.* Cambridge: Harvard University Press, 1964.

Thompson, Oscar. *How to Understand Music.* New York: The Dial Press, 1936.

Todd, R. Larry, ed. *Nineteenth-Century Piano Music.* New York: Schirmer Books, 1990.

Trachtenberg, Alan. *The Incorporation of America: Culture and Society in the Gilded Age.* New York: Hill & Wang, 1982.

Waldo, Terry. *This Is Ragtime.* New York: Hawthorn Books, Inc., 1976.

Walters, Ronald G. *American Reformers, 1815–1860.* New York: Hill & Wang, 1978.

Watts, Steven. *The Republic Reborn: War and the Making of Liberal America, 1790–1820.* Baltimore: Johns Hopkins University Press, 1987.

Wiebe, Robert. *The Search for Order, 1877–1920.* New York: Hill & Wang, 1967.

Wilentz, Sean. *Chants Democratic: New York City and the Rise of the American Working Class, 1788–1850.* New York: Oxford University Press, 1984.

Wood, Gordon. *The Creation of the American Republic.* New York: Norton, 1969.

Woodward, C. Vann. *Origins of the New South, 1877–1913.* Baton Rouge: Louisiana State University Press, 1971.

————. *The Strange Career of Jim Crow.* New York: Oxford University Press, 1974.

Workers of the Writers' Program of the Works Projects Administration. *Arkansas: A Guide to the State.* 1941. Reprint. St. Clair Shores, Michigan: Scholarly Press, 1977.

Wright, Gwendolyn. *Moralism and the Model Home: Domestic Architecture and Cultural Conflict in Chicago, 1873–1913.* Chicago: University of Chicago Press, 1980.

Ziff, Larzer. *The American 1890s: Life and Times of a Lost Generation.* Lincoln: University of Nebraska Press, 1966.

# INDEX

## ABOUT THE AUTHOR

Susan Curtis is Professor of History and American Studies and Director of Interdisciplinary Studies at Purdue University. She is the author of several books, including *A Consuming Faith: The Social Gospel and Modern American Culture* and *The First Black Actors on the Great White Way* (University of Missouri Press).